Rudolf Sohm, C. W. (Charles Wesley) Rishell

A history of Christianity

Rudolf Sohm, C. W. (Charles Wesley) Rishell

A history of Christianity

ISBN/EAN: 9783742896711

Hergestellt in Europa, USA, Kanada, Australien, Japan

Cover: Foto ©Lupo / pixelio.de

Manufactured and distributed by brebook publishing software
(www.brebook.com)

Rudolf Sohm, C. W. (Charles Wesley) Rishell

A history of Christianity

A

HISTORY OF CHRISTIANITY.

from the German

OF

PROF. RUDOLPH SOHM,

(LEIPSIC,)

BY

CHARLES W RISHELL, M A.

WITH

REVISIONS, NOTES, AND ADDITIONS.

CINCINNATI: CRANSTON & STOWE.
NEW YORK: HUNT & EATON.
1891.

PREFACE.

THE little book herewith given to the public is based upon the "Kirchengeschichte im Grundriss," by Professor Rudolph Sohm, professor of jurisprudence in the University of Leipzig, the many excellencies of which are enhanced by the fact that here Church history is written from the stand-point of a lawyer. The aim has been to preserve every thing of value to the American reader which the original work contains, and to add much which it omits or barely mentions. Thus §§ 17, 18, 37, 38, 39, 53, 54, 55, 56, are all additional, as also the supplementary and explanatory notes, and the chronological tables. In the translated portions, omissions and additions were made, and statements of opinion altered whenever it was deemed necessary. The book in its English form, therefore, is practically an independent work.

The notes are intended for the lay reader, and were prepared with reference to questions which will be likely to present themselves to the inquiring

1

mind. The effort to limit the book in point of size necessitated the restriction both of their number and length. The same influences operated to prevent the extension of Chronological Table No. 1 beyond the fifteenth century, and the introduction of other tables, which would have materially increased the size of the book.

The following works, in addition to others, have been carefully consulted and found specially helpful in the preparation of all the additional parts, as well as in the translation: Gieseler, "Kirchengeschichte;" Kurtz, "Lehrbuch der Kirchengeschichte;" Moeller, "Kirchengeschichte;" Hefele, "Conciliengeschichte;" Harnack, "Dogmengeschichte," and "Das Mönchthum;" Zöckler, "Geschichte der Askese;" Schaff, "Creeds of Christendom," and "Christianity in the United States;" Rothe, "Vorlesungen über Kirchengeschichte und Geschichte des Christlichen-Kirchlichen Lebens;" Piper, "Zeugen der Wahrheit;" Uhlhorn, "Die Christliche Liebesthätigkeit," and "Der Kampf des Christenthums mit dem Heidenthum;" Schaefer, "Leitfaden der Inneren Mission;" Lecky, "History of European Morals;" Gibbon, "Decline and Fall of the Roman Empire;" McClintock and Strong, "Cyclopedia of Biblical, Theological, and Ecclesiastical Literature;" Herzog and Plitt, "Real-Encyclopaedie;" Smith and Wace, "Dictionary of Christian Biography;" Weltzer, and Welte, "Kirchen-Lexikon;" Ersch and Gruber, "Encyclopaedie;" Meyer, "Konversations-Lexikon;" Brockhaus, "Conversations-Lexikon;" "The New American Cyclopedia;" and the "Encyclopædia Britannica." In the treatment of Methodism the works of Dr. Abel Stevens ("History of Methodism") and Isaac Taylor ("Wesley and Methodism"), were principally employed. The first chronological table is taken, with modifications, from Professor Dr. Uhlemann's "Zeittafeln der Kirchengeschichte," and Tables No. 2 and 3; also, with modifications, from McClintock and Strong's "Cyclopedia."

In the hope that they may contribute to an interest in, and a knowledge and understanding of, the history of Christianity, these pages are now sent forth.

CHARLES W. RISHELL.

CONTENTS.

FIRST CHAPTER.

ORIGIN OF CHRISTIANITY AND ITS INSTITUTIONS.

SECOND CHAPTER.
THE MIDDLE AGES.

THIRD CHAPTER.
PERIOD OF THE REFORMATION.

FOURTH CHAPTER.

THE CHURCH IN GREAT BRITAIN AND AMERICA.

APPENDICES.

THE CHRISTIAN CHURCH.

FIRST CHAPTER.

ORIGIN OF CHRISTIANITY AND ITS INSTITUTIONS.

INTRODUCTION.

§ 1. THE ROMAN WORLD.

IN thought we transport ourselves backward to the first century of our era. In Strasburg the legions stood on guard and Roman military orders rang on the air. As on the Rhine, so also on the Danube, the Euphrates, and the Nile, at the foot of the Atlas and the Pyrenees, the Roman eagle[1] held sway. With the establishment of the empire[2] was developed the energy of the Roman national character. A wise administration developed the resources of the provinces. An undivided authority controlled the imperial arms. With the energy of military measures against external foes were united peace and welfare at home. Trade flourished. The rich culture of the Greek Orient spread itself over the Latin Occident,[3] distributing blessing, bringing life, and lifting art and science to a new development.   A golden age had dawned. The Roman Empire was there with all its splendor.

What could humanity yet desire?   Was not every earthly and spiritual good poured out upon mankind with prodigal hand?   Here must men say to the passing moment: Pause awhile; thou art so glorious!   And yet, amid all the riches and all the culture, the greatest good was wanting.   The old gods were disenthroned.   The temples of Jupiter and Apollo[4] were yet standing; but the faith which once honored them had departed.   The Olympian heaven[5] had become empty.   Its inhabitants, whose forms the ancients had once clothed with so much sensuous vigor and ideal beauty, were now seen to be the product of poetic fancy.   The educated world turned away from the gods of Homer to the many-tongued philosophies, whose systems knew but one refrain: There are no gods.   The masses thronged the temples of Isis and Serapis, or satisfied themselves with the jugglery of Etrurian diviners, the secret, intoxicating solemnities of the mysteries, or the sense-confusing festivals of the great mother of gods, Cybele.[6]

Not that heathenism, whose dissolution was preparing, was wanting in the consciousness of religious needs or of religious ideals.   On the contrary, we observe in the first and second centuries a constant and ever higher development of the religious spirit, whose steps are marked by the appearance of such men as Seneca and Marcus Aurelius.' Philosophy, which had robbed the gods of their glory, was at the same time a guide to the true God, as the law was a schoolmaster to bring the Jews to Christ. The Stoic philosophy, which, with its requirements of a severely virtuous life of self-control, represented the faith of the majority of the educated classes, was increasingly influenced by the Platonic philosophy,[8] whose search for the ideal which lies behind the sensuous rose, in the philosophers of the imperial period, in an ever higher degree to a longing for the divine, for revelation, and for redemption. Side by side with the countless local deities, the monotheistic idea[9] lifted itself in might, seizing and ruling the Roman world. But this monotheism, toward which the ancient philosophy pressed, was able neither to banish polytheism nor to become the popular faith; and above all, it was unable to secure what was chiefly desired,—that is, certainty. Here the power was not given to regenerate a world grown old. The outcome of this philosophy was not possession, but desire; and that a desire which at the same time carried beneath its heart doubt of the existence of the longed-for good. The world had become empty because heaven had become empty.

Humanity was filled with the desire to discover the kingdom which is from above. The mighty movement of civilization which, within the Roman Empire, was borne onward by the united power of the Latin and Greek character, harmoniously grew until it culminated in the production of the world's desire which greeted the world's Savior at his coming.[10]

§ 2. CHRISTIANITY.

Over the wide domain of the Roman Empire Christian congregations, as yet unobserved, were here and there scattered. The new faith had its point of departure in Jerusalem. As early as the middle of the first century it had reached Rome and Alexandria. Between these cities, in Greece, Macedonia, Asia Minor, and Syria, was a series of congregations, founded chiefly by the apostle Paul between 50 and 60 A. D. Among the as yet not very numerous members of these congregations the Jewish nationality was represented by a large and increasing proportion. Along with these were Hellenic slaves and freedmen.[11] There were not many rich nor many educated, but many lowly people, artisans, soldiers, shop-keepers, fishermen, tax-gatherers,—the ignoble and despised in the eyes of the world. Upon this small and insignificant company, devoid of external aids, overlooked in the confusion of the great cities, rests the eye of history. It contained within itself the power which was to overcome the Roman world.

Looked upon from without, the Christian congregation appeared merely as a new society, like countless others then in existence. The Roman

Empire of the first century was satiated with religious associations. There was no fixed religion;
but there were religious forms of faith and worship, ceremonies of every variety. There was no
one, especially among the more lowly classes, who
did not belong to some society of this kind. There
was a divinity of these societies, though it were indeed but the deified emperor of the day.[12] This
deity was worshiped in common, regular, monthly
assemblies. Here were performed mysterious con-
secrations and washings, in outer appearance not
unlike Christian baptism. The members partook
also of common meals, similar to the love-feasts
and the Lord's Supper of the Christians. Indeed,
there was also a feeling of brotherhood among the
members. In these fraternities, as among the
Christians, distinctions of rank were unknown; the
slave was equal to the free, the freedman to the
free-born. The assemblies and festivities of the
brotherhoods were the periods in which the most
miserable slave enjoyed for the time freedom and
equality with his fellows, where the lowly man, at
least for the moment, could shake the burden of
life from his shoulders. As an advantage of connection with these unions, needy members received
assistance, and especially such as would secure to
them a decent burial. Even the idea of beneficent
brotherly love did not seem to be peculiar to the
Christian congregation.* If one viewed the Chris-

* But see ₹ 18.

tian Churches externally, they would appear as merely another effort at association upon the part of the lower classes. They might come and go unmolested.

But what a difference! Where are the other countless associations which the needs of the masses in the Roman Empire called forth? Where are they to-day? The winds of history have blown them away. For many centuries no trace of them has been found. Of all these religious unions of the Roman Empire but two yet live: The Jewish Synagogue and the Christian Church,—the synagogue chiefly in consequence of the inherent vitality of the Jewish nationality; the Church, behind which no one national life stood, solely as the result of the power of her religion.

The world-history is the world's judgment. No other religion but Christianity was able to be the leader of the developing civilization. On this account she won the victory. With her were not the legions nor the culture of the ancients; but she had the power of truth, which is mightier than all the forces of our earthly life. By the power of the spirit which was living within her, the Christian Church, steadily growing, was able to outlive the great Roman Empire, unite the new with the ancient time, and to become the teacher of the coming generation.

FIRST DIVISION.

THE PERSECUTIONS.

§ 3. Judaism and Christianity.

The enemy with which the Church was born was Pharisaic Judaism. Pharisecism, which sprang up with the heroic struggles of the Maccabees,[13] was Judaism newborn. It attempted to separate itself from all that was heathenish and unclean, and concerned itself with a legal righteousness in daily servitude to constantly new and severer precepts. The masses of the Jewish nation were Pharisaically disposed. In Pharisecism it found its inborn zeal for the law and its deep national self-consciousness, united with burning hate toward the heathen conqueror,[14] and wild hopes of a world-wide Judean kingdom to be established by a coming Messiah. In sharpest contrast with this servile zeal for the law came Christianity, with its freedom for all God's children; and in opposition to the false conception of the Jewish Messiah came the Crucified, who called both heathen and Jews without distinction to membership in his heavenly kingdom. In Pharisecism was the consummation, in Christianity the overthrow, of national Judaism.

Hence the immediate conflict. Stephen died a martyr's death (36 or 37 A. D.), because he taught that Jesus of Nazareth had come to destroy the temple service and to set aside the ceremonies of the Mosaic law. (Acts vi, 14.) The apostle

2

James, brother of the apostle John, was beheaded under Herod Agrippa (A. D. 44); Peter left for a time in prison; and James, the brother of the Lord, stoned to death (A. D. 62). So far as the power of Judaism extended, it poured itself out in violence against Christianity. For a time the Church at Jerusalem was scattered by the flight of its members before the enmity of the Pharisees, the apostles alone having the courage to remain at their posts. In Phariseeism, the Jewish people fought against Christianity all the more bitterly just because the issue concerned moral convictions attacked by the new religion. So even Paul, full of the noblest and most sacred enthusiasm, went forth to protect the law of the Fathers against dissolution.

The effect of the Jewish persecution was to hasten the spread of Christianity. From the eyes of the persecutor himself the scales suddenly fell. Christ, the Risen One, revealed himself to Saul. He saw Him whom he had persecuted, and the zealot for the law and for Judaism became the apostle to the heathen, to preach with power to Jews and Greeks justification by faith, and not through the law. The conflict of Christianity with Judaism was, however, but the preliminary to a greater struggle upon a broader field.

§ 4. HEATHENISM AND CHRISTIANITY.

Christianity applied itself not only to Judaism, but to the world. The world was Roman. In the

Roman Empire must the decision for the future be worked out. But the Roman world was also heathen. What attitude would heathenism take toward Christianity?

Scarcely was the Church founded when it was attacked by heathenism. The burning of Rome[15] was attributed to the guilt of the Christians (A. D. 64). A large number of the members of the infant Church, painfully executed, fell victims to the thirst for revenge among the masses of the people. Among those who sealed their testimony with their blood were Paul, who had long been a prisoner in Rome, and perhaps Peter. The flames of the capital of the world and the living torches of the martyrs' bodies in the gardens of the Emperor Nero light the entrance of the Christian Church into the history of the world. Until then the Christians had been confused by the masses with the Jews. Now, for the first time, the distinction found its way into the general consciousness. Only the Christians, not the Jews, were accused of setting fire to the city.

In the investigation which followed, the Christians were found innocent of incendiarism. Nevertheless they were executed because they were found guilty of "hatred against the whole human race." The religion of love appeared to the Romans as a religion of hate; and, strange as it may seem, from their stand-point not altogether by mistake. The Romans believed in the eternal continuance of their city[16] and empire. Their patriotism consisted in this faith. The Christians believed in the downfall of the city and the imperial power, and in the destruction of the earth. They believed only one kingdom to be eternal—the kingdom of Christ, the kingdom of God. Not only so, the first Christians believed that the end of the world was at hand. The disciples had seen the risen Lord ascend. They were of the conviction that during their life-time they would also see him come again in divine splendor and power to overthrow the terrestrial world, and to judge the living and the dead. They hoped for this day as the bride waits for the coming of the bridegroom. They longed for the overthrow of the Roman kingdom, that the kingdom of God might come. In this consisted their high treason, their "hate" against the Roman Empire, and therewith their "hatred against the whole human race."

Rome (heathenism) and Christianity stood face to face with one another. To the ancient heathenism the State was the highest good. Moral virtue was identical with that activity which served the State. To live and to die for the common good was the sum of existence. Hence heathenism found in the worship of the emperor, which the Romans had adopted from the ancient customs of the East, the final and most perfect manifestation of its character. The emperor of the Roman Empire was the incarnation of the idea of the State. The altar which was erected to the emperor was dedicated to the adoration of the power of the State, which, to heathenism, was the highest moral power. In Christianity a view of religion came to the front which abhorred, with uncompromising decisiveness, not only the adoration of idols, but also of the emperor—that is, of the power of the State. The highest and best for the Christian was not this all-powerful Cæsar,[17] nor this Roman Empire, nor the Roman nation. For the Christian the highest and best could not be found in this world. His longing was directed toward something better. A new view of the world entered into history with Christianity—a view which emphasized the relative valuelessness of everything earthly in comparison with the heavenly; which gave to Cæsar what was his due, but which proposed to give also to God what belonged to God. It laid claim to being the only valid view of the world, and challenged all opposers to conflict. While Judaism, in the spirit of exclusiveness, cherished its promises and convictions only for itself, and the philosophical systems sought entrance alone among the educated classes, Christianity came forward with the avowed purpose of conquering the world for itself. This was the reason why Christianity was, in the judgment of ancient heathenism, dangerous to the State. The foundations of the ancient theory of national existence, with its unlimited and illimitable claims upon the outer and inner life of man, were threatened. Even virtue, in the sense of the ancients—the love of the community as the greatest good—was attacked. Rightly did the ancient idea of the State feel its innermost life threatened; and in the violence of the Emperor Nero, and the blind rage of the heathen masses against the Christians, the national instinct gave itself its natural and necessary expression.

§ 5. LEGAL PROCEEDINGS AGAINST THE CHRISTIANS.

The Christian, as such, appeared to the Romans as an enemy of the State; on account of his sentiments under suspicion of high treason, and therefore, according to justice, worthy of death. Under the pressure of this principle of penal justice, the Christian Church asserted itself during three centuries. It would be indeed an error to represent this long period as one of unbroken persecution. On the contrary, the principle was only now and then really put into operation, and generally for some special cause. With times of persecution alternated long periods of tolerance. The persecutions of the very first period were wholly local in their character. When pestilence, famine, or fire excited the masses of the people; or when a violent provincial governor found it agreeable to vent his passions upon the Christians; or when the Christians stubbornly set themselves in opposition to the masses, there were persecutions, now in one place, now in another. Thus the burning of Rome gave occasion to the Neronian persecution, but only against the Roman Christians. So Ignatius, bishop of Antioch, died a martyr's death, and Polycarp, bishop of Smyrna, sealed his faith at the stake (about 155)—both under Antoninus Pius.[18] Under Marcus Aurelius (161–180) occurred the bloody persecution in Southern Gaul, in which so many of the Church at Lyons fell as victims (177). Under Septimius Severus[19] conversion to Christianity was formally forbidden (202), and persecution raged against the Christians in Egypt and in the Latin province of Africa. Notwithstanding, there was no general persecution until the middle of the third century. In the broad area of the Roman Empire the Church had room enough to unfold, although now this, now that, congregation passed through conflicts more or less severe.

Nevertheless, the statement remains true that to be a Christian meant to be devoted to death. The characteristics of a Christian were a sufficient basis for a deadly accusation against any member. The principle remained, although it was but imperfectly carried out. What an advantage it gave, not only to the heathen priests and makers of images who might feel their craft in danger (Acts xix, 27), but also to the money-loving procurator, the jealous neighbor, or the revengeful enemy, to strike a deadly blow at the chosen victim by accusing him on account of his Christianity! Justin Martyr, a philosopher, who had become a Christian, was beheaded in Rome (165) at the instigation of a literary rival, the cynic Crescens,[20] who vented in this manner his spite upon his enemy. The number of the martyrs is not limited to the names preserved by history. Justin's chief motive for adopting Christianity was the sublime courage with which its professors died for their convictions. To the heathen, death came with all its terrors; to the Christian it was gain. The moral power of Christianity was, above all, opposed to heathenism in this courage in death; a courage which went to the stake, the block, or the lions—not in the spirit of stubborn determination, nor yet with stoical indifference, but with victorious confidence in Christ and immortality. Here was the faith which more than overcame the world in the certain possession of the heavenly. The faith of Christianity was her only power over against enmity and assault; but it was a most victorious power, and it worked with mighty effect upon its enemies, even though externally it was overpowered.

Proceedings against Christians were first regulated by Trajan[21] (112). They must not be sought out by the officers, but could only be executed when accused by others. Until far into the third century this remained the principle. Marcus Aurelius ordained (176 or 177) that the officers might proceed against Christians only when Christianity gave occasion to public disorder. In the apparent mildness of Trajan's order lay both calculation and cruelty. If the accused Christian offered to the image of the emperor, he was set free; if not, he was put to death. But if he offered, he had discarded Christianity in order to escape the penalty of death. How subtle the temptation, and how many fell a victim to it! Pliny, the governor of Bithynia and Pontus, whose letter of inquiry to Trajan gave occasion to the order, was convinced that under this arrangement Christianity would soon come to an end. If the Christian refused to offer, he was accounted worthy of death—not ostensibly on account of his religion, nor on account of his conduct prior to his accusation, but on account of crime against the emperor which he had committed after his arrest, in refusing to sacrifice to the image of the emperor. Procedure against the Christians was distinguished from every other judicial process, in that it was aimed at making the accused guilty through a refusal to offer as demanded. What cruelty! As such, the Christian was suspected of high treason. The process was so conducted that the accused, in case he clung to his faith, must become guilty. In fact, it was not a crime, a deed already done, but a sentiment, the faith of Christianity, which was pursued by the power of the State; although that faith refused the adoration, not only of the power of the State, but also of everything and every person not divine. The form of procedure against Christians which Trajan introduced made it unquestionably clear that the heathen State, with its claim of being the highest moral power, had undertaken a warfare against Christianity.

§ 6. The Decisive Struggle.

Still the Church grew, and grew without cessation. As early as the second half of the second century, Christianity had become a noticeably advancing and aggressive ingredient in the life of the people throughout the entire empire. By the middle of the third century, heathenism sensibly felt that it was threatened in its very existence. The Church at Rome, at this time the largest in Christendom, must have numbered at least twenty thousand members. Indeed, by its constitution, which meantime had been developed (§ 10), the Church had become a match for the State. If the old, traditionary, national character was to be maintained, the last moment when interference was possible had come.

At this point began, therefore, the systematic Christian persecutions over the whole empire, the carefully planned attacks of the heathen State upon the Church, and carried on with every possible means. The Emperor Decius (249–251) made the beginning. He ordered a universal Christian persecution. By virtue of their office, and without waiting for accusations, the authorities throughout the whole empire were to step in and require the Christians to sacrifice to the emperor's image. It was a frightful period, and demanded numberless martyrs. Even the death of Decius brought only temporary relief. Under his successor Gallus,

(251–253), after two years of peace, new measures against the 'Christians were employed (253). But above all was it Valerian (253–260) who again took in hand the work of Decius (257). He commanded that all bishops, priests, deacons, Christian senators, and judges, so far as they did not recant, should be executed. There came to be method in the attack. No longer was it the plan, as under Decius, to destroy the whole body of Christians, for this was found to be impracticable; but the organization of the Church must be annihilated, with all the families of the more influential classes in the Church. The formless, uneducated mass which might remain would be unable, so it was hoped, to maintain Christianity. As victims of this persecution Cyprian, bishop of Carthage, and in Rome the deacon Laurentius (the St. Laurence of the Roman Catholic Church) fell,* and with them many others. But among the first measures of the reign of Gallienus, who ruled as sole monarch after the death of his father, Valerian, belongs the abrogation of the edict of persecution (260, 261). Not that the Christian religion had now obtained legal recognition and tolerance; rather was it true that even under Gallienus and his successors the Christian profession was punishable with death; and it was liable to be so punished whenever the refusal to worship the image of the emperor was officially fixed upon any one; for example, upon a Christian

---

* Compare ₹ 18.

soldier. But the direction to the authorities, which had necessitated them to seek out the professors of Christianity, and ascertain the fact of a refusal by legal process, was no longer in force. A condition of actual tolerance, with only occasional exceptions, was brought about. A period of rest, which continued forty years, entered in. It was the stillness before the storm. Under Diocletian (284–305) the Roman Empire roused itself once more against the hated enemy, in order to bring back the old undivided authority of the State in all its splendor. It was the severest persecution the Church had yet seen. It was a struggle for life and death. Toward the end of his reign, after he had permitted the Christians to live in peace under his sway for eighteen years, Diocletian allowed himself to be persuaded to an attack upon the Church by his son-in-law, Galerius, a brave, stern, but uneducated soldier, and fanatical enemy of the Christians.

Nicomedia was the residence of the emperor. The destruction of the Church in Nicomedia (on the 23d of February, 303,) was the signal for the attack. On the following day the edict appeared. All Christian officers were to be dismissed from the army, and all Christian civil office-holders from the service. All Christian churches were to be destroyed, and all the sacred books of the Christians were to be delivered up and burned. A second edict followed, according to which the clergy of all ranks were to be cast into prison in order to com-

pel them to offer.   A third edict (304) commanded
even private Christians to offer under penalty of
death.   The most comprehensive plans were
adopted to carry out these edicts.   But in vain.
In 305, seized by a deadly ailment, Diocletian laid
down the imperial crown.   Galerius now proceeded
in the execution of his plans unhindered.   At this
instant began the bloody persecution in the Orient.
A senseless slaughter was begun.   Whatever the
means, the Christians must be compelled to offer.
Even the food in the markets was sprinkled with
wine dedicated to sacrifice, in order in this way to
necessitate the Christians to submit or starve.   A
tremendous excitement spread throughout the empire.   Here and there, indeed, there was active rebellion.   After four long, anxious, frightful years
(306–310), Galerius, severely ill, recognized that
he would be compelled to retreat.   On the 30th of
April, 311, on his death-bed, he issued a universal
edict of tolerance.   He was obliged to confess that
the Christians had conquered.   Constantine,[22] the
son of Constantius Chlorus, Cæsar in the Occident,
completed the work.   After he had conquered the
usurper Maxentius, and taken Italy from him, by
the sign of the cross, he issued from Rome, in 312,
his edict of tolerance for the Western Empire; and
from Milan, in 313, in conjunction with Licinius,
another for East and West alike.   Christianity was
placed on an equality with heathenism in the eyes
of the State.   Every one should have " freedom to

choose and worship a deity as he would." Freedom to hold public worship was granted to the
Christians of the whole empire. The time of trial
had been met and borne. The Church breathed
afresh. A dark night was followed by the bright,
clear light of day.

§ 7. The Church and Her Victory.*

To what power must Christianity ascribe its
victory? Was it the faithful perseverance or the
heroic courage of its professors? By no means.
As in the time of Pliny, in the beginning of the
second century, so in the Decian, and if possible,
still more in the Diocletian, persecution, the defection of the Christians was enormous. That is a
false picture which represents the Christians of the
first three centuries as being, one and all, types of
willing martyrdom whose memory the Church has
rightly glorified. The masses of the Christians
were then, as at all times, cowardly, of little faith,
weak in confession before men, and incapable of opposition in the midst of danger. When persecution
came, how many were ready to abjure this faith in
order to save property, position, or life! The
Church had already grown large. As the mass of
Church members grew, the inner strength of the
Church declined. The Church no longer expected the immediate end of the world. She estab-

---

* Many of the statements of this section need qualification.
Compare §§ 17, 18.

lished herself in this world; but not without, at the same time, receiving something of the world into herself. She opened her doors wide, a:d with the multitudes all that was ignoble and weak in human nature found unhindered entrance. It is evident that the mutual relations of the members of the Church were different in the first decades, when a more limited circle united as brothers, from those of a later period, when the half of the people had accepted Christianity. That brotherly love which showed itself in works disappeared. It was handed over to the clergy. Church discipline became constantly weaker and more negligent. A double morality arose—one for the clergy, from whom the full energy of the Christian life was still demanded; another for the laity, for whom in general it was enough if they refrained from the coarser offenses. From the middle of the second century forward a constant secularization of the Church was in progress. The world received of the spirit of Christianity; but, in return, Christianity partook of the spirit of the world. If we look at the masses of the believers in the third century, or even at many of the best of them, how much nominal Christianity, how much falsehood, hate, enmity, envy, ambition, and worldly desire, is visible in the Church! As early as the middle of the second century a Roman Christian saw in spirit the picture of a Church full of wrinkles, blemishes, and weakness. When the Roman State, of the times of Decius and

Diocletian, proposed itself to wage a war of destruction against Christianity, it saw itself opposed by a Church from which the spirit of the first witnesses had departed—a Church which had become worldly, and which had fallen from its ideal. Hence the many apostasies, hence the fearful desolation, which, especially in the last great persecutions, broke upon the Church.

And yet the Church was unconquerable. That is just the wonder—that Christianity could not be destroyed; and that, on the contrary, it conquered, notwithstanding it was so miserably represented by many of its professors. Not even so many denials, nor so many weaknesses and sins, were able to overcome the indestructible power of Christianity. Christianity had become conformed to the world, and yet it remained the leaven which was able to leaven the whole world. It was betrayed by a large number of its adherents, and yet the spirit remained in it by which a little company of the faithful were able to overcome the world, and even to awaken, by its examples of martyrdom, the power of opposition in the ranks of the lukewarm, the hesitating, and the cowardly. Christianity was no longer that unknown religion concerning which, as in the first and second centuries, the most abominable and lying reports were circulated. The spirit of Christianity had become visible, and it spread its protecting wings over its professors. In wide sections of heathenism the true God of the Christians

met a monotheistic hope which lifted itself in power
out of the ruins of the old worship. When, therefore, the State opened the campaign against the
Church of the third century, it no longer found the
old popular hate of the masses on its side. Numerous Christians found shelter in the houses of the
heathen, and the execution of the edicts of persecution, issued by Diocletian and Gallerius, was, in the
Occident, impossible. The State had the convictions of the very best people of the period against
it, as well as the spiritual might with which Christianity worked upon those outside of its pale, as soon
as its operation was really understood. And this
spiritual might found expression, and unfolded its
full energy, notwithstanding the weaknesses of its
adherents. Through all the shadows and darkness
observable in the history of the Church there broke
at all times the inextinguishable light of true Christianity. There was enough good grain among the
tares to exhibit the striking contrast. The light,
where it did shine, appeared all the brighter. And
God had established his Church in the world, not
to be conquered, but to conquer. The power of the
gospel, which is the power of God, could not be
hindered, though it might be delayed, in its progress,
either by defections and sins within, or by foes
without the Church.

3

SECOND DIVISION.

INNER DEVELOPMENT.

§ 8. Jewish Christianity.

The persecutions which attacked the Church from without, constituted her slightest dangers; far more ominous was the fact that forces with which the Church had to fight found entrance to her own bosom, and then threatened to deteriorate her faith, and therewith to weaken, if not destroy, her power.

This was the case first of all with Judaism, and afterward with heathenism. Pharisaic influences were not long in making themselves perceptible in the youthful Church. Not every Pharisee, in passing over to Christianity, met with the change which so completely transformed the apostle Paul. Hence there arose a Pharisaic tendency in the Church, known as Jewish Christianity, whose object was to Judaize Christianity. The Pharisaic Christians believed that Jesus, the Crucified, was the Messiah, but asserted that salvation through him was only for the Jews. Whoever would become a Christian must first become a Jew by circumcision, and take upon himself the whole burden of the Mosaic law. Such a Christianity was simply a renewed form of Judaism. A universal religion was to be transformed into a national religion. Jewish Christianity stood in open contradiction to the words of our Lord, who had repeatedly called the heathen, as well as the Jews, into immediate membership in his kingdom. (See, *e. g.*, Matt. xxii, 43; Luke xiii, 29, 30.) As plainly did it stand in contradiction to the Christianity of the original Church. What had inflamed the hate of the Pharisees to the point of persecution but the fact that Christianity, from the first, preached the dissolution of the temple-service and the doing away with the Pharisaic conception of the Jewish law? (Acts vi, 14.) What was it which had filled Saul with holy indignation but zeal for the law of the fathers? (Gal. i, 14.) And was there not in Antioch, as a result of the missionary zeal of the earliest years of Christianity, a congregation of heathen Christians who had received Christianity without circumcision and without the observances of the Jewish law? (Acts xi, 20; xv, 1.)

Heathen Christianity was not created by the apostle Paul. Yet he defended it, and by his efforts it found a broad acceptance. His contest was not directed against the original apostles; on the contrary, they gave him the hand of brotherly recognition. (Gal. ii, 9.) His conflict was with the "false brethren," who had "come in privily," and who formed a later element in the Church. (Gal. ii, 4.) As the water of a river partakes of the color of the bed over which it flows, so Christianity was tinctured with the characteristics of the peoples who accepted it. And the first people upon whom Christianity wrought—indeed, from whom it went forth—were the Jews. How reasonable, then, to expect that Judaism would exercise an influence upon Christianity! Out of this influence, and representing a modification of the first form of Christianity, the narrow-hearted Jewish Christianity had sprung. It contained sufficient energy to cause the original apostles at least to hesitate. All the natural instincts of national Judaism came to its assistance. Nevertheless the apostles Peter and John, and even James, who was so favorable to the observance of the law, gave Paul the right hand of fellowship in recognition of his gospel—the gospel set free from the burden of legal observances which he preached to the heathen. Opinions as to whether the Jewish law was obligatory upon converted Jews were divided. James took the affirmative, while Peter, at least temporarily, hesitated. (Gal. ii, 11, 12.) The negative answer lay in the character of the first form of Christianity and hence it won in the Church. A sort of treaty was concluded between Paul and the other apostles; he was to preach the gospel to the heathen, they to the Jews. (Gal. ii, 9.) The division of missionary territory pointed to opposing convictions as to the validity of the Jewish law for Judaism. Notwithstanding, this opposition must have been of short duration in leading circles. In the very next period of the Church's history no trace of a division of missionary territory is observable. On the contrary, even if Peter was not in Rome, according to tradition, it is exceedingly probable that he at least appeared in Corinth, where the Church had been founded by Paul (1 Cor. i, 12), and the apostle John lived and labored in Asia Minor, and especially in Ephesus. In spite of the manifold differences of opinion which, for example, produced during the life-time of the apostle Paul no less than four parties in the Corinthian Church (1 Cor. i, 12), from the very beginning the mighty stream, in its onward movement, had been harmonious. As early after the close of the first century as we are able to trace the life, not only of prominent individual personalities, but as well of the Church as a whole, we find a Christianity free from the Jewish law ruling the entire Church. Yet it by no means bears such peculiar marks of Paulinism as to suggest that it was the work of the apostle Paul alone. The incidental fact that the epistles of Paul hold so prominent a place in the canon of Scripture might easily lead to an erroneous overestimate of the influence of Paul in the molding of Christianity. Church history shows that the ruling power in Christianity from the beginning was neither Jewish Christianity nor a Christianity with an individual Pauline coloring. These were merely antitheses which, along with others, arose in the Church. Powerfully as Paul labored as an instrument in the hands of God to assert victoriously the universality of Christianity, and to turn the relation of Christians of all nations to God into one of sonship, rather than one of slavery to the Jewish law, we have not Paul, but a greater than he, even our Lord Jesus Christ, the Son of Man and the Son of God, to thank for the blessings of the gospel as it has been handed down to us from the early Christian fathers.

§ 9. HEATHEN CHRISTIANITY.

From Palestine Christianity went forth to conquer the Græco-Roman world. If in the first period the influence of national Judaism made itself manifest, in that which followed the life-vigor of heathen ideas proved themselves operative also. In the second century Christianity flowed far and wide over heathen soils. Hence the mighty uprising of Gnosticism, which represents both the operation of Christianity upon heathenism and the operation of heathenism upon Christianity. The heathen religion was the outcome of the ancient natural religion, or religion of nature. Heaven and earth, and all the powers which they contained within them, had been transformed by poetic fancy into the forms of gods, in which man worshiped at once nature and his own ideal. The memory of its historical origin was never fully lost to heathenism. This was preserved in the mysteries.* Here, in the mysteries, in the circle of the chosen few, the memory of the ancient sacred worship of both the dark and the joyous powers of nature was firmly adhered to, while the faith in the more easily com-

---

* See Note 6 to page 10.

prehended gods of human creation was left to the masses. Here also a series of thoughts of deeper moral significance could be preserved, which in the popular religion could only be expressed in material figures, such as idols and images. In contrast with the depth and wisdom of the mysteries, the religion of the masses appeared as mere allegory. The initiated saw and looked upon the unveiled Truth herself; the masses saw but the hem of her garment.

From heathenism the mysteries found their way into Christianity. In this consisted Gnosticism. *Gnosis* means knowledge. Gnosticism promised its adherents the knowledge of that which was really truth in Christianity. It sought the secret (mystery) which hid itself in Christianity as in the heathen religions. Such a conception of Christianity weakened the distinction between it and the religion of the heathen. Even in Christianity the truth was supposed to lie behind the facts with which the common faith contented itself. And this truth was to be discovered by the Gnostic through his philosophy, which was compounded of traces of the old natural religion, heathen mythology, and facts of Christian faith. The key-note which runs through the most prominent of the Gnostic systems is the philosophical idea of the opposition between spirit and matter, and the prominent thought in the old heathen religion of nature, of the opposition between light and darkness.

God is the light-god, who brings forth a series of light-spirits (*æons*), each standing higher in order than the other. Matter, chaos, with the lower spirits of darkness, stand in opposition to him. The world was created out of matter by one of these lower spirits (the Demiurge), a wicked being. Hence the imperfection of this world, and evil, whose seat is in matter. Gnosticism anticipated modern pessimism :[23] the worst possible world had been created. But Christ was the light-æon (or spirit), who, by assuming a body of matter, overcomes the kingdom of darkness. In Gnosticism we see the monotheistically directed philosophy of the Roman Empire making its first splendid attempt to conquer the world which then existed. It gave eloquent expression to the felt need of revelation and redemption, and to the desire for the one true God, among the educated classes. It indicates, at the same time, the attitude of power which Christianity had assumed for the spiritual life of the people of the empire during the second century. These philosophers gave to Christianity the first place in order by the help of the saving facts which were believed, preached, and defended by the Christian Church, to win that which above all was desired; namely, the certainty that there really is a God, and that over this imperfect terrestrial kingdom rises a higher one, which the spiritual man can win, if by the power of knowledge (*gnosis*) he frees himself from the dark power of matter. But the

Christian faith was to Gnosticism merely a means by which to win the conviction of the truth of the *philosophical* faith. In order to this, the historical facts upon which the Christian faith was founded must be allegorically accepted. But in the same moment in which that which was historical was treated as mere symbol, the convincing power which lay in the facts as such was irrecoverably destroyed. Gnosticism was philosophy, although joined to Christianity, and shared the common fate of all mere philosophy by ending at last in doubt and uncertainty. In a certain sense, Gnosticism was the rationalism of the second century. It set in place of Christianity a philosophical religion presumed to be clearer to the understanding, but which was founded upon the supposed knowledge of the coherence and powers of the world, upon traditions of heathenism, ideas of ancient philosophy, and the old heathen worship of heaven and earth. The god of the Gnostics was the "abyss," the "silence," the "non-existent," the "incomprehensible," and the "unapproachable." The living God of Christianity was to be changed back into the unknown god of the philosophers and of the mysteries.

The Church perceived that here, in spite of all its professed friendliness, was a power which in its last analysis was inimical to her welfare. The Church was conscious that her power lay in the fact that her faith was not philosophy, and that the moral life which made individual Christians appear as the "true philosophers" did not rest upon the knowledge or recognition of philosophical ideas, but upon the experience of the divine love, which had been made manifest in Jesus Christ.

In the Gnostic philosophy the Church was brought face to face with the mightiest power of the period. If we take into consideration that Gnosticism satisfied the common masses by mysterious customs and ceremonies, the whole heathen world by the charm of its perpetuation of the ancient mysteries, its promise to satisfy both mind and heart, and its harmony with traditionary views; and at the same time satisfied the better disposed by a severe morality, firmly held by most of the Gnostic systems,—we can understand the danger which threatened the Church from this source. The whole of the second, and even of the third, century was taken up with the struggle of the Church against Gnosticism. The struggle meant the saving of the simple truths of salvation believed by the Church from the results of an allegorizing heathen speculation. Gnosticism was the treaty of peace which the culture of the second century offered to Christianity. Had Christianity accepted the offer, it would have gone to pieces with the civilization of the period. From such a result it was necessary to preserve the Church. But the victory was won with terrible inner conflicts, the significance of which we see in the consequences which they had for the Church. In the struggle with Gnosticism was finally fixed the canon of New Testament Scripture; that is, the books which the Church recognized as authoritative witnesses of Christian truth in contradistinction from Gnostic error. In this conflict also was formed the Christian theology, and at the same time the future constitution and government of the Church. The Church asserted itself not only against the heathen State, but also against the far more dangerous foes of heathen philosophy and the doctrines of the mysteries; but she did not come forth as the same institution which entered the struggle. While it was repelling the assaults of Gnosticism, Christianity transformed itself from the original form of its first epoch into the Catholicism of the second.

§ 10. The Constitution of the Church, and Catholicism.

The development of the Church and her constitution proceeded from the unity of the believers in Christ—the unity of a great brotherhood. We call this entirety of all Christians the Church. The early Christians called it *ecclesia*, that is, people of God. To them Christendom[24] was the chosen people of God under the new covenant. The presence of Christ in their midst, and therewith the presence of God, was promised to this people. In the *ecclesia* each individual Christian enjoyed full fellowship with God in Christ, and therewith the fullness of the gifts of divine grace. The Christian must be a member of the *ecclesia*, the Church. Hence the question, Where is the Church, and what constitutes it?

The apostolic period replied, Where two or three are gathered together in the name of Christ, there is the *ecclesia*, the Church—since Christ had said: "Where two or three are gathered together in my name, there am I in the midst of them." (Matt. xviii, 20.) The Lord was risen and was alive for evermore. That was the victorious faith of Christianity. The Lord was in the midst of his believers in divine omnipresence—He who is, and was, and is to come, the Almighty. Hence he was, and lived, and worked, wherever two or three were assembled in his name. Where Christ was, there was the Church. It was the Church which was gathered and which acted in every assembly of believers. No human priesthood was needed. In each assembly of believers existed the right of baptism, and of administration of the Lord's Supper. There was the perfect communion with Christ, the only High Priest and Mediator between God and the believer.

A formal organization of the Church, binding upon all Christians, was unknown. The Church confided in the power of the Spirit, who raised up men from her midst, to whom God intrusted the gracious gifts (charisma) of proclaiming divine truth, together with the control of the congregation.

In the apostles the word of God was living, not only
for purposes of edification, but as well for the direction of the Church; and equally so in other spiritually gifted men, as the "prophets" and "teachers."
But from the beginning the number of such men
among the Christians was none too great. Where
men·thus specially distinguished of God were entirely wanting, the "elders" (presbyters), Christians
already matured and approved, came forward of their
own accord as heads of the congregation. These
"elders" were not always the eldest in years; they
were sometimes "elders" by reason of earlier
entrance into the Church, or because of a higher
development or strength of personality. In these
"elders" the Christian charism, the gift of grace,
was operative, a gift common to all true, genuine,
adult Christians. They placed themselves in the
service of the congregation, as, for example, Steph-
anas and his house in Corinth, the "first-fruits of
Achaia." (1 Cor. xvi, 15.) Because of their
activity in leading, superintending, and admonish-
ing the congregation, they received the honorary
title of "bishop;" that is, overseer, minister, pastor
(shepherd). Not every "elder" was a bishop; but
in the eldership lay the call to be, if necessary, a
bishop, pastor, minister, to the brethren. The
bishops were those elders who labored in the
Church with a real superintending, ministerial
activity. They were a selection from among the
elders, and the title elder was bestowed upon them

in a special sense. These presbyters, in the narrower sense, those who exercised the office of elder in the Church, are identical with the bishops of the apostolic period. There was therefore, as a rule, more than one bishop of a congregation. All the elders, or presbyters, who labored as ministers in the congregation were its bishops. (Comp. *e. g.* Phil. i, 1.)

Thus at the head of the Church was an office; but an office not provided by men, nor by the Church, but by God through the *charisma*, and which manifested itself variously in the apostles, prophets, teachers, and bishops or elders. None of these men had any formal, constitutional commission. It was their work which entitled them to their office and to the loving obedience of the congregation. (1 Thess. v, 13; 1 Cor. xiii.) There was a selection in the Church assembly, which was followed by the laying on of hands and prayer for those selected, an election to the office of apostle (Acts xiii, 2, 3), evangelist (2 Tim. iv, 5; comp. 1 Tim. iv, 14; vi, 12; 2 Tim. i, 6; ii, 2), elder (*e. g.* Acts xiv, 23). But as little as the choice of the congregation constituted one an apostle, so little did it constitute those chosen elders or bishops. It was God who gave apostles, prophets, teachers, and also bishops of the Churches (1 Cor. xii, 28; Eph. iv, 11; Acts xx, 28), and the choice of the Church was merely the recognition of the choice of God. The choice by the congregation had not the signif-

icance of a formally valid, constitutional commission. Such a choice was neither necessary nor
sufficient to constitute an apostle, an evangelist, or
a bishop. The ministry of the apostolic period was
a product of divine power, which was and is
operative in the true Churches of Christ. It was
not the constitutional officiary of the Church.
Notwithstanding the ministry, the Church was not
constitutionally organized.

Hence the ministry had no exclusive right to
perform spiritual functions. In each assembly of
believers was Christ the Lord, and hence the Church.
Therefore in every assembly of believers existed
the authority, conferred by Christ, to baptize and
to administer the Lord's Supper. According to the
conviction of the apostolic Christians the presence
and co-operation of the ministry was unnecessary
to the existence and functions of the Church.
Even where no apostle, or prophet, or teacher, or
bishop was present, baptism could be validly administered and the Lord's Supper celebrated. The
ministry was, indeed, the usual medium by which
the functions of the Church were discharged; as a
rule, a bishop of the congregation would baptize or
conduct the celebration of the Lord's Supper. But
the ministry did not possess the authority of the
Church. That authority existed in every assembly
of believers. As every Christian could preach the
Word in the assemblies of the Church, so every
Christian could validly baptize and conduct the

Lord's Supper. In this equal right to perform churchly functions consisted the truly apostolical Christian doctrine of the universal priesthood of believers.

During the second century a change took place. What was an actual practice, the exercise of churchly functions by the ministry, came to be a constitutional provision and right. All the more because confidence in the free operation of the *charisma* decreased, and the need of order in the growing Church became constantly stronger. Not seldom was it necessary to protect the congregations against swindlers who traveled about in the guise of "prophets" and stirred the benevolent activity of the brethren into motion in their own interest. Election by the congregation won legal significance. But one was now chosen with authority to perform the functions of the Church. To him, in consequence, was given the name bishop in a special sense. He was now *the* bishop of the congregation, *the* minister, teacher, preacher, superior to the others. Now, in the second century, for the first time, there was constitutionally *one* bishop of Rome, *one* bishop of Corinth, etc. The Church assumed the monarchical form of government. The other elders of the congregation took a subordinate relation to the one bishop chosen by the congregation.

This one bishop—and that is the most important—had now, as the one called of God through the congregation, the exclusive right to act as the organ of the Church, through whom alone the Church could act, and hence came to be regarded as necessary to the existence and functions of the Church. To him belonged first the right to speak in the assemblies of the Church, and only with his consent to others; and so was it also with regard to the performance of the rite of baptism and the administration of the Lord's Supper. Without the bishop, or his authorized representative, the sacraments could not be administered; no one could be consecrated to an ecclesiastical office; nothing could be done to which the authority of the Church was necessary. Only where the bishop was, was the Church. The bishop alone possessed the capability of exercising ecclesiastical functions. The universal priesthood of believers, in the apostolic sense, had passed away. As assistants and representatives the bishop had the presbyters (elders) under him. Thus the presbyters partook of a share, although limited, of the priestly character of the bishop. In the plan of the universal priesthood of all believers there had grown up a special priesthood of a priestly order, the order of bishop and of presbyter.

The Church was now no longer represented in every assembly of believers, but only in an assembly where the special priesthood was present. Christ was no longer believed to be present everywhere with an assembly of two or three in his name, but only when the bishop was with the elders. In order to have full fellowship with God, and to

4

receive the valid sacraments, the Christian now needed fellowship with the priesthood.

Besides this change in the constitution of the Church, there was a change in belief also. Personal communion with Christ is the secret and the power of the Christian life. This communion with Christ and the Father was now made dependent upon external forms and conditions. In this consists the nature of Roman Catholicism. Adherence to the external organism, which was represented by the bishops and elders, was the new law which was laid upon each individual Christian. The Church was no longer the communion of believers, but was built upon an office which was now necessary to constitute the congregations members of Christ. The Church, the body of Christ, had now a formal episcopal constitution, and to this formal, visible Church it was necessary to belong in order to belong to Christ. The Catholic conception of the Church had appeared; the foundation of the later Roman Catholicism was laid.

This stupendous alteration was brought about during the struggle of the Church with error. There were the Gnostics, who claimed to possess the real truth of the gospel. Where was the authority which could defend the genuine truth against them? The canon of the New Testament was yet undetermined; a Christian theology had not yet been produced. The only power which could successfully withstand the encroachments of Gnosticism was the living tradition of the Church. But where was the true Church? The Gnostics, too, claimed to be the true Church. The only resource was to fall back upon an ecclesiastical authority. The doctrine of apostolic succession was brought into requisition. The bishop was believed to stand in the line of unbroken succession from the apostolic time. It was believed that the first bishops had received their office and their doctrine from the apostles; and that the office and doctrine of the bishops was in turn handed down to their successors; hence, where the bishop was, the true Church and the genuine apostolic tradition were to be found. The Gnostic heresy was not destroyed by any proof of its falsehood, nor by the strength of a true theology, but by means of the natural respect which the officers of the Church attracted to themselves. The bishop was the only one whose charismatic gifts[25] and divine call to the administration of the ministerial office had been formally recognized by the choice of the congregation, and whose authority was thereby raised above doubt. The original free exercise of the ministry was made to serve the errors of Gnosticism, but it was driven from the field by a ministry which had the advantage of formal recognition by the Church. The bishop, as the one endued by the Spirit with the true knowledge (*gnosis*), and as the teacher of the congregation according to the true apostolic doctrine, was able to overcome the Gnostic philosophy; and as the episcopacy had de-

fended (though it had also altered) the faith of the
Church, authority over the Church fell to it as the
reward of its victory.

At the same time, with Gnosticism, the episcopal
office had another enemy, Montanism, to drive from
the field.   About the middle of the second century
Montanus appeared in Phrygia as a Christian
prophet, announcing a new revelation of the Holy
Spirit.   The second coming of the Lord was near.
At Pepuza, in Phrygia, the New Jerusalem, the
place of assembly for all Christianity, was to be
found.   All formal constitutions of the Christian
Church were worthless.   It was sufficient to prepare
a Church of the holy,—the pure, spotless bride of
the Lord.   In opposition to the Church, which
had already established itself contentedly in the
midst of this temporal world, burned once more the
fire of old Christian hope of the near end of the
world.   With this was united an enthusiastic renunciation of everything earthly.   Far and near, the
new prophet was received with the greatest enthusiasm.   Had the movement been victorious, Christianity would have been transformed into a little
flock of ascetics,* with their backs turned to the
world of sinners; and the mighty progress of the
conquest of the world for Christ would have been
brought to a stand.   For this was the spirit of Montanism, however much of good might be recognized
in it.   The first point of attack was the episcopal

* See Note 35 to p. 81.

office. The authority of the bishops was denied by the Montanists; only the prophet, as the immediate organ of the divine revelation—not the bishop, the mere bearer of an office—could have authority to receive back again into the congregation of the holy those who had fallen into mortal sin. In Montanism, also, the old Christian order of Church government, which had recognized no privileged office, was set in opposition to the power of the episcopacy. But the episcopal form of government had already struck its roots too deeply into the convictions of the Church to be thus overcome. The priesthood of the bishop, resting upon its power over the being and functions of the Church, and especially upon its power in the eucharistic feast,[26] won the victory over Montanism. The result was the complete triumph, by the beginning of the third century, of the authority of the episcopal office, and the establishment of the principle that the bishop alone has the power to exercise the office of the ministry, and the right to bind and to loose (the power of the keys) in his congregation. The apostolical Church had been transformed into the Catholic Episcopal Church.

The episcopal constitution was the armor which enabled the Church to withstand the stormy attacks of the approaching period. If the Christian faith lost in the purity of its contents, the Church gained by strength of external organization. The Church was preparing to conquer the world for itself. She organized herself in the monarchical constitution according to the pattern of the world. Over the growing mass of believers she set a visible and efficient governing head. By her episcopal form of government she was able to lead, guide, and correct the movements of the hesitating masses, and thus to overcome. The Constitution of the Church received its power to perpetuate itself directly through the fact that the position of the bishop came to be regarded, not only as a right in custom and law, but also as an object of faith. Only in the belief that the bishop alone was the divinely called teacher and pastor of the congregation, that alone where the bishop is the Church is, and that only in communion with the bishop one can have communion with Christ, lay the power which gave the Church[27] her victory over the world, and produced the papacy of the Middle Ages. The original, genuine apostolic conception of the Church passed away, that the external rule of the Church might be established. Only after long centuries, when the Roman Catholic conception of the Church had fulfilled its historical mission in the world, could the true conception of the Church and the universal priesthood of believers be established through the Reformation. Perhaps only after such an experience, under the providence of God, could a true Christianity and an enlightened Church be again produced, whose might is not in external power, but alone in the energy of the divine truth and the

Holy Spirit. Like the prodigal son, the Church could only come to itself when it contested its own want with the plenty freely offered in the Father's house.

THIRD DIVISION.

THE CHURCH ESTABLISHED.

§ 11. STATE AND CHURCH.

IN the year 313, Constantine, comprehending with the vision of a statesman the requirements of his day, had given the Church recognition and freedom. At the same time he restored her property, and bestowed upon her numerous privileges. Heathenism he left as yet untouched. It was subsequent to his time that heathenism was first persecuted. He even remained high-priest of the heathen worship, although he accepted the Christian faith as a catechumen,* and, having received proper preparatory instruction, was baptized in the year of his death (337). Heathenism still stood out mightily against Christianity, and that not alone because the majority of the population of the empire was still heathen in the beginning of the fourth century. On the basis of heathenism a new power had grown up. It was Neo-Platonism,† which, springing out of the third century, turned the old heathen religion into philosophy by a distortion of its myths,

---

* See Note 43 to p. 94. † See Note 8 to p. 11.

and philosophy into religion by giving to the myths a fundamental position. It was a *renaissance* of heathenism, which united mysticism and speculation, and which lent it in many circles, especially among the educated, a new splendor. The greatest result of Neo-Platonism was that it led the Emperor Julian to turn away from Christianity to the heathen gods. Julian the Apostate (361–363) once again presented the spectacle of a Roman emperor as a believer in heathenism, following the religious ideals of the heathen fathers. He undertook to oppose heathenism to Christianity; but it was the heathenism of the educated classes, restored, as one might say, in imitation of Christianity, emphasizing morality and practicing benevolence. But he did not persecute Christianity. He limited himself to securing to all creeds their freedom. It was the last hope of heathenism; but it too was vain. The inner power of heathenism had departed. Even Neo-Platonism was unable to restore to it the living power of religion. Under the succeeding emperors Christianity was again established as the recognized religion of the State. Heathenism was unable to offer any effective opposition. Christianity was the religion of the future. In the course of the fifth century heathenism disappeared as an element in the civilization of the empire. The empire had become Christian; the Church had conquered. Out of a forbidden, persecuted society she had been transformed into the mighty, all-commanding established Church, supported by the power of the State.

What a triumph! But in the very triumph lay hidden danger. Not only that now, along with freedom, honor, and authority, the desire for place and for wealth entered the Church; but chiefly because the State maintained certain claims on the Church. No longer an enemy, the State had become an ally. But, as a reward, it demanded rulership in the Church. The ancient State was not accustomed to tolerate any other might along-side of its own. The Roman emperor looked upon it as his right to fill personally the highest office in the official worship. What he had possessed in the heathen religion he was inclined also to demand of Christianity. The Church had grown up in conflict with the State. She had been able to assert herself against its almost omnipotent power. The State had been obliged to yield. But now that it had recognized her, and granted her so many privileges and so much wealth, it demanded all the more the right of control. The friendship of the empire threatened to be more dangerous than its enmity. In the embrace of the emperors the ecclesiastical spirit was in danger of being smothered. The legislation of the Church, the calling of the general councils, and the confirmation of their decisions, the filling of the most important episcopal chairs, the highest jurisdiction in ecclesiastical courts, a deciding influence in the doctrinal disputes raging in the Church—in a word, the highest authority in the Church—was claimed by the Roman emperor as his natural right, and, in the main, with effect. All the struggles of the first three centuries appeared vain, if now, at last, the Church was to be degraded to the position of an involuntary servant of the Byzantine emperor.[28]

One thing, however, the Church had won which remained secure. She was able, under the protection of the State, to give to her constitutional organism, over the whole broad circumference of the empire, a harmonious, united form which should control with authority the whole being of the Church. Catholicism could now unfold itself in molding the Church into a constitutional form. In the main, the ecclesiastical constitution was patterned after that of the empire. The town was the lowest administrative unit of the empire. It became the fundamental administrative unit also for the Church. It appeared in the Church constitution as the diocese of the bishop, his diocese being limited at first, like his episcopate, to his own city or town. Above the town, in the imperial constitution, stood the province, with the provincial governor. The episcopal dioceses of the imperial province were united, accordingly, into the ecclesiastical province, under the authority of the metropolitan; that is, the bishop of the chief city of the province. After the fourth century several provinces came to be joined together into an imperial diocese, under the imperial constitution, with an imperial governor (vicar) at its head. This imperial diocese appeared again, at least in the Greek Oriental Church, as a part of the Church constitution, and formed the domain of the patriarch, to whom the metropolitans of the provinces were subject. To the entire empire corresponded again the entire Church, whose legitimate organ was the Imperial Council, the so-called Ecumenical Council. The Church of the empire was an externally visible, harmonious, imposing representation of the Christianity of the whole world.

It was its last great legacy to the future that the already decaying Roman Empire handed its form of constitution over to the Church, which was striving upward with new power. In the form of the Church constitution, the imperial constitution outlived the fall of the empire. Even to-day the diocese of the Roman Catholic bishop is the copy of the old Roman town, the province of the archbishop the copy of the old Roman imperial province, and the whole Roman Catholic Church, under the unlimited control of the pope, the copy of the old Roman empire, with its emperor, who demanded control of the whole world. In stamping itself upon the body of the Church, the ancient, powerful, wide-reaching imperial constitution perpetuated itself, and gave to the Church its organizing power. In a world-comprehending organization the imperial Church could display with imposing effect her unity.   Was she able to save her inner freedom and her faith?

§ 12. The Council of Nice.

Ever since the close of the second century, the Synods—that is, the assemblies of the bishops of several congregations—had taken control of the development of the Church.   The provincial Synods had become the usual organ of the Church; and these, since the beginning of the fourth century, had been called and led by the metropolitan. Thus these Synods formed the basis of the power of the metropolitan over the province.   When greater and more difficult questions were to be solved, it was customary to call larger Synods.   Now, after the recognition of the Church by the empire, it was possible to have an Imperial Synod, or, as it was later called, an Ecumenical Council.   Such a Council was composed of bishops from all parts of the empire, in a sense a parliament of the whole Church, an assembly which effectually represented the unity of the Church.

A few years after Constantine had recognized Christianity, he called (325) the first Imperial Council, the first of those afterward recognized as ecumenical, and which were supposed to represent the whole Church.   It was the famous Council of Nice. The moving cause for the calling of the Council was the great doctrinal dispute which was agitating the Church.

From the very beginning the question, What think ye of Christ? took first rank in Christianity. Is he only David's son, a mere man, or is he not rather David's Lord, the true God, the Lord of hosts? (Matt. xxii, 42–46.) The secret of the divinity of Christ was the first and the greatest problem for the Christian educated mind. It included in itself the secret of the Church. The Church is not only the work of Christ, but the body of Christ. She had him himself, the Risen One— him who sitteth at the right hand of God, in the midst of her assemblies. As the nature of Christ, so is the nature and dignity of his Church. In reflecting concerning Christ, the Church also reflected concerning itself. From the Pauline and Johannine writings, on through the centuries, the creed of the Church had been that the Lord Jesus Christ is "the first and the last" (Rev. i, 17), the "beginning of the creation" (Rev. iii, 14), "the Word of God," by whom God had created the world (1 Cor. viii, 6). He was living and operating in divine glory before the foundations of the earth were yet laid (1 Cor. x, 4; Phil. ii, 6–8). In this sense he was the Son of God, and at the same time God himself (John i, 1, 14). The difficulty for human thought which lay therein—that the Son of God, who had become man, and had taken upon him the form of a servant (Phil. ii, 7), should be distinguished from God, and yet made equal with God—must be expressed, and at the same time solved.

Christian theology, whose fundamental outlines were then determined, grew to the height of this difficulty during the second and third centuries.

Was Jesus Christ a mere man, although distinguished by his gifts, power to work miracles, and by his righteousness? Then the difficulty does not exist. There were those who favored this solution, although they never played an important part in the Church. In the beginning of the third century, when this view was advanced in Rome, it was expressly rejected and pronounced heretical by the Church. Paul, bishop of Antioch, who adopted this faith about the middle of the third century, found it necessary to veil his opinions from his congregation by the use of orthodox forms of speech. Nevertheless, on account of his doctrine, he was deposed and excommunicated by a great Oriental Council. The universal presupposition of theological thinking was the divinity of Christ. But God is one. Hence some inferred that God the Father was made flesh in Jesus Christ, and suffered on the cross; that God the Father, God the Son, and God the Holy Ghost represented only different and temporary revealed manifestations of this one God. These are known as Monarchians. In reality they gave up the distinction between the Son and the Father, since the Son was merely God the Father come in the flesh. Others saw in the Divine Being who appeared in Christ a spiritual nature, created, indeed, before the world, yet created, and hence lower than the Deity. These are known as Subordinationists. Here the equality of the Father and Son, as to nature, was renounced. Neither of these attempts at a solution, although satisfactory to human reason, passed for orthodox. The predominating conviction, and that which was more and more decidedly pressed to the front, was, that with the unity of God it was possible to unite the distinction of Father and Son, and their equality of nature.

The decisive conflict broke out in Alexandria, in the beginning of the fourth century. Alexandria was the last great nursery of Greek culture, and at the same time the birthplace of Christian theology. Here Origen (born 185, died in the Decian persecution, 254) had grown to his greatness. He was the greatest theologian of the third century, but united and confused philosophy with Christian belief. Here was the place where the great question found prepared soil. And here was also the place where the great separation between Greek philosophy and Christian theology must be completed. Arius, a presbyter of Alexandria, spoke out unequivocally (313) for the view of the Subordinationists. He asserted that the Son had been created by the Father, that he was like God, but not equal with God, nor of the same substance, and hence not very God, but a being intermediate in nature between man and God. As with the Subordinationists in general, so here the divinity of Christ was, in principle, given up; although Christ was declared to be, not a mere man, but the human manifestation of a higher, godlike being. In opposition to Arius appeared Alexander, bishop of Alexandria; and soon after Athanasius, then deacon, and, after 328, bishop of Alexandria. The conflict soon extended to the whole Church, and became very excited. Constantine, in passing over to Christianity, had hoped to find in the Church the most important means of uniting his empire. If the Church itself were divided, he was destined to be disappointed. After all other means of deciding the controversy had failed, he proceeded to call the Imperial Council of Nice for the settlement of the dispute. In an assembly of bishops from all parts of the empire, he proposed that a decision should be reached which should determine the future doctrine of the Church. The faith which Athanasius represented won, but not without the influence of the emperor on his side. But it was not mere conformity to the imperial wish, which had been of decisive weight, was soon to be made clear. Constantine himself changed his opinion. His successor in the Eastern Empire adopted Arianism. That decided Arian, Constantius, ruled for eight years (353–361) over the West, and fought the Nicene doctrine with all possible means. In the East, Arianism came off victorious; but in the West, the Nicene Creed sustained itself, although under persecution and in the face of denials. Here the fundamental doctrines of the Church asserted themselves, uninfluenced by Greek thought. Arianism was not able, however, to maintain itself in power in the Orient. Even after it had attained supremacy by imperial aid, it dissolved into various parties. The second Ecumenical Synod, in Constantinople (381), with the assistance of the Athanasian Emperor Theodosius, was able to proclaim the Nicene Creed anew, as the creed of the whole Church. Arianism expired within itself. It did not possess the requisite power of resistance to stand the storms of time. It was the first vain attempt to substitute for the Christian faith a doctrine formed by rationalistic processes of thought. The Nicene doctrine of the distinction between the Father and the Son, and at the same time their sameness of substance, was victorious, because it left that which is incomprehensible to remain incomprehensible; and while indicating the wonderful secret of the person of Christ, at the same time did not attempt to lift the veil. The doctrine thus established naturally led to the expression of the related doctrines of the threefold personality and the trinity (tri-unity) of God. The divinity of Christ had been the faith and hope of the Church from the first. It had now been simply averred that this wonderful riddle must be given up. The secret of the person of Christ was recognized and designated, and in this very secret lay at once the nature and a great element of power in the Christian religion.

Still another process of development had reached

5

its terminus by means of Athanasius and the Nicene Creed. The soul of the old philosophy was the thirst for the knowledge of that which bound the world together. In this knowledge appeared even redemption to be included. Comprehend the world and you will free yourself from it, was the thought. Thus the ancient philosopher tried to redeem himself.* He thought himself in need of no other redeemer. This fundamental idea of ancient philosophy ruled even Christian theology at the first. Clement of Alexandria, the teacher of the great Origen, said that if it were possible to offer to the wise man in one hand knowledge and in the other redemption, he would cast away eternal redemption to gain the knowledge of God. And Origen, notwithstanding the decision with which he placed himself upon the platform of the Old and New Testaments, in order to develop a Christian theology which, based upon a fixed canon of Scripture, might be effective through the coming centuries,— even Origen held to the conviction that the historical Christ, with his incarnation, suffering, death, and entire work of redemption, was only a necessity for the great sinful mass of humanity. The wise man, the philosopher, needed no Divine Redeemer, according to Origen, but only the Divine Teacher to reveal the truth to him. This Hellenizing theology,[29] whose first office was to satisfy the desire of the understanding for knowledge, found its suitable

*See Note 10 to page 12.

expression in subordinationism. To this theology, as to Origen, Christ was the incarnation of the ruling, reasonable, creative law, active in the world, the "Logos" of the philosophers.[30] He was the law of nature embodied, the law both of material and of spiritual moral being. He was the union of all the thoughts which were operative in the world, the "idea of ideas." This Christ was thought of, first of all, as the effectual divine power in creation. In this Christ, this "Logos" which came out from God, this world-thought, the whole created world is supposed to have existed; and the interest of the wise man and even of the philosophical theologians, Clement of Alexandria and Origen, was exclusively directed toward this eternal, creative, ruling, refulgent, and clarifying Logos. In the contemplation of this divine Reason, living in the world, the sages, such as the Alexandrian theologian of the third century, and the old Stoic and Platonist, found rest of soul, which freed him from the world, and in this sense redeemed. The theology of Clement and Origen, like the old philosophy, reached its summit in this self-redemption of the "Gnostic," or wise man. It is plain that this theology must range itself by the side of subordinationism. As the ideal beginning of the creation of the world, as the principle of the world, as he who comprehended the world with all its contradictions in himself, Christ must be subordinate to the **Father.**

Christian theology was in danger, in the third century, of being transformed again into a new Gnosticism, a new Hellenistic philosophy; and that by means of Clement and Origen. Hence it was the great work of Athanasius to oppose this mighty stream of development with all the power of his convictions, and with all his scientific culture. Athanasius was the first to raise Christianity to the sphere of true scientific theology, by showing that it did not come to bring self-redemption by a knowledge of self and the world, but redemption through Jesus Christ. The thought of redemption through Christ, by an act of God, and not through ourselves, is the central point of the whole Athanasian theology. The theology of Athanasius, like that of Paul, rested, not on the thought that where the knowledge of the world is, but that where the forgiveness of sins is, there is life and salvation. In the theology of Athanasius the Logos (Christ of Greek thought), the Creator of the world, gave way to the Logos of the Gospel of John, the Son of the living God, who redeemed the world. The redemption of the world can not be accomplished by any being not in essence divine; and Christ, the Redeemer, must be of the same "substance" as God. If God himself were not the source of our redemption, we should all be yet in our sins. This non-philosophical, but religious and genuinely Christian, longing after a redemption wrought by God is the strength of the Athanasian-Nicene doctrine. And it is by this

power that it conquered the world. The nature of
the great controversy which was settled by the Nicene Council was not that of a strife about words.
It did not aim merely at introducing into theology
a new, or another, speculative conception, that of
the *homoousia*.[31] It was aimed rather at driving the
heathen philosophy from the soil of Christianity,
and at preventing the nature of Christianity from
being conceived as an explanation of the world, and
the effect of Christianity from being turned into
the mere possibility of a reasonable meditation concerning the world. Speculation was to be shorn of
the power which the entire ancient philosophy,
aided by the Alexandrian theology, had given it,—
the power which was supposed to be able to place
men in possession of the divine by their own reflection. The Hellenizing (Grecizing) of Christianity was effectually resisted by Athanasius and
the Nicene Council. The great danger which had
lain in the fact that Christian theology had begun
to work scientifically with the methods and by the
means of heathen philosophy, was now happily
overcome. In making redemption through Christ
the central fact of theological thought, the contents of the Christian system were scientifically conceived; and yet Christianity was not transformed
into philosophy. Christianity was preserved as the
everlasting, comforting truth, as the revelation of the
grace which God had in store for sinful men. In this
sense the Nicene Council was the regeneration of

the gospel, and hence the firm foundation for the entire development of the Church, which was to follow.

§ 13. THE PATRIARCHAL SYSTEM.

The Council of Nice busied itself also with the organization of the Church. The power of the bishop of the capital of the province—that is, of the metropolitan—together with the Provincial Synod, was the principle of Church order adopted by the Nicene Council. But there were individual episcopal chairs of such importance that their power had already come to extend beyond the narrow limits of the imperial provinces. The Council confirmed the traditionary privileges of these individual Churches. The three Churches of Rome, Alexandria, and Antioch were especially named. These were the Churches of the three great capitals of the Roman Empire. Alexandria possessed authority over Egypt and the adjoining lands; Antioch over Syria and the neighboring portions of the Orient; and Rome over Italy. In the course of the fourth century the power of these bishops attained a still more fixed form. The empire (from the time of Diocletian) was divided into dioceses, each diocese being administered, as a rule, by a vicar of the emperor. Thus there was a diocese of Italy, of Gaul, of Spain, etc. As the power of the metropolitans, so that of the greater bishops in the imderial dioceses, was fixed in the course of the fourth century. The Eastern diocese (Syria, Palestine, Arabia, etc.), was subject to the bishop of Antioch as the chief bishop; the diocese of Egypt to the bishop of Alexandria; the diocese of Rome (with the greater part of Italy) to the bishop of Rome. The imperial dioceses were divided into provinces. Hence the domains of these bishops of Alexandria and Antioch were divided into ecclesiastical provinces; and the bishops of these great cities came to have authority not only over the bishops of congregations, but over the metropolitan bishops of the provinces in their dioceses. The name patriarch, which originally could be bestowed upon the bishop of a congregation, came to be reserved (in the fifth century) for these bishops of Rome, Alexandria, Antioch, etc.

The bishop of Constantinople now came forward as a new element in the realm of ecclesiastical affairs. Constantinople had come to be the second capital of the empire. It was natural that its bishop should demand a place along-side of the bishops of the other great cities. All the more was this natural since the immediate contact with the imperial power elevated the authority of the bishop of Constantinople (Byzantium), and this was in the interest of the emperor. At the Council of Constantinople in 381, the bishop of that city was raised to the second rank in the Church, and placed only below the bishop of Rome. In 451, the Council of Chalcedon gave him authority over the imperial dioceses of Thrace, Asia Minor, and Pontus, so that the bishops of Theraclia, Ephesus, and Cæsarea fell into a subordinate relation to him. The Council of Nice had also made honorable mention of the bishop of Jerusalem. The Council of Chalcedon, one hundred and twenty-five years later, in order to set upon the mother Church of Christendom a mark of distinction, gave its bishop the rank of Patriarch of Palestine. Thus it was the five patriarchal chairs of Rome, Constantinople, Alexandria, Antioch, and Jerusalem, which in the second half of the fifth century were intrusted with the guidance and control of the Christian Church. Which of them should outrule all the others and become supreme in the whole Church?

§ 14. Rome and Constantinople.

The bishop of Constantinople rose rapidly in authority. From a position of subjection in the first part of the fourth century he rose before its close to be one of the first bishops of Christendom. Indeed, the Council of Chalcedon (451), which subjected their imperial dioceses to him, at the same time awarded to him the highest authority over the whole of Christendom. The great question was already decided. None of the great, ancient, celebrated, apostolic episcopal chairs, but a later one, the bishop of Constantinople, was to be the bishop of bishops, the first of Churches.

But how could this come about so suddenly?

Not in vain was the bishop of Constantinople the bishop of the second capital of the empire. More and more, as the Western Empire fell to pieces, it became the first capital. By the end of the fifth century the Western Empire had fallen. The Eastern emperor in Constantinople was now the emperor of the whole world. Should he not make his rights as ruler of the world secure? To the rights of the ruler of the world belonged, however, according to general imperial agreement, the power over the Church. The bishop of Constantinople was the court bishop of the emperor, in the immediate sphere of the imperial power and majesty, a creature of the imperial will. But he was not ecclesiastically independent. His chair lacked all the traditions and privileges of the ancient Church. What the bishop of Constantinople was and represented in the Church, he owed to the emperor. All the more was it necessary to elevate him. What the bishop of Constantinople won, was won for the emperor. As the imperial power rose, it carried the bishop of his capital upward also. In the person of the bishop of Constantinople the emperor's power over the Church was represented. The conclusions of the Councils of Constantinople and of Chalcedon showed that not the bishop of Rome, nor of Alexandria, nor any other bishop, but the emperor himself, was the chief head of the Church. The whole development of the constitution of the Church appeared to have been in vain. A secular head controlled the structure of ecclesiastical organization. Where was the power in the Church, prepared and capable for the task of withstanding the emperor and defending against the master of the world the Church's right to govern itself by a spiritual chief? Such was the great historical position in which the bishop of Rome appeared. He it was who took upon himself the struggle for mastery with Constantinople and the emperor. Rome naturally possessed great advantages in such a contest. To these were added the fact that the concern of Rome was that of the freedom of the Church from the secular arm.

After the second half of the second century the Roman congregation was believed to have been founded by the apostles Peter and Paul. The Roman bishop was believed to be the successor of Peter, the prince of the apostles. If Peter was the rock upon which the Church was founded, the successor of Peter must hold the same relation. Where was another bishop comparable to him? It soon became the custom to take advice from this great Church in all difficult questions concerning congregational life. The decisions of a Church founded by the apostles possessed special authority. There the true doctrine was supposed to be preserved in its utmost purity. Rome was the only apostolic Church in the entire West. Standing in unbroken contact with Africa, Spain, and Gaul, its decisions were enforced in the face of all opposition.

It assumed the first place among the Churches. Above all, Rome was the capital of the world, the Eternal City; bluntly, *The* City.   From the time of the apostle Paul, forward, who thought his great mission to the heathen imperfect until he had labored in Rome and had had fellowship with the Church there, through all the centuries, the overpowering position of the Roman Church as such, not of its bishop, is observable.   This, notwithstanding at the time of Paul's visit in Rome neither Peter, nor his representative, much less one of his successors, was to be found there.   Yet the Roman Church was unquestionably the first, most influential, and most important of all Christendom, even for the Orient.   The large number of members in her fold, together with the great wealth of some of them, added to her spiritual might a background of temporal strength.   As in the West, so also in Greece and Asia Minor, the fame of her readiness to assist the needy and her steadfast orthodoxy was spread abroad.   It was but natural that after the rise of the episcopal form of government the influence of the congregation should belong also to her bishop.   Even as early as the end of the second century, the Roman bishop was in a position to threaten the exclusion of the Church in Asia Minor from ecclesiastical fellowship on account of a departure from the Roman conception of the celebration of Easter.

As the first-born of the Church, the Roman bishop entered the lists against the claims of Constantinople and the emperor. The elevation of Constantinople to the position of second capital of the empire was the first great blow which the rising power of the Roman bishop experienced. Rome had ceased to be the capital of the empire, the center of the world. The more completely the center of gravity was shifted from West to East, the more must the bishop of Constantinople become the clerical head around whom the Greek Orient gathered. The decisions of Constantinople (381), and of Chalcedon (451), indicated this fact beyond the possibility of misunderstanding. The protests of the Roman legates resounded unheeded in the East. That Rome was not chiefly indebted to the apostles Paul and Peter for its position in the Church, but to the fact that it was the capital of the world, became clear the instant that a second capital of the Roman Empire was established.

Nevertheless it was just in this time of conflict with Constantinople that the foundation was to be laid upon which the later history of the Roman see [32] was to rest. Even in the fourth century Rome was able to reap some results. At the Council of Nice the Arian controversy was to have been settled. But the hope was vain. Under the leadership of the Arian successors of Constantine, the whole East rose up in favor of Arianism. Athanasius was deposed from his Alexandrian bishopric, first at a Synod in Tyre (335), and a second time at a Synod of Antioch (340). The West alone,

under the leadership of Rome, remained true to
the Nicene Creed. Athanasius fled to Rome, there
to prosecute his cause; and the Roman Bishop
Julius, at a Synod in Rome (341), refused to recognize the justice of his deposition, and reinstated
him in his episcopate. The Roman bishop, with
his Synod, exercised authority over all Christendom.
Athanasius was not the only one who appealed to
Rome. The conflicts which continually arose between the Arian East, and the few bishops there
who remained true to the Council of Nice, gave
Rome repeated opportunity to act as arbitrator,
even for the Eastern Church. It mattered but
little that the decisions of Rome (as in the case
of Athanasius) were by no means accepted as binding by the opposing bishops of the Orient. The
fact remained that the oppressed bishops of the
East called upon Rome as an arbitrator,—that the
Roman Church, with her claims, became known to
the whole Church. She even succeeded in obtaining
the decision of a Council in her favor. In the year
343 an Ecumenical Council was again called at Sardica (Sofia, in Bulgaria). The controversy concerning the faith resulted in a split in the Council.
The Arian bishops of the East seceded and withdrew to Philippopolis, and there held a Synod for
themselves. The Council of Sardica had thus become a Council of Western bishops, with a few orthodox bishops from the East. It recognized the
right of the Roman bishop to hear the appeals of

deposed bishops, and to secure the assembly of a
new Synod (a provincial Synod, that is) which
should give a new decision concerning the deposition. The Occident was the fortress in which the
power of the papacy resided, and the Occident, at
the Synod of Sardica, recognized the right of its
chief bishop to exercise authority over the entire
Church. The great dispute concerning the faith
ended at the close of the fourth century, in the
overthrow of Arianism. The victory of the Nicene
Creed was at the same time the victory of Rome.
All the greater episcopal chairs of the East had de-
filed themselves with the accursed heresy. Where
was the Church, which, like Rome, had borne
aloft the banner of orthodoxy in the midst of all
conflicts?

And now, when Rome felt itself justified in undertaking the government of the entire Church, an
upstart, the bishop of Constantinople, and he in the
interest of a secular power, dared to contend for
the prize of superiority. The imperial dignity had
already begun to lose its terror for Rome. Great
masses of Germans were flooding the already unde-
fended West. The fall of the Roman Empire was
at the same time the release of the Western Church
from the oppressive power of the State. The Occident, the immediate domain of authority for the
Roman bishop, withdrew from the authority which
ruled in Constantinople. A time came indeed (the
sixth **and seventh centuries**), when the bishop of

Rome, whose city became again a part of the Eastern Empire, fell into a position of undignified dependence upon the emperor and bishop of the East, the bishop of Constantinople. But the Franks would establish an empire which should free the Roman bishop, and give him finally the primacy over the Latin half of the empire. At the Council of Chalcedon the primacy of Constantinople was decreed. The legates of the Roman bishop present had solemnly protested against this decision. The conflict was formally declared. The opponents stood face to face. The course of the world's history would decide between them. The foundations of that great opposition had been laid which later divided the Roman Catholic and the Greek Catholic Church.

Such was the discord with which the development of the first Christian centuries closed. Christianity as yet formed an ecclesiastical unity. The giant tree, which had grown up from the grain of mustard-seed, lifted itself ever higher, bringing forth fruit, and giving nourishment to the people, so that the nations came and dwelt under its branches. But already, upon the horizon, appeared the storm-clouds from which the lightning would descend and cleave the majestic trunk in two. Not merely on account of the ambition of two bishops,—not because the Roman Empire had been divided into the Latin and the Greek sections, and a second capital set up as a rival to the greatness of Rome. Far

from it!   In the division of the Church was made
the first great step leading to its own continued
development.   The division was necessary, if the
Church of the West was to be set free from the influence of the Oriental Church, which was now
sinking into a death-like stupor.   The schism left
one-half of Christendom free to develop.   As often
in the providence of God, so here, that which
seemed to be an evil was overruled for good.

§ 15. The Rise of Monasticism.

The ecclesiastical separation of the West from
the East proclaimed itself.   At the same time, the
spiritual forces appeared which were to give the
Western Church an independent character, and become the efficient principle of its development.   In
the course of the fourth century, monasticism
sprang into existence.   It was a movement among
the masses which had inscribed upon its banner
the legend, "Flight from the world."   There had,
indeed, been ascetics before, who professedly and
sincerely, for Christ's sake, denied themselves marriage, property, and the use of meat and wine.
The "gift" of asceticism was believed to be a
charism (a gift of the Holy Ghost).   But it was
classed along with other gifts of the Spirit, and was
not supposed to have any special worth above others.
That which was new in the monastic asceticism,[33]
was that to asceticism, as such, the highest merit
was ascribed.   The fundamental ideas of the heathen

philosophy that the sensuous, as such, was the immoral, and that the body must be mortified in order to overcome it, and that this process led the spirit of the sage to God, took even Christianity captive. Asceticism was now declared to be the highest, noblest task of life, since it enabled the ascetic to see and possess God. Monasticism originated in the very instant in which this thought came to pervade the masses, and vast companies of people fled to the solitude of the desert, there to choose asceticism as their life-calling. The movement took on organization, and out in the wilderness organized asceticism rose up as the rival of the organized Church. The two great forces of the future Church had appeared upon the stage of action, supported by fundamentally opposing ideas, yet designated for each other. The Church had developed into an institution in which all salvation went out from the organization, and which sustained, purified, and sanctified the life of the individual by means of its priesthood and the virtue which resided in its sacraments. On the other hand, monasticism represented the free energy of the individual, who struck out his own path, in order to secure salvation for himself. Monasticism was recognized by the Church. Indeed, the Church was compelled to recognize, in order to control, this movement, which, in its last analysis, signified a contradiction to the pretense that alone in and by the Roman Catholic Church salvation was possible. Catholicism recognized monasticism, although it fled at once from the world and from the Church.

There was in the Church a surplus of spiritual energy which she had not adequately employed. Monasticism became, in a measure, the vent for this energy, thus giving it opportunity for development without shattering the existing ecclesiastical body. Above all, monasticism was the form in which the individual found at once his peace with God, a goal of effort, a way to higher ideals, and a means of broadly effective activity. The organization of the Church was, like its doctrines, fundamentally unchangeable. In monasticism alone did the individual, as such, find a way for the development of his gifts, a domain in life, in which the power of his own personality found room for action. In the Church the principle of conservatism prevailed; in monasticism, the principle of progress. Monasticism irresistibly attracted individuals of special spiritual energy, and was therefore, from the beginning, in spite of its flight from the world and the Church, destined to leadership in ecclesiastical affairs.

By the middle of the fourth century, monasticism had appeared in Lower Egypt in an organized form. From there it soon found its way to the Orient. By the end of the fourth century it had obtained entrance to the Occident, under the guidance of St. Jerome, but not without a struggle. Over against the self-torture, self-neglect, filthiness, and the disregard of culture inherent in monasticism, stood, in the fourth and fifth centuries, the love of the educated classes for a tasteful form of existence, for science, and for art. Hence monasticism was met with contempt and decided opposition. It was felt that Christianity had for its object, not the distortion and enslaving, but the perfection of the personality. But the clear, religious conviction that monasticism was to be utterly rejected, was still wanting. This was not won until a thousand years later, by Martin Luther. Then, for the first, was it clearly seen to be a contradiction of the gospel. The causes of the opposition to monasticism in that early day were far more worldly than religious; hence they were overcome. The might of the religious life in those days was with the adherents of asceticism. They were working out their soul's salvation with fear and trembling. In them was a living power of conviction which was really prepared to count all the good things of this world but naught for the sake of Christ. For this reason the Church must embrace the movement. In the sixth century the contest was already decided in favor of monasticism. The Church had adopted the monastic ideal. Church history took upon itself the stamp of monasticism, and therewith the Catholicization of Christianity was made complete.

In the Orient, monasticism has remained true to this day to that form of asceticism which turns away from the world and culture to a life of religious contemplation. Only exceptionally has it en-croached upon the history of the Church, and then, as a rule, solely by reason of its sluggishness and the force of fanatical opposition with which it has opposed every innovation, whether in doctrine or in worship. The effort of the Oriental emperors, during the eighth and ninth centuries, to banish the worship of pictures from the Church, was finally rendered fruitless by the monasticism of the East. In the monasticism of the West, however, the ener-gies of the individual unfolded their full might. Latin monasticism became the great power which conducted the further development of the Church, founded the papacy, and then gave birth to the Reformation. Benedict of Nursia gave to the mo-nasticism of the West its characteristic form. He was the builder and the first abbot of the monastery of Monte Casino, near Naples, founded in 528. The Benedictine rule became the rule of the West-ern monks. All later rules, of whatever orders, proceeded out of those of Benedict. That which was peculiar to his rule was the adoption of labor as a part of the monastic program. Labor was looked upon as an ascetic means. The monk must work, not for the sake of what he can produce thereby, but for his own sake, for his own moral self-discipline, and for his own moral health. But this toil of the Benedictine monks had the result of turning the desert which surrounded the monastery into cultivated soil. Monastic labor prepared in the monasteries a place for science and art. It turned the cloister into a center of education, from which the mighty impulse toward a thrifty, a mental, and a spiritual life went forth into the world. As a society of laborers, Benedict's monasticism turned its face again toward the world. It irresistibly pressed these ascetics toward the transformation of the world, instead of flight from it, and made them leaders, through the fellowship of toil, in reformatory movements in the temporal, governmental, and ecclesiastical life of the people.

§ 16. AUGUSTINE.

Along with monasticism, which in the fifth century was preparing to conquer the Occident, arose at the same time an individual personality, likewise destined to rule intellectually the development of the Church in the West. It was Augustine, who died as bishop of Hippo, in Africa (430). To him it was given to measure in himself the depths and heights of spiritual experience, to prove in his inmost soul the power of the gospel, and, like Paul and Luther, to pass from sin and anxiety of conscience into blessed fellowship with God. The lust of the world and the lust of the flesh had fastened their chains upon him. But he early sought, with giant effort, to attain his freedom from the burden of sin, and to find favor with God. He had explored, one after another, the religious systems which then prevailed in the world. He became a pupil of Manicheism, the last form of Semitic heathenism; then of Neo-Platonism.* Manicheism,[34] which offered to the perfect ascetic, as the final secret, the doctrine of the Light-god, and of light as the power of the good, left him disappointed and in despair. Neo-Platonism, which gave to those who despaired of winning the truth new hope of redemption and communion with God, led him to Christianity. Here he found what he had so long sought with burning desire—the living God who forgives the sinner. The divine truth revealed in Jesus Christ, the power of divine love, found entrance to his heart. On Easter-night, 387, at the age of thirty-three, he was baptized in Milan by the great Bishop Ambrosius. His life-task, from that time forward, was twofold—to proclaim the gospel of grace for the sinner, and the glory of the Church. In opposition to the British monk, Pelagius,[35] he developed the doctrine of original sin, and the further doctrine that man is saved by grace alone. To him, as to Luther at first, this doctrine and that of predestination were inseparable. In opposition to the Donatists,[36] of Africa, who taught that the benefit of the sacraments was dependent upon the worthiness of their administrator, he established the idea of the Church as an objective and holy institution through which men must be saved. The highest dignity of this external, visible Church he expressed in the statement that it represents the

---

*See Note 8 to p. 11.

kingdom of God upon earth. From the fellowship of this Church salvation flows to the individual. To subserve the interests of this communion of saints is the highest task and duty of the State. It was the duty of the civil power to force the erring Donatists back into the Church. By such a service the State would receive a value which it could not otherwise have. The Middle Ages began to announce their coming. Catholicism, Western Catholicism, striving for the rulership of the Church over the world, first embodied itself in Augustine's powerful personality. Even in his monasticism he was by conviction a Catholic. To him, flight from the world and entrance into a monastery was the perfection of the Christian life. Yet this man carried also the Reformation of Luther in his heart. Together with his idea of a hierarchical Church, he had also that of a true, invisible Church of the redeemed. In direct contradiction to his doctrine of salvation by means of the authority of the Church, he lived in the belief in the freely bestowed grace of God as the only source of salvation. His doctrine of the Church prepared the way for the Catholicism of the Middle Ages; his doctrines of sin and grace prepared the way for the Reformation. The contradictory doctrines, which he knew how to reconcile for himself, have made themselves felt in two great historical ecclesiastical bodies—Romanism and Protestantism.

In the Augustinian theology the Occident had

gained a treasure which freed it intellectually from the East. Out of the depths of a Christian personality, which had, in truth, experienced its redemption through Christ, broke in breadth and fullness a stream of religious ideas and problems, which rendered fruitful the ecclesiastical life of the West for the centuries which followed. He wrought upon the succeeding generations, by the power of a mighty subjectivity, which, struggling with unceasing desire for the possession of God, attained at last a personal experience of the love of God in Jesus Christ, and to rest of soul in the certainty that he had been made the recipient of the grace of God. At the same time he established, with dogmatic decisiveness, the great objective authority of the Church, which he declared to be the final hope of all certainty of salvation. The West was about to attain to its ecclesiastical majority. The two powers which were to undertake its guidance were Western monasticism and the theology of Augustine. When we meet the stream of the Church's external historical development again, it will be at the beginning of the Middle Ages.

§ 17. Christian Life and Worship.

The rapid progress of Christianity early attracted the attention of the Roman authorities. In the beginning of the second century (107), Pliny, the governor of Bithynia, found the heathen temples comparatively empty, and the sacrificial animals without purchasers. This was in part due to the indifference of heathenism to its own religion, but still more to the influence of Christianity. City and country were full of believers in Christ, and all classes and conditions in life were included. Even thus early Pliny looked upon Christianity as a dangerous rival of heathenism. As it was in Asia Minor, so was it in the entire Roman world. The number of Christians in the time of Maximian is variously estimated at from one-twelfth to one-tenth of the entire population. The highest testimony to the innocence and purity of the lives of the Christians was forced from the lips of their enemies. Even under torture, Pliny could extort nothing but what appeared to him as a stupendous superstition. According to his testimony, they came together on a stated day, and sang hymns to Christ as God, and pledged themselves to commit no sin or crime. So great was the change in the moral character of the converts to Christianity, that the Christian apologists were able to point to this as a proof of the general innocence of the lives of the Christians, and of the truth of the Christian religion. Salvation was by faith; but the Christian must obey not only the moral law, but also the new law of Christ to forego the pleasures of this world, in the belief that he would find his reward in the next. If there was any fault in the then existing conception of Christianity, it was in the fact that the Christian was supposed to have no moral obligation toward the world, since his citizenship was alone in heaven. This was a natural consequence of the expectation of the immediate end of the world, and the coming of Christ to judge the living and the dead. Still, the principle of the Christian life was not only love to God, but also love to man. The latter found expression in brotherly helpfulness. In Jerusalem it was carried to the extent of establishing a community of goods (Acts ii, 44, 45); in the gentile Churches it resulted in liberal collections for unfortunate brethren. Brotherly love was not, indeed, new to the Romans, either in theory or practice. But among the Christians it appeared as one of the most prominent features of life, and by its steady and systematic exhibition, excited the constant wonder of the heathen world. Such a system of life was the more easily realized, because, while the Christians were taught that all things were theirs (1 Cor. iii, 21–23), yet even in the Gospels a mild form of asceticism is taught as valuable for the individual. Both benevolence and self-denial were the natural result of the principle that it is more blessed to give than to receive. As early as the first half of the second century the ascetics formed a special class in the Church, and were regarded as worthy of special honor.

Prayer recognized God as the Creator, besought his assistance in times of need, and especially for the strengthening of the weak, and the lifting up of the fallen. But these blessings were besought, not alone for their own sake, but also that God might be recognized as the true God, Jesus Christ as his Son, and they as his people. They prayed for forgiveness of sin, for cleansing through the truth, strengthening in all goodness, and unity among themselves and all the inhabitants of the earth. At the same time, according to the Word, of Christ, the stress was not laid upon saying "Lord, Lord," but upon doing the will of God. Church membership involved holiness of life. Those who had been baptized and purged of their sins were in duty bound not to forsake the way of life, that is, the commandment of the Lord. Sin was believed to separate from the Church. It was soon discovered, however, that there were those in the Church who did not live up to these high demands. A higher and a lower morality, adapted respectively to clergy and laity, began to develop. There were some commandments which it was sin to break; there were some advices (evangelical counsels[37]) in the Bible which might indeed be neglected without sin, but which it was especially meritorious to observe. The first compromise with sin had been made; the first step in the development of the doctrine of the merit of works had been taken.

That there were those who did not succeed in breaking with their sins, or that some fell victims to temptation, and forsook Christ under persecution, should cause no surprise to one who knows the fickleness of human nature. And it is a tribute to the sanctity of the Church in those early days that such apostasies were regarded as so serious. It was believed by many that those who sinned after baptism could not be renewed in the grace of God. In baptism they had received that grace which was purchased by the death of Christ. In subsequent apostasy they renounced it. Christ would never die again to purchase fresh grace, but would, instead, come to judgment. Only those who were found without fault at his coming would enter his heavenly kingdom. Others, however, believed that once, but only once, the Church should receive again into its arms those who had fallen away. But those who had thus sinned could not expect to be received back without the most satisfactory evidence of their sorrow and desire for reconciliation with the Church. Exclusion from the Church was exclusion from the possibility of grace. Satisfaction to the Church was satisfaction to God. Penitence must therefore be exhibited by all manner of signs of humility; as fasting, wearing sackcloth and ashes, lying upon the earth; prostrations, especially before the clergy; tears, sighs, and deprecations, especially to the more honored members of the Church, such as the confessors.[38] These things were at first the natural expression of the penitent heart; but in course of time they came to be demanded, and thus were degraded into a mere form. A considerable number of years must elapse before the penitent could be received back into full fellowship with the Church, in order to which he was required to pass through four distinct steps or stages. First, he must stand at the entrance to the church, beseeching those who entered to invoke the mercy of God and the favor of the bishop in his behalf. Second, he was permitted to hear the Scripture reading and the sermon, but must sit in a place apart reserved for penitents. Third, he could participate kneeling in the prayers of the Church. Fourth, standing, he might look on while the Lord's Supper was being administered. Having passed through all these stages, and having spent the requisite number of years in penitence, he was once more admitted to the table of the Lord.

From the first, the public religious services consisted of the reading of portions of Scripture, prayer, preaching, the administration of the Lord's Supper, and the love-feast,[39] which latter, however, was finally abandoned. The liturgical forms first employed were very simple, even for the administration of the sacraments; but as these, especially the eucharist,* came to form the principal feature of the service, and were regarded as having in and of themselves a special merit, the ritual employed became more complex. In the apostolic and post-apostolic ages[40] there was no secrecy connected with the Lord's Supper. Later, however, it came to be regarded as a Christian mystery, only to be partici-

---

* See Note 27 to p. 62.

pated in, or witnessed, by those who had passed the initiatory stages of the catechumens.[41]   Hence, by the end of the third century, it was customary to dismiss the catechumens, penitents, and others not entitled to commune, as soon as the public services were ended, and proceed to the eucharistic feast, with the use of collects, the sign of the cross, the prayer of consecration, and the elevation of the consecrated elements, all accompanied with hymns, doxologies, and responses.

The spontaneous and loving impulses of the first Christians prompted them to daily assemblies.   It was impossible, however, to maintain this custom, and Sunday,[42] in commemoration of the resurrection of our Lord, was chosen as the day of special services, although for several centuries Jewish Christians, in places, observed Saturday (Sabbath) also. At the Sunday services it was the custom to stand in prayer, in token of Christian joy; but on other days it was proper to kneel, as a sign of humility. The first cycle of special festival days was formed in connection with the annual celebration of the resurrection and ascension of Christ.   There is no evidence of an independent festival of the birth of Christ until the middle of the fourth century.   Regular fasts were held on Wednesday and Friday, and the significance of fasting is seen in the fact that they fasted as well as prayed for their enemies. The beautiful inner sentiment and life, of which many of these forms of worship were at first but the expression, died out in proportion as the form came to be the looked-for fruit of a Christian experience. Religion became external. More and more was saving merit attributed to good works. Almsgiving was supposed to be a means of redemption. To suffer a martyr's death insured entrance to heaven. At the same time asceticism, in all its forms, developed with great rapidity. Second marriage fell into greater disfavor; celibacy, at least for the clergy, was looked upon as more seemly than the married state; the holding of property, if not a sin, was at least dangerous to the welfare of the soul; army and civil service were inimical to the Christian life, since they required participation in heathen worship, loaded the Christian with the cares of this world, and might stain the hands with human blood. But if some erroneous tendencies began at so early a period to exhibit themselves, it was alone the result of an imperfect understanding of what Christianity required. In their private lives the Christians were still a pattern to the heathen world, and the homes of the Christians were controlled by the spirit of God's Word and of praise.

From the time of the recognition of Christianity by Constantine, great changes took place in the life and worship of the Christians. The first effect of the imperial favor was to attract vast throngs to baptism. However, as baptism was supposed to wash away all one's sins and fit the soul for heaven, many postponed that rite until the last days or hours of life. Constantine himself was not baptized until he was on his death-bed. The danger of such a movement of the masses toward Christianity, as a result of royal recognition was perceived, and the Church made stringent regulations to prevent the admission of unworthy applicants. Persons in certain callings must disentangle themselves from their dangerous affiliations. Slaves must have the recommendation of their masters. The time of catechization must extend through two or three years, although exceptions might be made. If a catechumen fell into sin, his period of preparation was lengthened, and his baptism might well be delayed to the hour of his death. Reception into the class of catechumens was attended by the use of the sign of the cross and laying on of hands. As the time for baptism approached, the real nature of Christianity was made known to the candidate. The ceremony of exorcism[43] was performed upon him, to destroy the influence of the evil spirits and to purify the soul. Immediately prior to baptism, the candidate, standing in the entrance to the Church, with uplifted hands and face directed westward, said: "I renounce thee, Satan, and all thy works, and thy pomp and thy service." Then turning eastward, he confessed his belief in the Father, the Son, and the Holy Ghost, and in one only baptism to repentance. This renunciation of the devil was the solemn breaking with heathenism, its worship and customs, and especially with theatrical exhibitions and circuses. Baptism was by a threefold immersion. Holiness consisted in the greatest possible separation from the natural life. Those who were perfect must give themselves only to God's service, desire neither property nor children, and take no part in the usual occupations of life. Orthodoxy of faith had special merit. Prayer, fasting, and almsgiving were Churchly services of the highest worth. Augustine taught that fasting and almsgiving were the two wings of true prayer. In prayer the grace of God was sought, in fasting the desires of the flesh were exterminated, and in almsgiving redemption was purchased from sin. The original design of Church discipline, to prevent open sin in the members, was changed to that of improving the morals of believers by punishments. Hence the idea that only one repentance was possible fell away. Public repentance was no longer a necessity. One could confess his sins and receive his punishment in private. Thus arose the confessional, in its first form. But such confession was left voluntary. Each must decide for himself whether he were fit to go to the Lord's Supper or not. External requirements multiplied; Churchly functions attained increasing value. Reverence for martyrs, relics, and the Virgin Mary became almost, if not quite, a kind of worship. The long night, which was to break centuries later in the Reformation, had fallen.

7

§ 18.   BENEVOLENT ACTIVITIES.

Even before the apostles had left Jerusalem for the various portions of the earth in which they closed their labors, the care of the poor and dependent had grown to such proportions in Jerusalem as to demand regulation. (Acts vi, 1, *seq.*) But while the apostles gave over this work to the deacons thus appointed, they did not lose their interest in it. When the division of missionary territory (§ 8) was made between Paul and the earlier apostles, the latter expressly stipulated that the former should remember the poor. (Gal. ii, 10.) How zealous he was in this particular, is testified by many passages of Scripture. (Acts xi, 29, 30 ; xxiv, 17 ; Rom. xv, 25, 26 ; 2 Cor. viii, 1–15 ; ix, 1–7.) The fearful poverty which later oppressed the masses had not yet fallen upon the empire.   Hence the benevolence of the first three centuries was of a somewhat private character.   Every Christian house was open to brethren in need, and benevolent institutions were the less necessary.   Besides, it was a period of persecution, and every such institution would but call fresh attention to the despised sect.   The love-feasts became more and more occasions for feeding the hungry poor.   But the gifts of the congregations were administered by the bishops and deacons with such effect, that under Urban I, bishop of Rome (223–230), there was not a Christian beggar in his city.   The number of those for whom the Church cared, grew constantly, and about the middle of the third century there were in the Roman congregation alone about fifteen hundred widows and others who received aid. Benevolence was not bestowed indiscriminately, however; and the beneficiaries were led to feel that they had no claim upon the charity of the Church, but that it was bestowed as an expression of pure Christian love. Those who were capable of work were provided, so far as possible, with suitable employment; and the relatives of the needy were encouraged to give them aid. The spirit of brotherly love prompted large numbers, not only to sell their property and bestow the proceeds upon the poor (as Cyprian, bishop of Carthage, who died a martyr in the Valerian persecution, 258), but led them also to active labor for the relief of the suffering. Especially did Christian women participate in these works of mercy, and Tertullian[44] has given us a charming picture of the activity of one such, as she went from street to street, and carried blessing to the poorest huts. But the benevolence of the Church was not confined either to the congregation which gathered the funds, or to those who belonged to the household of faith.

The Roman congregation sent its assistance to Cappadocia, Arabia, and Syria. Cyprian collected money in Carthage to purchase the freedom of some Numidian Christians who had been imprisoned. And in a time of pestilence in Carthage, when the heathen were beside themselves with terror, it was the Christians, under the leadership of Cyprian, who took up and buried the dead bodies of the victims, and thus saved the city from further contagion. Similar courage and Christian love were exhibited by the Christians of Alexandria under similar circumstances. The poor and unfortunate were, as such, the objects of a real affection. When the secular authorities, during the Valerian persecution, demanded that the deacon Laurentius (died a martyr, 258,) should deliver up the treasures of the Roman Church, he assembled the objects of charity and said: "These are our treasures."

Such was the pure and beneficent stream of charity in the first three centuries of the history of the Church. From the beginning of the fourth century two important changes made themselves manifest in Christian beneficence. The first has to do with the motives which prompted it. These suffered a marked change for the worse. The doctrine of the merit of good works overshadowed the motive of Christian love. The bishops sought by every means to incite the believers to zeal in benevolence. The chief stress was laid upon the merit of almsgiving. It was a favorite saying that as water quenches fire, so almsgiving blots out sin. Chrysostom,[45] Augustine, and others, protested, indeed, that gifts without the true spirit of love availed nothing; and Augustine was particularly vehement in opposing the custom of bestowing upon charity what was needed by poor relatives. But by the majority, and in the main, the custom of making the Church the beneficiary in wills and by gifts was encouraged. Gifts of property were expected from ministers, monks, and nuns; or at least it was expected that at death their property should fall into the treasury of the Church. The greater bishops, with some exceptions, set the example, not only of willingness to give their wealth to the Church, but also to live in the simplest manner that they might help the poor. Ambrosius, bishop of Milan (died 397), did not hesitate to call almsgiving a kind of second baptism, which, it will be remembered, was supposed to wash away sin. Salvian, bishop of Lyons (died 480), appealed to the motive of reward without reserve. He said that whoever had done *few* good works ought all the more in the hour of death to make good his negligence for the sake of the heavenly reward. Whoever *had* done good works should not be content therewith, since one can never do enough. But if one had done evil all his life, he should at least in his last hours seek the salvation of his soul by giving away all his property. He would have no one consider his children or relatives. One must, first of all, love himself, and show it by seeking his salvation. What advantage had a rich man in making his sons rich if he himself fell thereby into the fires of hell? Those who were rich and adopted children to whom to leave their property, he censured. Better that the children should be poor in this world than the parents in the next.

It was also taught that the power of these gifts reached even into the next world. Hence the offerings for the dead. Even Augustine said: "It is not to be doubted that the dead are benefited by the prayers of the Church, by offerings for their salvation, and by alms which are given for their souls, so that God will deal more mercifully with them than their sins deserve." If one had done good works he was entitled to the cleansing of purgatory, and hence the benefit of these offerings, and good works done for the dead. Besides, it is the works of mercy which blot out the small sins of daily life, which otherwise would have to be suffered for in purgatory. But no one can know whether he has done the requisite amount of good works; hence he ought to do as many as he can. Such was the doctrine, and such the motives to which appeal was made; although we must not suppose that the motive of true charity was altogether excluded from those who endeavored to relieve the sufferings of those in distress.

Far as the motives to which the bishops appealed were removed from those of Christianity, yet the stream of wealth which flowed into the treasury of the Church in response was truly magnificent and blessed. And yet there was none too much. For the times demanded and produced a change in the method of relieving the suffering. Enormous taxes had consumed the property of many, and some were even obliged to sell their own children in order to meet their taxes as they fell due. This, and other causes combined, brought about such a general state of poverty as greatly to increase the demands upon the benevolence of the Church. In Antioch, in the life-time of Chrysostom (Patriarch of Constantinople, died 407), there were three thousand persons cared for by the Church of that city. Chrysostom cared daily for seven thousand seven hundred persons in Constantinople. During the patriarchate of John the Almsgiver (Patriarch of Alexandria, died 620), the register of the Alexandrian Church contained the names of seven thousand five hundred who received aid at the hands of the congregation. Such increasing numbers of needy or unfortunate made necessary a change in the provision for their support. One new measure consisted in the districting of the larger cities and the appointment of a deacon for each district, whose duty it was to look after the poor in his territory. In these, district houses were established in which the poor might be fed. It was not possible to carry the needed assistance to scattered individuals. Those who were to receive aid must be brought together. Hence the monasteries became places of refuge. There the dwellers were free from taxation. There the poor of the neighborhood were fed. There children could obtain the best education which the times afforded. In many of the monasteries lodging was provided for the poor, the stranger, and the distressed. Along with these institutions were founded those known as hospitals, although they were open not only to the sick, but to the suffering and needy of every class. It was only gradually that special institutions were established for each special class of sick or unfortunate.

Thus, while the theory of a universal brotherhood of all mankind was not unknown to the Roman world, the natural spirit of selfishness prevented it from being more than a theory. It was the spirit of Christian love which first prompted men to the carrying out of the principle in its highest conceivable form. And if the motive became somewhat mixed in later centuries, enough of the original principle remained to give the results their true value as works of Christian charity. Indeed, the very breadth of the demands elicited a broader sympathy. It was no longer the special case of distress, which fell under his own observation, which appealed to the heart of the Christian. The effort was now directed, not toward the relief of the sufferer, but of suffering in general. Men came to love, indeed, not only the welfare of those whom they knew, but also of those whom they did not know. There was suffering in the world, and it was Christ-like to alleviate it, even though the sufferers were separated from the benefactor by distance, lack of acquaintanceship, and religious faith. Nor did this have the result of making men feel that they could do their works of benevolence by proxy. The motive was not to escape personal responsibility, but to provide in the most effective manner for those in need. It was in this spirit that the first hospitals were erected, to the astonishment of the heathen world. While heathenism was theorizing, Christianity was acting. It is one of the differences between true Christian love and the spirit of speculation. The latter may sit and weave all manner of beautiful dreams; but the former puts them into actual practice. Thus Basilius the Great, bishop of Cæsarea in Cappodocia, established (370) a hospital, consisting of a number of houses where the sick and miserable of every kind were received, and provided with medical aid and the care of nurses. About the same time Ephraem Syrus (died 378), the greatest hymnist, and father of the Syrian Church, established at Edessa a hospital of three hundred beds, supported by the Christians of the city. Fabiola, a Christian lady of the noble Fabian race, and of great wealth, established, with her own funds, a hospital for the sick, in Rome, the first of the kind in the West. These hospitals were served by officers of the Church, especially the so-called *Parabolani*,[46] and by many who volunteered their services, not infrequently ladies of high rank. Of such, Fabiola deserves to be especially named. She herself frequently carried the sick into the house, washed and bound up, with her own hands, wounds so sickening that others could not even bear the sight of them, and refreshed the sufferers with food and drink. The faith of the period may have been in many things erroneous. Ideals of life may have been perverted. But the spirit of Christian love was not dead, and the faith, such as it was, was effective in leading men to live in accordance with it. Even in its partially fallen condition, Christianity was far above any system of faith and practice the world had ever seen.

SECOND CHAPTER.

THE MIDDLE AGES.

§ 19. INTRODUCTION.

WHEN we pass from the history of the Church in the first six centuries to that of the Middle Ages, our thought fixes itself upon events and personages of less importance. The circle of vision of the Church history of the Middle Ages is no longer the entire Christendom, but only the Western world. The center of gravity in the world's history is shifted westward to Italy, Spain, Gaul (France), Great Britain, and Germany, where, with severe struggles, the Occidental Germanic-Romanic nationality is produced, which is destined to rule the future.

The Middle Ages began with a tremendous upheaval. In the Orient the Greek Church and the Greek nationality and culture received their death-blow in the invasions of Islam.[1] Like a stream of fire, consuming everything living, the hordes of Mohammedan conquerors were poured out upon Asia and Africa. The movement had its beginning in the seventh century (the first public manifestations of Mohammed fell in the year 611); in the beginning of the eighth century it had already reached Spain. (The fall of the Spanish kingdom,

under the assaults of the Moors,[2] occurred in 711.)
A few years later (732), when Charles Martel,[3] with
the entire force of the Franks, threw himself against
the Mohammedans, they had already reached the
banks of the Loire, prepared to overflow the entire
West, and to wipe out the Romanic-Germanic
Church and culture, as they had destroyed the
Church and culture of the Greeks.

The Greek nationality had been robbed of its
life-forces. It was a nationality incomparably rich
in gifts; a nationality in which even porters in the
streets philosophized; in which disputes concerning
the mysteries of faith were heard in the barber-
shops and ale-houses, on the streets and in the
markets; in which not only religion, but even theology, were matters of popular interest, and were
able to throw the masses of the people into boister-
ous agitation; in which the energy of the mental
life, sustained by the strength of the entire nation,
appeared inexhaustible. This most splendid, this
intellectually richest and most wonderful nationality
had been thrown to the ground, trampled under
foot, crushed, never to rise again. In place of the
Hellenic culture in the Orient, came the Arabic,
which also was mentally vigorous, superior to the
Middle Ages in mathematics, natural science, and
philosophy, and of the greatest influence upon the
West, producing the scholastic education * of the
Middle Ages. It was a culture surrounded by an

---

* See ₹ 37.

imperishable splendor on account of its sober and
acute understanding, and, at the same time, on account of its glowing and fairy-like shimmer of Oriental poesy ; and yet a culture of the second order,
not equal to that of the ancient Greeks, lacking
purity of form, the Promethean[4] strength of genius,
and, above all, the historical sense which preserves
at once the power and the freedom of investigation, and gives it strength of vision and an immeas-
urable horizon. It was necessary that Europe
should free itself from this Arabic culture of the
Middle Ages, in order that at their close the science
and the spirit of the present should be awakened by
the newly awakened interest in the literature and
civilization of the ancients.

The Greek nation was no more. It never re-
covered from the terrible blow. With the Greek
nation fell the Greek Church. The patriarchates of
Alexandria, Antioch, and Jerusalem indeed remained ; for Islam exercised toleration toward the
remnant of the Church. But the power for further
development was broken, in Byzantium as in Alexandria. The one event which yet convulsed the
Greek Church was the stormy attempt at its reform
by the Greek emperors of the eighth and ninth centuries. The worship of images, which almost
amounted to idolatry, was to be repressed by a complete removal of them from the Churches. The
emperors believed that they could the more easily
win the Jews and Mohammedans[5] of the kingdom

to a Church so purified. There was to be one faith and one Church as the bond and firm support of the empire. In this thought, Leo, the Isaurian (717–741), opened the attack. But the power of the monks and the superstitious needs of the masses were stronger than the emperor and his army. The united declaration of the great bishops of Jerusalem, Antioch, and Alexandria, led on by the bishop of Rome, in favor of the worship of the images, was decisive. A great Synod at Nice[6] (the seventh Ecumenical) in the year 787, decided the conflict against the iconoclasts. But the worship was declared to be that of the object for which the picture stood, and was distinguished from the worship of God. Both Roman and Greek Catholicism has ever since adhered to this position. About the middle of the ninth century the emperors of the East ceased to oppose the Church in this respect. The last iconoclastic emperor was Theophilus (829–842). After this conquest, both monasticism and the Greek Church sank back again into apathy. John of Damascus (died 754, as a monk in the monastery of St. Saba, near Jerusalem), one of the leaders of the party in favor of the worship of the images, framed the dogmas of the Greek Church into a systematic, philosophic, theological work, which was final for the East, and which became one of the foundations of the scholasticism of the Middle Ages for the Western Church. It was the last significant intellectual product of Greek Christianity.

Since then the Church has been mute, and, with the extinction of its intellectual life, it fell into a final position of dependence upon the power of the State. The Byzantine emperors conquered, notwithstanding the outcome of the contest with the authorities of the Church concerning the images. The Greek Church had been able to maintain its essential character, its dogmas, and its forms of worship; but its strength became subsidiary to the power of the State.

The candlestick of the Greek Church was removed out of its place. (Rev. ii, 5.) What was still left under the scepter of the Eastern emperors was just sufficient to make over to the onstreaming Slavonic' tribes, as a last inheritance, the art of writing, the elements of education, and the doctrine of the Church. But the Slavonic peoples lacked the vigor necessary to regenerate the Greek world. It, together with the Church, remained dead. The Greek Church of to-day, as we have it in Russia and the lands bordering on the Balkan peninsula, is the Church of the seventh century petrified. Not one step in advance has been taken. Exactly as the history of the world left the Church of the East at the time it received its destructive blow in the seventh century, do we find it to-day, after the lapse of more than a thousand years. The Greek Church, once so glorious, lies rigid in death. When shall the Spirit from above awaken her to new life?

The West also presented, at the beginning of the Middle Ages, a scene of dissolution. That mighty empire which once ruled the world was fallen. The hordes of Germanic[8] invaders streamed over the West, carrying with them desolation and destruction, and spreading the barbarism of their primitive forests over the civilized countries of the Occident. That which was once so glorious, great and beautiful; that which had once filled up the cup of life, and made life worth living—art, science, the all-comprehending power of the empire—all had been lost. The night had fallen, and nowhere was visible a sign of the coming day.

And yet there was one ground of hope remaining. The kingdom had indeed fallen; but not the Church. In the Orient the Church and empire had both been devastated, and therewith the last root of culture deprived of its vigor. But in the Occident the Church remained. In a world of ruins, in the midst of universal destruction, she was the one witness of the past. She brought her organization, her traditions, and her faith, in a measure, unharmed from the wreck of the ancient world into the period of the new, and, by her preaching and her constitution, transformed the conquered into conqueror. The hordes of invading Germans entered into the. Christian Church, to revere, as Remigius, bishop of Rheims, said at the baptism of Clovis,* king of the Franks, what they had persecuted, and to persecute

---

* See ? 38.

what they had revered. The Church was saved, and with her was saved also civilization. The entire education of the ancients, the great riches there heaped together for posterity, remained. In quiet cloisters, under the protecting wings of the Church and Churchly investigation and science, was the precious treasure guarded, until the time should come again when it could once more go out into and enrich a world.

The German tribes adopted Christianity with the entire vigor and cordiality of their emotional life. The German blood was noble enough, and possessed sufficient life-vigor, to regenerate the Church of the Occident. Upon the Germanic-Romanic people, produced by the blending of Latin and German character, rested the progress of the world's history. In the first period the Greek Church had been the leader of Christianity. Now the scepter was bestowed upon the Latins. The Church history of the Middle Ages, comprising only the Christianity of the West, has a more narrowly limited sphere; but it is a sphere which includes within itself all possibilities for the future.

FIRST DIVISION.

THE KINGDOM OF THE FRANKS.

§ 20. The Primitive German Tribes.

Upon the ruins of the Roman Empire we see a series of German tribal kingdoms growing up. To which shall fall the victor's palm? Which should succeed in erecting anew what had been destroyed, in reproducing upon Roman soil, but in the form of a German State, that great, world-comprehending, splendid, and never-to-be forgotten empire? The empire had been overthrown; but the sun of the imperial idea shed its rays over the horizon throughout the whole of the Middle Ages. Through long centuries the Roman Empire remained to the on-streaming barbarians the ideal of all that ever had been great and glorious. With the power of magic it held them fast, and after the empire had disappeared, the desires of those who had destroyed it followed it. That empire was to them the State, the only, the ideal, the incomparable, the everlasting, the one necessary State. To them the history of humanity and the history of that empire were synonymous. To re-establish it, to give back again to mankind its forms of existence, must be the greatest and highest good of German statesmanship. Not alone in the minds of scholars, but in the phantasy of the people lived the imperial idea, the immediate effect of what had been seen, experienced, and received, never to be lost, in the time of the Roman Empire. The dream wove mysterious and brilliant pictures, incited men with intoxicating power to immortal deeds, and produced first the empire of the Franks and then that of the Germans. Which of these German tribal kingdoms will be able to establish again the empire? The Ostrogoths or the Visigoths, the Vandals or the Burgundians? The answer of history was that the Franks,[9] and none of the others, should succeed in this effort.

One fact was decisive from the beginning. Without exception, the German tribes who had up to that time come into contact with the Roman Empire, had received Christianity in the Arian form. The Eastern Empire had been Arian during the greater part of the fourth century; and it was just at this time that the Goths and their related tribes, the Vandals, Burgundians, Alans, and Suevians, had received Christianity from the East. Thus Arianism, even after it had been extinguished in the Roman Empire, lived on for a time in these converted German tribes. Not as though the masses of the Gothic or Vandal peasants had a deeper insight or a more lively interest in theological questions. It was merely an exhibition of the German character of faithfulness to traditions. Hence the German conquerors were Arian, while the subject Romans of the West were orthodox, and to the national opposition was added that of religion. This inner division consumed the kingdoms of the Goths and their

related tribes.   One only of these early kingdoms—
that of the Franks—had been orthodox from the
beginning.   Clovis had received Christianity in the
Roman Catholic form.   The Frankish conquerors
held the same faith with the Roman population.
Not only so, but they had the same faith with the
Romans of the provinces in the kingdoms of the
Burgundians and Visigoths in Southern Gaul
(France).   Hence all who hated the Arian heretics
would rather be subject to the king of the Roman
Catholic Franks than to the rulership of the Arians.
It was only necessary for Clovis to touch the kingdom of the Visigoths (at the battle of Buglé in 506)
and it fell to pieces.   Under his sons the conquest
of Burgundy took place.   It had gone over to
Catholicism too late.   Gaul belonged to the Frankish
conquerors, and therewith the heart of the Latin
West.   It was only a question of time when the
empire of Charlemagne should follow the kingdom
of Clovis.

§ 21. THE MEROVINGIANS.

The epoch of the Merovingian[10] kings, which
covers the sixth and seventh centuries, is the time
during which the Romanic-Hellenic culture ceased
to be felt.   As yet the time of the new civilization
of the Middle Ages had not come.   Humanity
rejoiced in the last rays which the rapidly descending
sun yet threw over the horizon.   There were still
schools of rhetoric in Southern Gaul, which spread

abroad an education in harmony with that of the ancients. There was still a literature which joined itself to the types of the fifth century, and still further developed its forms. The Church, too, was the immediate continuation of elements inherited from the old empire. The (national Roman) portion of the clergy, especially of the bishops, enjoyed the preference for a long time.

But the culture of the ancients, upon which the Merovingian period sustained itself, was in process of extinction. Its hour had come. In the sixth century the mental energy was still sufficient to produce literary works which are worthy the attention of history. But when we examine even the works of Venantius Fortunatus, the most important poet, and Gregory of Tours, the most important author of the period, how rude the language has already become, and how weak the thought! Bishop Gregory of Tours, the more prominent of the two men just named, was a personality full of noble simplicity, of true nobility of soul, and of masculine strength. Yet how limited his mental powers, how poorly educated, how wanting in intellectual gifts, and, above all, how barbaric he had become under the influence of the coarse world which surrounded him!

The education of the ancients was approaching its end. In the seventh century it uttered its last word. In the beginning of the eighth century its death hour had struck. It had become mute. A time had come which was no longer in a position to

give any information concerning itself. A culture-
less atmosphere surrounds us. The education of the
ancients was dead; it would awaken to new life
during the time of the Carlovingian kings.[11]

What was true of the history of education in
the Frankish kingdom, is true also of the history of
the Church. Churchly vigor died out under the
Merovingians. In the sixth century the contact
with freedom which the German State secured both
to the individual and to the Church produced a
vigorous Frankish National Church. But in the
seventh century this Church was already smothered
in the earthly interest which it felt in riches and
power. The bishop played the part of a great
landlord and took the lead in the opposition of the
aristocracy against the royalty. Spiritual interests
retreated to the background. Synods were seldom
held. In the beginning of the eighth century the
dissolution of the great ecclesiastical organization
was almost complete, and Charles Martel could deal
with the Church as he would, because it had lost its
spiritual strength. In the necessities of his kingdom he found it convenient to re-establish its power
by the help of the Church's possessions.

Not very different was it with the Church in
Italy, in Spain, and in Great Britain. In Italy the
life of the Church suffered from the hate of the
Arian Lombards,[12] and after their acceptance of
Catholicism (middle of the seventh century), under
the disfavor of their royalty, who were at enmity

with the Roman bishop. In Great Britain the Roman Catholic and the Celtic forms of Christianity were opposed to each other. (See p. 118.) In Spain, where the Latin education and the Churchly life had maintained themselves in far more energetic forms than in France, the Church, from the time of the conversion of the Visigoths to Christianity (587), was entangled in the intrigues which resulted in the complete overthrow of the Visigothic throne in the middle of the seventh century.

The Church of the West was in need of reform. But who should be the reformer? Did she look to her natural head, the bishop of Rome, as her helper? The bishop of Rome was oppressed between the Greeks and the Lombards. Still more he was cut off from the immediate authority over the Church by the German kings, by the Visigoths in Spain, the Franks in Gaul (France), and the Lombards in Italy. None of the German kings would tolerate within their own dominions the authority of a foreign bishop. The Church of the West dissolved into a number of National Churches; the Spanish, the Lombard, the Frankish; and the kings of the Anglo-Saxon kingdom, who had at first received Christianity from Rome, claimed exactly the same authority over the Church of England which the German kings claimed over the Churches of their respective kingdoms. Western Christianity had fallen to pieces. Its Churchly unity had been destroyed. The Roman bishop was disrobed of his one-time power.   The papacy was not in a position to check the decay of the Church.   The papacy itself lay calling for help.   Who was to be the reformer?

§ 22. The Frankish Reformation.

Germany in the sixth century was still chiefly heathen.   Although the Allemanians, Bavarians, and Thuringians[13] had been incorporated in the Frankish kingdom, Christianity was, with them, still in its beginnings.   The kingdom did not recognize it as one of its tasks to propagate the gospel. That was an affair of the Church.   But the lack of life vigor in the Frankish Church showed itself exactly in its lack of propagating force.   Not from the Franks, but from Ireland and Scotland, after the close of the sixth century, came monks of a strange tongue to preach the gospel to the Germans. The most important of them were Columban (died 615) and Gallos (died 646).   Along with strange manners and customs they brought a Christianity in many respects foreign, and of a peculiarly Celtic[14] stamp.   They reckoned the Easter period differently from the usual custom in the West.   The marriage of the priests was still current among them.   But above all, the regularly ordered episcopal form of government, which was the form everywhere else recognized, was to them unknown.   Monasteries were at once the middle point of their mission and their government; and along with the usual episcopally organized Church, a Church of another character appeared in Germany—a Church patterned after that of Ireland and Scotland, whose chief aim was to found monasteries and make monks. So that this newly originated German Church introduced a new element of dissolution into Western Christianity.

In the beginning of the eighth century even the political existence of the Occident was threatened. The Moors had overthrown the kingdom of the Visigoths in Spain (711). The dukedom of Aquitania (from the Pyrenees to the Loire) then became an easy booty. The foreign conquerors, filled with the animosity born of their faith, already stood within the heart of the Frankish kingdom. It was the same time at which the Slav emigrants from the East pressed forward toward the Main and the Rhine. Where was the kingdom which should secure protection? The kingdom of Clovis had fallen. Its king was a boy of the house of the Merovingians. The Allemanians, Bavarians, and Thuringians had, under their dukes, refused further subjection to the sinking kingdom. Aquitania had fallen away and formed an independent duchy, when it was overtaken by the Moorish invasion and swallowed up. In the remnant of the kingdom, anarchy ruled. The great lords, counts, dukes, abbots, and bishops had taken authority into their own hands. Royalty had become a mere name. Not merely the Church, but Christendom as well, was threatened; so also the German nationality.

At this fateful moment two men became the saviors of the threatened Church and State, the one politically, the other as a Church reformer,—Charles Martel and Boniface. The battle of Poitiers (732), in which Charles Martel defeated the Arabs, was the sign of the beginning regeneration of the kingdom. Upon the battle-field of Poitiers the Carlovingians won their right to the kingly and imperial crown. The appearance of Boniface (719), who is honored by the Roman Catholic Church as a saint, in the capacity of missionary to Germany and ambassador of the apostolic chair, was the sign of the beginning regeneration of the Church.

Boniface (whose original name was Winfried) was one of the Anglo-Saxon[15] missionaries, who, as early as the end of the seventh century, began to go over from England to convert Germany. Gregory the Great (pope, 590–604) had sent the Benedictine monk, Augustine,* to England, thus taking in hand the conversion of the Anglo-Saxons directly from Rome. Augustine landed in England in 596, spread Christianity throughout Kent, and founded the Church of Canterbury. After many struggles the Roman form of Christianity had triumphed over the Celtic.† Now the Anglo-Saxon Church paid to Rome her debt of gratitude. The Anglo-Saxon missionaries who went to Germany were preachers at once of the gospel and of the authority of the

---

* Not to be confused with Augustine of Hippo. (See § 16.)
† Compare section on the History of Christianity in England.

Roman papacy. The Anglo-Saxon Willibrord had (695) received the episcopal consecration in order to undertake his mission to the Frisians.[16] Boniface (Winfried) received his missionary commission from Gregory II, in the year 718, when he first fixed the full significance of his missionary work in his mind. Different from the Irish-Scottish monks, he came to preach the gospel to the Germans in the name of the Roman episcopal chair. In the year 722 he was consecrated bishop in Rome, and took the formal oath of obedience to the Roman bishop. He believed, with all his heart, that salvation was to be received in connection with the Church of Rome alone; and to this faith and its propagation he dedicated his life. It was he, and no other, who established the papacy of the Middle Ages.

His work was at once that of a missionary and a reformer. The sacred thundering-oak[17] of Geismar fell by his stroke, a type of falling heathenism. The Celtic (Irish-Scottish) form of Christianity he replaced by the Romish. He organized the regular episcopal form of government in Bavaria, and founded a series of new bishoprics in Hesse and Thuringia. But most important of all was it that he succeeded in reorganizing the Frankish Church. After the death of Charles Martel (741), whose iron hand had lain heavy upon the Church, and whose iron will had opposed the reformation, Boniface succeeded, in a short time, in introducing the regular forms of Church government throughout the entire

Frankish kingdom.   The canonical law was en-
joined; the Synods of the provincial bishops, with
the metropolitan at their head, were re-established
as the governmental and supervisory authority over
the bishops of the provinces; and, above all, the
Frankish and German Churches subjected themselves, through his influence, to the pope.   The
pope was recognized as the chief head of Western
Christianity, his decisions met with respectful obedience, and thereby the unity of the Western Church
was once more restored.

The re-establishment of the papal authority was
the corner-stone and the cap-stone of the Frankish
reformation.   It had become evident that at that
period the dissolution of the Church into national
Churches had operated unfavorably for the mainte-
nance of ecclesiastical life.   There must be a power
which, as the highest authority, could at once lead
the whole Church and secure its unity.   The power
and full splendor of the Church was necessary in
order to render sensibly visible to the people of the
Middle Ages the power and splendor of the gospel.
Whatever served to give power to the Church
served to give effectiveness also to the gospel.   The
papacy was destined and necessary,[18] the all-comprehending organization of the Church, that the dominion of Christian ideas over the life of the people
of the Middle Ages might be secured.   In giving to
the Roman chair its power, Boniface had not sold
the German Church as a slave to Rome, but gave

to German, as to the entire Western Christianity. the decisive, mighty, and fruitful life-impulses out of which the splendor of the Church and the civilization of the Middle Ages proceeded.

§ 23. The Empire of Charlemagne.

In the empire of Charlemagne the work of Clovis was completed. The totality of the Roman and German tribes of the Western continental countries were now united in a world-controlling community. The great task which had filled the imaginations of the hordes of wandering tribes was now fulfilled. A new empire was established, equal in glory and power to the Roman Empire of the West; and when Charlemagne, on Christmas eve (800), received the imperial crown at Rome from the hands of the Roman congregation, and the Roman bishop (Leo III) as the head of this congregation, he gave a visible and imposing expression to far and near of the vigorous and glad self-consciousness of his people, that now the great achievement had succeeded, and the rulership of the world had passed over to the Germans.

The new Roman Empire was to be, at the same time, a Christian world-empire. The emperor was to be, at once, head of the State and the Church. With this purpose before him, Charlemagne placed himself at the head of the government of the Church, setting the Roman bishop in the shade, presiding over councils, giving to bishops and ab-

bots their spiritual rights and duties, superintending the Churchly life; and by the assistance of his
friend, the Anglo-Saxon Alcuin (died as abbot of
Tours, 804), and by requiring a Latin education,
and the establishment of new centers of education, gave the impulse to a rich, fresh life.

Charlemagne accomplished great results for the
Church by means of the so-called Carlovingian
books (*libri Carolini*), which were composed by his
order and published in his name. The bishop of
Rome had expressed himself in favor of the worship of the images (see page 108). Pope Hadrian I
sent (790) the Acts of the Nicene Synod of 787,
in favor of the worship of the pictures, to Charlemagne for observance, and through him to the
Frankish Church. The answer which Charlemagne
made to this communication from the pope of the
conclusions of an Ecumenical Council, was a warlike protest on his own part and that of his theologians, in the form of the Carlovingian books
(composed between 790 and 794). In this " Work
of the Distinguished King of the Franks against
the Foolish and Arrogant Conclusions of a Greek
Synod in Favor of the Worship of Images," as the
official title ran, both the worship of the images and
their destruction were rejected with genuine Christian decision and a learning worthy of respect. The
images were objects toward which Christianity was
indifferent. They deserve no kind of worship nor
do they deserve any kind of opposition. Let hu-

man art unfold all its powers in the interest of the service of God. Neither the having nor the not having of images in the churches has anything to do with Christianity. Both the Greek emperors with their iconoclastic spirit, and the Greek Church with its worship of the images, are wrong. The pope also is wrong when he proposes to subject the empire to the decision of the recent Synod of Nice. The document was laid before the Synod of Frankfort (794). The assembled Frankish bishops expressed themselves with one accord in its favor and against the spurious Greek Synod. The royal book was officially delivered to the pope (Hadrian). He answered in a diplomatic document, in which he emphasized the necessity of adhering to the tradition of the Roman Church, and of condemning all who repudiate the worship of the images. Notwithstanding, the Frankish Church remained true to its convictions during the whole of the ninth and tenth centuries; and only with the strengthening might of the Roman Church in the course of the Middle Ages did the worship of images (to which also the Tridentine[19] Council adhered) press itself upon the Western Church. Until then the spirit of Charlemagne, whose judgment was sustained in the German Reformation, protected the German people from the entrance of Greek-Roman superstition. The Frankish Church followed the lead of the emperor, not of the pope.

Under Louis the Pious the great empire fell to

pieces. The papacy itself, in the person of Gregory VI (833), entered into alliance with the sons of Louis the Pious to assist in the destruction of the empire—the empire which had made possible the re-establishment of the papacy over the West. But with the unity of the empire fell also the great imperial power, which had been superior to the papacy, and which Charlemagne had established. With this destroyed, the Church, if it would maintain its unity, must build solely upon the power of the pope. It was in this knowledge that the *Pseudo-Isidor* was produced, about the middle of the ninth century. It was the work of a Frankish clergyman, and was the most unblushing, and at the same time the most fruitful, forgery of the Middle Ages. An old collection of decisions of Councils and of papal decrees was, in the *Pseudo-Isidor*, enlarged by a great mass of forged decrees, which the originator sent forth under the names of the old Roman bishops, especially those of the second and third centuries. The continually recurring thought of the forged portions was, on the one side, that the bishops should be free from the secular authority, even to the extent of altogether preventing the laity and the lower orders of the clergy from making an accusation against a bishop; on the other side, the subjection of the Church to the pope. This second thought was brought prominently into the foreground. Not only that every bishop deposed by a provincial Synod should have the unconditional

right of appeal to the pope, but the universal principle was maintained in the *Pseudo-Isidor* that *all*
more important matters were to be brought before
the pope, and that no decision of a provincial Synod
should be valid without the papal confirmation.
What an unheard-of change in the law of the Church!
It was the program of the Frankish party of reform,
which was here brought forward in the form of law.
The fate of the Church was to be disconnected from
the fate of the empire, which was falling asunder.
The constitution of the Church was to be founded
upon an episcopacy which was free from all local
authority, and upon the papacy. The unity of the
Church was to be preserved in spite of the dissolution of the empire. Hence the tremendous consequences of the forgery. In the year 864, Pope Nicolaus I openly declared in favor of the principles of
the *Pseudo-Isidor*. He even ventured, although in
tortuous expressions, to give official assurance that
the forged decrees, which, however, he did not
name, would be preserved in the archives of the
Roman Church, thereby making the papacy a party
to the deception. With these forged decrees he destroyed the power, as metropolitan bishop, of the
most important, learned, and ambitious of the Frankish bishops, Hincmar[20] of Rheims. Supporting
himself upon these forged decrees, he reinstated
(865) Rothod, bishop of Soissons, whom Hincmar
had deposed. By the end of the ninth century all
opposition to the genuineness of the false decretals
9

of the *Pseudo-Isidor* was silenced. Throughout the
entire Middle Ages they passed for genuine. Repeatedly did they find acceptance in the *Corpus Juris
Canonici.* In the fifteenth century, Cardinal Nicolaus, of Cusa, expressed a doubt of their genuineness.
This doubt was raised to certainty by Protest-
tant research, as, for example, in the Magdeburgh
Centuries.[21] Meantime, however, the false decretals
had done their work—not that they had produced
the papacy of the Middle Ages, but that they had
been an important ally of the rising papacy in
founding its claims to rulership over the Church
and the world. The empire of Charlemagne dissolved and fell. If the unity of the Church was
to be maintained, it could only be accomplished
through the papacy. With the fall of the Carlovingian Empire the first foundation was laid for the
papal power of the Middle Ages.

And already the papacy announced itself to the
future. Nicolaus I (858–867) became one of
its most important representatives. He checked
the power of the Church of the West Franks
(Hincmar). He took measures against King
Lothair II because he had put away his queen,
and subjected him and the archbishops of Cologne
and Trier, who had made themselves serviceable to
him, as well as the entire episcopacy of Lorraine,
to the papal authority. He even broke with
Photius, Patriarch of Constantinople, because he
failed to recognize the decision of the Roman chair

that Ignatius, and not Photius, was the rightful Patriarch (863). By means of him the division between the Latin and the Greek portions of the Church came to open rupture. He and Photius mutually excommunicated each other. He proceeded against the power of the metropolitans, the kings, and his great rival in Constantinople. The papacy lifted itself up to conquer the Occident, and to separate the refractory Greek Church as schismatic from the body of the true Church. The papacy entered upon the inheritance of Charlemagne. On its way to the rulership of the world, the papacy will have only one more opponent to overcome—the German Imperial power.

SECOND DIVISION.
THE GERMAN MIDDLE AGES.

§ 24. THE GERMAN EMPERORS.

GERMANY first succeeded in producing a new national order. While France, Burgundy, and Italy were in process of dissolution, Henry I labored for the regeneration of Germany, which was finally secured under his great son, Otto I. The victory which was gained over the Hungarians (952) revealed at once to the invaders and to all Europe that a new and powerful State had been erected in Germany. To the first great power which arose upon the ruins of the Carlovingian

Empire, the Imperial crown naturally fell, and with
it the curse and blessing bringing rulership over
Italy. In the year 962, Otto the Great was
crowned Roman emperor by the pope. The crown
of Charlemagne once more had an heir who
was able to lend impressiveness to the Imperial
power. Yet how very different the political situation under Otto the Great from that under Charlemagne! Only a part of the former Frankish kingdom was subject to Otto the Great—the East
Franks on the Rhine, Elbe, Main, and Danube, •
and Italy. According to the doctrine of the
Middle Ages the world, or at least the Western
world, should be under the sway of the Imperial
power. But the world rulership of the German
emperors remained, for the extra-German countries,
a mere name. To this statement an exception must
be made of the rulership (how often contested and
fateful!) of Italy.

And even in Germany the power of the royalty,
upon whose shoulders the Imperial power rested,
was far less than that of the Frankish royalty.
The feudal system[22] had arisen meantime, and had
altered the constitution of the State. The count
was no longer, as previously, an officer and organ
of the royal will, but a vassal to whom the county
belonged in fee as his own right. Besides, over
the county there had arisen the dukedom—the
Swabian, Bavarian, Frankish, Lothringian, Saxon—
bearing within itself a power which was equal to that

of the royalty. The power of royalty was in danger of being transformed into that of a mere superior liege lord, instead of maintaining a real power. From this danger it was saved by Otto the Great by two means. First, by making members of his own family as far as possible dukes over the various duchies, and thus transforming the power which lay in the dukedoms into a means of royal power. This, however, was only imperfectly successful, since his own brother, as duke of Bavaria, and his own son, as duke of Swabia, showed far more inclination toward rebellion than toward obedience. The most successful means which Otto the Great employed was another; the founding of a new royalty upon the power of the Church. Under Otto the Great it was the outspoken policy to elevate the Church, and especially the bishops, by the presentation of property, the conferring of public rights, and even by making the bishops counts. The purpose was to erect a spiritual princedom in order to counterbalance the power of the secular princes. The king was more sure of the spiritual dignitaries than of the secular. The bishop and abbot of the royal monastery were nominated by the king himself by means of investiture[23] with ring and staff. He was more unfettered in his appointment of the bishop and the abbot than of the count and duke, because the spiritual office was not hereditary, and could not be. In case of the death of a spiritual prince, the king

was free to fill the place with one who suited his
mind.   Indeed, the property of the spiritual princes
passed as a kind of property of the kingdom.
Thus what was joined for the religious foundations
was not lost to the kingdom.   It was all the more
a sure possession of the kingdom, because it was
taken from the control of the great secular vassals.
Under the name of presents the king received taxes
from the property of the Church.   From the same
source the king received the larger portion of his
soldiers in case of war.   Over the property of the
Church the king set such bishops and abbots as
were agreeable to him.   Thus the German kingly
and Imperial dignity of the Middle Ages became
possible.   It found its material support in the
means which the Church had at its command, and
the means by which the Church was bound to the
king was the royal investiture.   It was a royalty
erected upon a broad foundation.   But this foundation itself must be shaken as soon as the Church
began to desire freedom from the control of the
State.

From the time of the dissolution of the Carlovingian Empire, the papacy itself had fallen into
decay.   It succeeded in individual cases in asserting
its authority.   But in.the main the German, French,
and English National Churches ruled themselves.
It seemed as though the era of National Churches
was about to be renewed.   But in the Imperial
power lay the decisive element which checked the

dissolution of the Church. According to the conviction of the Middle Ages a spiritual dignity, as well as a secular, attached to the emperor; and the Imperial Synods of the tenth and eleventh centuries, which were held under the presidency of the emperor, claimed to represent the whole Church. Above all, the emperor, as head of the Christian world, was immediately justified in elevating the papacy, and it was his duty to labor toward this end. At the close of the ninth century, and during the first half of the tenth, the papacy had been subject to the stormy agitations of the unbridled aristocracy of the city of Rome; and outcasts of a society which had fallen into rudeness of manners and morals disfigured the papal chair. It was necessary to free the papacy from the Romans. Repeatedly did Otto the Great and his sons interfere. The Romans had solemnly pledged themselves to Otto the Great to choose no pope without his consent. Several times the emperor interposed to lend new life to the papacy by his influence upon the choice of the pope,[24] but almost in vain. In the first half of the eleventh century, the great noble families of Crescens and Tusculanum fought for the papal dignity as for a family possession. In the year 1033 Benedict IX, a boy of twelve years, was elevated to the papal throne, only to be contaminated with all manner of crimes. An uprising of the people in 1044 drove him from the city, and Sylvester III was elevated as a rival pope. When, however, Benedict IX returned to Rome in 1045, supported by military power, he sold his right to the papacy to Gregory VI, without being really prepared to give up the papal power. The situation had reached its crisis. The only helper seemed to be the German emperor. Under the strong protection of Henry III the Synod of Sutri (1046) deposed both the rival popes, and a Synod at Rome in December of the same year gave the same sentence concerning Benedict IX. A German bishop (Snidger of Bomberg) was chosen in Rome as Pope Clement II (1046–1047). He conferred upon Henry III the Imperial crown. At the same time the emperor received the dignity and power of a Roman patrician, and thereby the right of nomination to the Roman bishopric. From this day forward it was a part of the duty of the German emperor to fill with his favorites the papal throne. Three more popes were named by Henry III: Damasus II (1047), Leo IX (1048–1054, an Alsatian of the race of Count von Dachsburg, chosen at the Imperial Diet at Worms), and Victor II (1054–1057, chosen at an Imperial Diet at Mayence). The popes were now no longer chosen in Rome, but in Germany. The Imperial power was at its height. The German Church did his bidding; the entire Church recognized in the emperor, as in the time of Charlemagne, its highest ruler, in so far that he had control of the highest spiritual dignities.

Yet it was only for a moment that this Churchly movement favored the authority of the emperor. For the time there was no other means by which to help the papacy and the Church out of their difficulties than the powerful arm of the emperor. But as a finally valid settlement of the proposed reforms, this solution could not be considered. The protection of the emperor was too insufficient. As long as the Imperial arm was respected, so long did the protection which he granted operate; but as soon as the immediate stress of the Imperial power ceased to be felt—and how often was the emperor distant, or engaged in other duties!—just so soon was the papacy anew the object of the small tyrants of Rome. The Church could not but desire the erection of a papacy upon the basis of its own power, and this the empire was not able to secure. For the moment, then, the assistance of the emperor was accepted. But just as soon as the re-establishment of a capable papacy was reached, the Church must make her freedom and that of the papacy from the emperor, the goal of her efforts. When the Church and the papacy had been truly reformed by the help of the emperor, the hour had struck for the founding of the supremacy of the papacy.

§ 25. The Reform of Monasticism.

While the world was thinking about the Ottos and the Henrys, an intellectual movement had begun in the quiet cells of the monasteries which was destined to change both the Imperial power and the papacy. The education of the tenth and eleventh centuries was the fruit of the revival, under the Carlovingians, of Latin culture. It was the time of Romanesque architecture,[25] in which the spirit of Christendom united with antique forms. ˙ As the Church edifices and the Imperial palaces bore the evidences of the Romanesque style, so did the entire education of the period. Virgil was the favorite author of the age. Latin was the language, not only of the Church, but as well of all persons of rank. It was the time when the nun, Hroswitha,[26] produced her Latin comedies in the presence of an audience of illustrious ladies; when the monk, Ekkehard[27] put the Song of Walthar into Latin verse, and thus secured its admission to the royal court; and when even the artless folk-song sometimes attired itself in the Latin tongue. The middle point and chief support of this Virgilian culture, was, together with the Imperial court, the monastery, which we may call the university of that day. The most important of the German monasteries was St. Gall, celebrated far and wide for its monastic scholars and artists. What later belonged to the court of the ruler, and after the sixteenth century to the cities—namely, the rôle of leader in intellectual development—then pertained to the cloister. The intellectual impulses which stirred the world here took their rise. There was no interest, either of art or science—and we may say, of national and political life—which was strange to these monastic professors. There was no power which was there thought unworthy of cultivation, no capacity which could not there have found a school for its complete development. Not the destruction, but the development, of individuality was the purpose of these monasteries and nunneries. The demand was for ears, not only for the singing of songs, but also for the melodies of the heroic legends of Germany; for eyes, not only for the letters which conveyed ideas to the mind, but also for that which adorned life; for art in painting, as well as for nature; for a heart, not only for the Latin of Virgil, but also for the then almost undiscovered German tongue. It was a monasticism which, giving and receiving, intellectually ruling the then existing world, stood in the midst of the stream of the national life.

But was it then the task of monasticism to rule the world, enjoy the benefits of life, and, with others, to live the national life? Was it not rather the ideal of monasticism to flee from the world, to count the noblest good which this earth affords as of no account and unworthy the immortal soul, and even to hold these things dangerous and as a part of the world, which is in and of itself wickedness, sin, and ruin?

The destruction or chastening, not only of the evil passions, but of every earthly impulse of humanity; not the development, but the destruction, of every earthly gift of the human mind,—this was

the special purpose of monasticism. But how far
were the monks of St. Gall, and of all the other
Benedictine monasteries of Germany and France,
fallen from this ideal! Without doubt there had
entered the monasteries of the time, not only a
sense of the noble and great, but also worldly-
mindedness of the lowest order. Monastic discipline had fallen into decay. Oversight of individuals had ceased. The abbot counted himself among
the guilty. The more the national spirit and devotion to a life of general culture won the supremacy in the monasteries, the more the old-style
monasticism, with its severities and self-discipline,
gave way. A luxurious and voluptuous life arose
in the monasteries, and the places dedicated to
asceticism were transformed into resorts of self-in-
dulgence. The interests of asceticism had given
way to those of education. It was evident that the
root of genuine monastic life was thereby endan-
gered. From the monastic stand-point, the salt of
monasticism had lost its savor. Hence, the monasticism of Ekkehard, of the Roman Virgil style, must
be cast out, that it might be trodden under foot of
men. The judgment which befell this monasticism,
which had so fallen from its own ideal, was executed
by the monastery of Clugny, situated upon Burgundian soil, near the French borders. Even during
the tenth century the old Benedictine rules had
been renewed and enforced by the abbot Odo (927–
941), of Clugny. Rules of the greatest severity,

and entering into the minutest particulars, were instituted with the hope of smothering every development foreign to the true purpose of monasticism.
The introduction of the requirement of silence for
given times and places was expected to contribute to
self-control and the artificial excitement of the spiritual life. In the monks of Clugny the old monastic
ideal of flight from the world and mortification of
the flesh asserted itself against the degenerate monasticism of the West. As soon as this ideal became apparent in the examples of its devotees, it
was destined to conquer the world of the Middle
Ages. These monks of Clugny, with their macerated
bodies, their glowing eyes set in their deep sockets,
and their lean and pallid countenances, became the
saints of the people ; for the Christian ideal, as the
Middle Ages conceived it, had come afresh to life
in them. Here the peasant who was held in the
chains of sensuality and rudeness, saw the spirit of
Christianity living before his eyes—the spirit which
is more than conqueror of this world. A mighty
and enthusiastic movement among the people favored this monasticism of Clugny. Numerous monasteries united themselves in a single congregation
with the mother monastery of Clugny, and were
singly ruled and superintended by the abbot of
Clugny. While monasticism reformed itself, it also
organized. The old-style independence, according
to which each monastery governed itself through its
own abbot, was displaced by a constitution which

placed in the hand of a single general officer the authority over a wide-reaching and powerful union of monastic institutions. This abbot of Clugny, this first general of a monastic order, was called the arch-abbot. Starting from Roman soil, the movement had there its first results. But in the eleventh century it swayed the whole West. The German emperors were favorably disposed toward the reform, and assisted one monastery after the other, including even the celebrated St. Gall, to transform itself from the old and usual form into the new and more severe. This new-born monasticism carried within itself the power which gave to the Church new life, won wide circles of the population to the Churchly idea, freed the Church from servitude to the secular authorities, and produced the hierarchical epoch of the Middle Ages. In the cells of the monasteries the world of the Middle Ages was to be produced, and from the same was to go out the individual—Martin Luther—who was to overturn the product. The decision for the future was rendered when Henry III, with all his power, prepared the way for the reform, and when, in the person of Gregory VII, the monk Hildebrand, the monasticism of Clugny ascended the papal throne.

§ 26. The Reform of the Church.

The ideals of Clugny referred by no means to the reform of monasticism alone. Rather was it the idea to unite the monastic and the Churchly reforms. Both monasticism and the Church were to be freed from the world. The freeing of the Church could be served in two ways, and both were tried. The one way was for the Church to renounce the world, its ecclesiastical benefices, its riches, its princedoms, its rights and prerogatives, and its magnificence. After renouncing all earthly authority the Church could, with propriety and right, demand her freedom from secular power, and especially her freedom from lay investiture, which was perceived to be a source of the secularization of the Church. This lay investiture was especially injurious to the Church because there was connected with it, in so many cases, the sale of the ecclesiastical offices (the so-called simony). Poverty was the real and peculiar ideal and consequence of the ideas which had their birth at Clugny. It signified the carrying over of monastic poverty and flight from the world to the sphere of the Church. Along-side of this ideal of poverty stood, naturally, the idea of the celibacy of the priesthood, likewise a Clugny ideal. Renunciation of the world, of necessity included renunciation of marriage. Here, as there, the question was one of realization of the imitation of Christ, which, according to the conception of the Middle Ages, consisted in poverty and celibacy. In a word, the secular clergy were to be monasticized. The Church was to be reformed by being subjected to monastic ideals.

The other way was the establishment of the authority of the Church over the world. The Church could in this way also be freed from the world, since the world would be her subject. Here, too, the setting aside of lay investiture was demanded. But the State was not to receive back from the Church its worldly goods. On the other hand, the Church held her worldly wealth with firm grasp, and demanded that her property should be free from the power of the State. The Church claimed the world for herself, and desired the State to give way, that she might enter upon its place. The leading thought here was the superiority of the Church to the State, even in worldly affairs. As the ideal of poverty was supported by the ideas of the monastic clergy, so this ideal of rulership was supported by the instincts of the secular clergy. When this Clugny movement seized the masses in the cities of Upper Italy, about the middle of the eleventh century (Milan at first, 1056), and excited the rabble against the ruling, wealthy, and luxurious secular clergy, it was this monastic ideal of poverty which controlled it, and set the masses of the citizens against the marriage, the wealth, and the rulership of the priests. And this ideal was never fully extinguished in the Church. Later, under the favor of the Church, it found expression in the form of the Mendicant Orders of monks. The complete carrying out of the ideal wrecked on the unconquerable opposition of the secular clergy. When Pope Paschal II, in the year 1111, was ready to purchase freedom from lay investiture, with the renunciation on the part of the Church of all her property and rights of rulership, a storm of opposition arose from the secular clergy[26] to which even the papacy felt compelled to give way. The celibacy of the priests was carried out, since it served not only the Mendicant ideal, but also the interests of the authority of the Church, by freeing the clergy from all bonds of family, in order to make them adherents and servants of the Church alone. Thus far the monastic idea won the victory. But secular power and rulership were not renounced. Here the interests of the secular clergy were mightier than the purely ideal interests of the Church.

The decision for the Church was given by the powerful Gregory VII, who, both monk and bishop, as monk forbade the clergy to marry, and as bishop became fascinated with the possession of worldly splendor. By him the ideal of rulership of the Church of the Middle Ages was brought to self-consciousness, and proclaimed with powerful voice, while the whole energy of his master spirit, so far superior to all his contemporaries, made real his desires. From him sprang the celibate law (1074), which forbade every married priest, under penalty of the ban of the Church, to serve at the altar of the Lord. From him sprang also the prohibition of investiture (1075), which forbade the German king, Henry IV, the right of investiture with ring and staff; that is, the bestowment of imperial bishoprics and imperial abbeys. Building upon the movement which went out from Clugny, which had grown to power, he could successfully challenge the German emperor. History confirmed his brave confidence. When Gregory VII (1076) laid the ban upon Henry IV, that monarch was compelled to exchange the garments of royalty for those of repentance, and in undignified humiliation, in the snow of winter, before the gates of the castle in Canossa, to the shame both of himself and his enemy, to beg absolution from the proud priest. The flood-tide of Churchly ideas was mightier than the loose structure of the State. By making and unmaking German kings; by his co-operation with the Norman duke, Robert Guiscard; by his co-operation in the undertaking of William the Conqueror against England; by his interference in the disputes for the crown in Hungary, Poland, and Dalmatia; by his opposition to Spanish counts and Sardinian princes,—he was able to realize, in all parts of the Western world, the idea to which he had dedicated his life—the idea of the secular power of the Church. The inheritance which he left to his successors, when he died, in banishment, fleeing from the presence of Henry IV, and surrounded by the hordes of the Normans, to whom he was more a prisoner than an ally, was the erection of the Church, the world-ruling theocracy. Thus, immediately upon the supremacy of the emperors was to follow the time of the supremacy of the papacy.

§ 27. THE CONCORDAT OF WORMS.

The ideas of Gregory VII, concerning secular rule, could not be fully realized, and never were fully realized. This was made plain in the disputes relative to investiture. These disputes were ended for Germany in the year 1122, by means of the concordat which was concluded between Emperor Henry V and Pope Calixtus II. Here the symbols of investiture were changed. The emperor was no longer to invest with the ring and staff, but with the scepter. Furthermore, the object of the imperial investiture was expressly designated as the worldly possessions of the Church. The chosen bishop or abbot was to receive only the "regalia," and not the spiritual office, by the royal investiture. The emperor also yielded his right of nomination, and parted the right of canonical election by the congregation under the leadership of the clergy and the nobility, or, according to circumstances, by the brothers of the monastery. But the presence of the emperor, or his legates, at the election, and the right of the emperor, in case of a contested election, together with the provincial Synod, to render the decision, again placed the deciding influence in the filling of bishoprics and the office of abbot in the hand of the emperor. And all the more so, since, according to the concordat, the investiture of the bishop or abbot elect was to be conferred before the consecration. If the emperor refused the investiture, the consecration, which was necessary to the exercise of the office of bishop or abbot, could not be bestowed. It was thus absolutely impossible that any not agreeable to the emperor should attain to the place of a bishop or an abbot. Repeatedly, in the course of the twelfth century, and later, did the German emperors refuse investiture previous to consecration. But the right remained and was exercised. For the outlying and adjoining lands of Germany, such as Burgundy and Italy, it was provided, by the Concordat of Worms, that the investiture should take place after the consecration. But even in such cases the right of investiture gave the emperor a great influence upon the choice, since it was with difficulty that any one could be elected and consecrated of whom it was certain that he would not be invested. Thus, only in form was the right of imperial investiture altered by the Concordat of Worms. The facts remained the same as before. All the more because that which the bishops and imperial abbots were required to contribute to the empire, such as soldiers and money, remained, according to the express stipulation of the Concordat of Worms, unchanged. It was impossible, and with reason, that the emperor should let the spiritual princes slip out of his hand. Thereby he would have neglected and renounced the foundation of his power. The settlement of the dispute concerning imperial investiture signified that the empire could assert its existence in opposition to the Church. It victoriously repelled the attack of the Church upon the very conditions of its existence.

During the whole of the twelfth century, and during the thirteenth to the time of the interregnum,[29] the right of investiture remained the most important source of their authority in the empire; and the splendor of the Hohenstaufen emperors rested, like that of the Ottos, first of all, upon the power which they exercised over the Church and her property. Only when, with and after the interregnum, the dissolution of the German royalty became complete, and the duties even of the spiritual princes toward the empire became less binding, did the significance of the royal investiture disappear. It then became a mere form. The knightly representatives of the congregations, who, in the twelfth century, had still participated, together with the clergy, in the election of the bishops, at the same time ceased to take part in these elections. The greater part of the ministry were also excluded. The canons, for most of the dioceses, became the electing body. They formed a closed, purely ecclesiastical body, far less accessible to the interests of the authority of the State. In place of the emperor, the pope now won the deciding influence. Not the Concordat of Worms, but the

victorious uprising of the sovereignty of the princes
in opposition to the emperor, together with the
growing power of the canons, was the cause which
emptied the emperor's right of investiture of its
former value.

The empire asserted itself in the eleventh and
twelfth centuries in opposition to the Gregorian
ideas, and would not allow the Imperial power to
be degraded to an empire controlled by priests.
The papacy passed through similar experiences in
the entire west of Europe. The right of nomination to ecclesiastical places, which to this day
inheres in the authority of State (in Europe), even
though in a variety of forms, is the after result of
the right of royal investiture which the law of the
Middle Ages had produced in Germany, France,
England, and in general in the Romanic-Germanic
State of the Middle Ages.

§ 28. The Crusades[30] and Knighthood.

The Church was not able to set aside the State.
Under Gregory VII, however, and his successors she
gained the advantage of it. Churchly and religious
interests arose like mighty waves to take possession of
the culture of the Middle Ages. Pilgrimages to the
Holy Land increased in the course of the eleventh
century with great rapidity. Notwithstanding all
the sensuality and rudeness of the times, the question, " What must I do to be saved?" came with
overpowering force to the front; and the inborn

longing of the human heart for the heavenly Jerusalem found expression in the Middle Ages in the desire of the Europeans to look with their own eyes upon the earthly Jerusalem. Toward the end of the eleventh century the complaints of the returning pilgrims against the violence of the Seljuks awakened a powerful response in the West. But it was not an emperor nor a king who called Christendom to arms; but Pope Urban II, at the Council of Clermont (1095). And with what results! The Crusades were the greatest military undertakings which the Middle Ages witnessed. The knighthood of the West rose up to answer the attacks of Mohammedanism upon Christianity with force. During two hundred years the idea of freeing the holy sepulcher stood in the forefront of European interests, and ever anew stirred emperor and king, and the blossom of the nobility to fresh endeavor. And the military service which was rendered in these Crusades to God and his Son, Jesus Christ, was at the same time rendered to the Church and her superior head, the pope. The Crusades, for which the knighthood of the West was ever ready to buckle on the sword, signified in fact that the pope was the greatest, mightiest, and highest soldier of the West.

Knighthood rested upon an international thought. The knights of the West, according to the conception of the Middle Ages, formed a harmonious and united society, not limited by the boundaries of countries and States, into which the young nobility were received after they had received the accolade and performed certain feats of arms. All the great institutions peculiar to the Middle Ages bear this universal character. As the Church, the empire, and the education of scholars, so the organization of the nobility. The idea of the Roman world-empire found its image reflected even in the phenomena of the knightly orders. The Christian, not the French, nor the German, but strictly the Christian, nobility was the accoutered knighthood of the empire, which was then first of all *Church.* The first knight is the emperor, the secular head of Christianity (of the empire). It was his honor, however, and his pride, together with the entire knighthood of the period, to serve the Church, the pope. Knighthood was a society whose interests included those both of the nobility and the clergy. The Crusades began at the close of the eleventh century, and at the beginning of the twelfth the orders of knights appeared. (The Templars in 1119, the Knights of St. John in 1120.) Knighthood assumed a spiritual organization that it might render to the Church the service due. Monasticism girt on the sword that it might fulfill at once the oath of the monk and the noble. And these proud orders of knights, embracing the domain of Christendom, recognized but one superior lord, the pope. A standing army of armed monk-knights stood at the behest of the pope, uniting the

States to which the commanderies locally belonged, and clearly revealing with how powerful a hand the Church was now able to employ the secular sword.

This clerical and military agitation against the East aided the pope to perfect his rulership over the West. The days came when, at the command of the pope, a crusading army of Northern Franks took up the march to quench in blood the heresy of the Albigenses* in Southern France (1209); and when King John of England received as a vassal his kingdom from the pope (1213). The papacy became the most important of political powers. And all the more strangely, because this, his power over the world, rested chiefly upon the shoulders of a monasticism which had at first its motive in flight from the world.

§ 29. Monasticism—The Mendicant Orders.

Monasticism had taken to the sword. At the same time it was engaged in continually renewed struggles to realize its own spiritual ideals, the ideals of Roman Catholic Christianity. The highest aim of the piety of the Middle Ages, as of the Roman Church of to-day, is, for the individual, asceticism—the effort to become free from the world and its goods. The ideal Christian of the Middle Ages and of Romanism is the monk who has fled from the world to the cell of the monastery, there to crucify his flesh, with its affections and

* See Note 46 to p. 197.

lusts. But the world followed the monk even into his cloister. The riches, the power, and the political and educational interests of the Frankish and Ottonian period had laid hold of monasticism and banished its original ideas. The monasticism of Clugny in the tenth and eleventh centuries, was the first great backward tide toward the genuine monastic spirit. But it was not until the twelfth century that the spirit of asceticism regained its full vigor. A large number of new forms of monasticism rose up, each in its way giving expression to the energy of the ascetic idea. Prominent among these were the Orders of Carthusians and the Carmelites. But the most important part in this movement was acted by the Cistercians,[31] and especially by their great abbot, Bernard of Clairvaux.

The period of Bernard's life fell in the first half of the twelfth century (1091–1153). By his word he ruled the world, popes, emperors, and kings. He it was who decided between Pope Innocent II and the rival Pope Anacletus II, and he it was who subjected the West to the former. By the power of his speech he compelled Emperor Conrad III to undertake the second great Crusade (1147). Pope Eugenius III (1145–1153), a Cistercian monk and a pupil of Bernard, was an instrument in his hand. Yet this man, who bent the world to the power of his spirit, experienced the satisfaction of his real nature only when he avoided everything

which belonged to the world, and lived alone in
solitude in the contemplation of Divine love and in
the bliss of intercourse with the Almighty. As
Augustine was the father of Western theology, so
Bernard of Clairvaux is the father of Western
mysticism.[32] In immortal song the glow of his
spiritual experiences broke forth from his innermost
being. His *Salve caput cruentatum*, which has been
translated in the English hymn, " O Sacred Head,
now wounded," is a specimen at once of his poetic
genius and his spiritual fervor. Under the stress
of his longing after God, and while yet a youth,
he forsook the noble Burgundian family to which
he belonged, and passing by the Order of Clugny,
which had grown wealthy, he entered the then
recently founded, poor and unknown Order of
Cistercians in the midst of the forest thickets of
Citeaux (1113). Through him the Order gained its
celebrity and power. After two years a second
monastery had to be founded, that of Clairvaux, in
order to satisfy the needs of the growing numbers
of those who sought admission. It was laid in a
wild and solitary spot, and Bernard was chosen as
its abbot. Countless other monasteries were then
founded throughout the entire West. Up to the
middle of the thirteenth century the leading monastic Order was that of the Cistercians. Bernard
placed his monasteries, which in their architectural
style aided the incoming of the Gothic, in waste
deserts, or in the midst of the primeval forests, in

order to prepare at once a place for Christian and temporal existence. The Cistercian monasteries of the Middle Ages were the pioneers, not only of monasticism, but also of a husbandry which labored to subdue the wilderness, and which covered the original silent country with the magic of loveliness. In Eastern Germany these monasteries became the central points from which the Christianization, the Germanization, and the civilization of heathen lands proceeded. What an abundance of life was set free by this single man!

After Bernard of Clairvaux, the Middle Ages produced another spiritually creative personality, whose significance was, if possible, still greater. It was Francis of Assisi (born 1182). The power of faith brought forth in this rare man its most beautiful fruit, that of love. Following the example of his Lord and Master, it was his wish to give all his goods to the poor, and to preach to all men the gospel of repentance and of love. And so far as it lies in the power of any one man, he did it, and brought others to do the same. It was out of the work of practical Christianity, which to him was the monastic-ascetic, and which he brought to perfection by the power of his irresistible love, that the Mendicant Orders proceeded; and it was these Mendicant Orders, especially the Franciscans (1209) and the Dominicans (1215), which controlled the history of the Western Church during the second half of the Middle Ages.

Francis of Assisi, from whom the Franciscans received their name, undertook to realize the ideal of poverty, not alone for the individual monk, but also for the monasteries and the monastic orders. These, too, were to be incapacitated for holding property, in order that riches, that constant foe of all monastic rules, should be entirely excluded. He proposed that the brothers should be mendicants in the true sense of the word, subject to want and poverty, so that, dependent upon the gifts which they could beg for their living, they might learn to lead lives of humility, self-denial, love, and devotion to others.* This thought gave most perfect expression to the ideals of piety in the Middle Ages, and consequently exercised great influence, although the actual realization of it was at all times but very partially possible. Almost from the beginning there sprang up within the Order of Franciscans a milder tendency, which admitted the holding of property, and favored art and science, and which, therefore, opposed the more severe ideas of the founder of the Order. The Dominicans followed the example of the Franciscans, although with certain reservations and limitations. But enough of the original idea remained to conquer the Middle Ages. The Mendicant Orders did not need to support their members, for they lived upon the gifts of believers. Hence these Orders had no need to bind themselves to any limitations in the recep-

*See ? 39.

tion of new members.   The principles of the Orders
also included the giving up of the old idea that the
monk must be shut up within the walls of the monastery, and thus shut out from the world.   Far
and wide went the hordes of Mendicant monks, and
as they asked for the gifts of the people, they at
the same time carried everywhere the spirit, the
doctrines, and the convictions of monasticism.
They soon became the favorite father confessors,
pastors, and preachers of the congregations.   Set
free from episcopal authority by papal privilege,
in order that they might be immediately subservient to the pope, they recognized no limits in reference either to the bishops or the lower clergy.   All
Christendom was to them one single congregation,
which, without any boundaries, was open to their
preaching concerning things political, ecclesiastical,
and spiritual; and whose masses were influenced
equally by the energetic preaching upon all these
subjects.   Indeed, the founder of the Franciscans
undertook to cast out the net of his Order and its
rules over the whole world.   He created the "Third
Order"* of St. Francis, whose adherents were designated as Tertiaries.   There was a branch of this
Order for males, and another for female members
of the Church.   These Tertiaries remained in the
world, in the married state, in their callings; but
in other respects they assumed the severe life of the
monks, denied themselves even of innocent pleas-

---

* See next section.

ures, and observed the oath of the most earnest morality. A gray garment, bound together with a rope, lent them externally the aspect of ascetics. If the Clugny reform had set for its goal the monasticising of the secular clergy, this movement under St. Francis undertook the monasticising even of the laity. If monasticism is the special and real calling of the Christian, then the ideal must be set for every Christian, that he free himself from the world and dedicate himself alone, in a monastic life, to God and Christ. If monasticism is truth, then it must seek to inclose all Christendom in monasteries. This attempt was made by Francis of Assisi, so far as it was practicable and possible. Monasticism conceived of itself as the one valid form of the Christian life. Once it had fled from the Church; but now it turned back to the Church, in order to change her into its own likeness. At this moment the principle of the Catholicism of the Middle Ages celebrated its greatest triumph. The principle which strove to merit salvation by works of the law, by mortification of the flesh, and by flight from the world, filled and ruled the Church and the world.

To this must be added that the Mendicant Orders, especially the Dominicans, who so rapidly and powerfully developed, made their interests identical with those of the papacy. The pope freed them from the authority of the bishops. By special privileges he opened to them the way everywhere for unhindered operation. Thus, the strengthening of the papal authority, which served as a protection against the ordinary ecclesiastical authorities, was in the immediate interest of the Orders themselves. Everywhere throughout the Church the Mendicant monks, with their privileges, were a living witness to the all-reaching power of the pope. As through the immediate subjection of the knightly orders to the pope the power of the ordinary secular authorities, as emperors, kings, and princes, was broken, so, by the immediate subjection of the Mendicant Orders to the pope, the power of the ordinary ministerial authorities, as bishops and archbishops, was broken. The authority of the papacy rose up everywhere, threatening danger to the entire traditionary order of Church and State.

It must be further added that it was by means of the Mendicant Orders, and once more especially by means of the Dominicans, that preaching won a continually increasing significance for the life of the people from the thirteenth century on. Up to that time the public worship had been chiefly liturgical. The clergy, and even the bishops, were seldom skilled in spiritual address. The services were, as a rule, silent. Only the solemnities of the mass, the brilliant garments of the priests, and the mysterious customs, awakened religious awe in the congregation, which observed, rather than participated in, the exercises. In the feeling of the immediate presence of the God-man, which threw the congregation upon its knees, lay the goal and culmination of the services, which nourished at once faith and multifarious superstitions. It was through the Mendicant monks that spiritual oratory first unfolded its full power in the congregations. Still, the preaching of the Word was not yet a regular part of public worship. But it entered into the plan, preparing the way of the Word along-side of the sacraments, so that by the Word the great reformation of the Church in the sixteenth century could be brought about. But the preaching during the second half of the Middle Ages was in the service of the papal hierarchy. There was no press, as to-day. The pulpit was the place from which public opinion was shaped. It was employed, in a measure, to do the work now done by the press. Think of a time when the means of forming public opinion among the masses was exclusively in the hands of the papacy. What tremendous power!

We can see how the world was ruled by the pope during the Middle Ages. From the eleventh century forward the mastery of the ascetic-Churchly (monastic) views made continually increasing progress. The State itself was claimed by the Church as her creature. According to the teaching of the Church (the doctrine is that of Bernard of Clairvaux), the two swords (Luke xxii, 38), the spiritual and the secular power, both belong to the pope. The emperor, therefore, receives his authority as the vassal of the pope. The State is in itself unholy. It must be sanctified by its connection with the Church. As the star of the Imperial power paled before the Church and her influence, so did even the splendor of the courtly knighthood. The nobility of the time lived in the traditions of the Church. Nevertheless, in the twelfth and thirteenth centuries it produced its own independent view of the world, which was directed toward a noble enjoyment of life and a lofty form of knightly existence. In the same period which brought forth the Crusades and the monastic knightly Orders, fell the period when this worldly knighthood most flourished, with its devotion to fair ladies, its chivalric poesy, its love-songs and artistic taste, its brilliant festivities and tournaments, its passion for noble war and adventure, its code of knightly honor and conduct of life. Over against the monastic ideal of flight from the world, there appeared here an ideal of the enjoyment of the world which, in its excesses in the domain of devotion to women and to feats of arms, not without reason, called forth the immediate opposition of the Church. But the Mendicant Orders were mightier than chivalry. The circumstance that the power of this courtly chivalry, whose classic period began under Frederick Barbarossa, was broken directly after the interregnum, when it had flourished scarcely a hundred years, must not be attributed least of all to the power of monastic preaching, which was energetically and everywhere practiced by the Mendicant Orders. The chivalric ideal yielded to the monastic.

§ 30. THE MENDICANT ORDERS AND THE THIRD ORDER.

The Mendicant Orders had a significance aside from that of spreading the ideas of the Church and the papacy. To them is due at the same time the beginning of that process which brought the "Third Order" upon the stage of the world's history. Up to that time the history of the Middle Ages had been the history of the nobility and the clergy; and the clergy, in its ruling elements, was chosen from the circles of the nobility, from the so-called higher classes of society, distinguished by the possession of wealth and by knighthood. It could indeed occur that the son of an artisan should become pope, as, *e. g.*, Gregory VII.[33] But as a rule the bishoprics and abbeys were filled from the members of the great noble families; and even among the simple monks the noble, or in other respects better-born, held the decided ascendency, whereas in the lower circles of the secular clergy the lower classes, and frequently even those who sprang from the enslaved elements of society, were the superiors. The Ekkehards and the Notkers,[34] who founded the fame of the monastery of St. Gall, belonged to the noble families of Germany. Bernard of Clairvaux, the pride of the Order of Cistercians, sprang from an old noble Burgundian family, and at his entrance into the monastery took more than thirty of his high-born associates with him. The entire movement which took its rise at Clugny, and which gave the key-note to the reform of monasticism in the sense of asceticism, had its origin in the circles of the nobility. And it was this relation to the noble and property-holding classes of the nation which became the foundation of the empire and the cause of the decay of the monasteries. Both in the Church and in the world these classes were the leaders of the historical development. The citizens and peasantry had as yet no existence for the history of the world. These were the great and uninfluential mass. They contributed to the temporal foundations of the national existence. But they represented no idea. The merchants and artisans of the period had no interest which reached beyond their own city walls. They lived in the interests of their own immediate surroundings, while the horizon of the nobility and the clergy was the Western world.

It was in the fourteenth century that the great agitation began in the Third Order, under the influence and in the form of the Mendicant Orders. These Orders were able to secure the entrance of large masses of the nations into the monasteries. They appeared as rivals of the aristocratic orders, and with greater popularity, and accessible to every one. The time now came when the monasteries and nunneries began to fill from the lower classes, and especially from the inhabitants of the cities. The power which the Mendicant Orders, and especially the Dominicans, exercised, was the first great expression of the power of the Third Order; and not without reason did the knightly, courtly chivalry fall before the instincts of the at once ascetic and civil Mendicants.

The Third Order made itself master of the power of speech, of preaching among the Mendicants. But not alone of the influence of speech. The literature of the thirteenth, fourteenth, and fifteenth centuries was predominantly in the hands of the Mendicants, and, in particular, of the Dominicans. The mighty intellectual movement, which had its origin contemporaneously with the Crusades in the twelfth century, produced the universities of Italy, France, and England, and then, in the fourteenth century, in Germany. The majority of the professorships were filled by Mendicant monks, and especially, again, by the Dominicans, who had the reputation of distinguished scholarship. In the professor's chair, as in the pulpit, in the field of literature, and of instruction, the Mendicant monks won the first rank, and the results which here were won by scholarly studies, literary activity, and oratorical gifts, were at the same time won for and by the Third Order, which, in the Mendicants, for the first time, learned and exercised the power of education.

The education which the Third Order thus re-

ceived and represented was the education of the
Church, which culminated in the confirmation of
the rulership of spiritual over secular interests, of
the papacy over the power of the emperor.   The
power of the Church appeared to be unshakably established.   Even the Third Order, which went forward in great masses to conquer the future for
itself, was filled with the spirit of the hierarchy and
of asceticism, and gave to the ideas of the Church
their full weight and unlimited rulership over the
life of the people. Nevertheless, just at this moment the fall of the Church of the Middle Ages,
and of the whole structure erected by it, was prepared.   The complete victory of the Church included in itself the necessity of the return current.

§ 31. Excesses of Papal Power—Abuses.

In the mighty struggle during the course of the
thirteenth century the papacy had victoriously overcome the proud race of the Hohenstaufen.* Hence-
forth the power of the papacy knew no bounds, either
of secular or clerical justice.   The sum of earthly
might seemed to be united in the pope as in a single
point.   But this surplus of power must inevitably
prove a source of danger to its possessor.   The
rulership over the Church was manifested chiefly
in the filling of the clerical offices.   He who had
the right to fill the places of the Church had also the
Church.   He had the right to fill the places of the

---

*See Note 29 to page 147.

Church, had further the benefices at his command—
the untold riches of the Church, which were spread
over the whole world.

After the twelfth century, the papacy proceeded
upon the principle that, as a matter of right, all
power to fill offices in the Church belonged to
it, and that therefore the pope was justified in re-
serving places according to his wish—such as can-
onries, episcopacies, and pulpits—which he might
fill at pleasure. Especially did he choose the rich
cathedral benefices. The pope controlled such benefices in England, Germany, France, and elsewhere,
at first in the form of a request to the one who was
really entitled to fill the place, and soon in the form
of a command. What an enormous increase of papal
power! No monarch of the earth had such an
inexhaustible supply of offices, honors, and incomes
at his command, with which to win or reward men.
The possessions of the Church were open to him,
but not to the advantage of the Church. The filling
of the parish churches and the cathedrals within
a diocese, which naturally seek the most suitable
candidates, demands a degree of local and personal
information which the pope, at such a distance,
could not possess. The claim to the immediate
right of filling such places throughout all Christendom meant the failure to discharge that duty according to its true purpose. Not the Church and the
congregation, but the power of the pope alone, was
thereby served. The places were not bestowed upon

the most worthy, nor upon the natives of the country in which the Church or episcopacy, or prebendary was located, and who were acquainted with the congregations and their circumstances; but they were bestowed upon strangers who had never seen the country or the congregation, and who, perhaps, never came to administer their offices personally, but who sought only to make sure of the incomes, and who sent starving vicars to represent them in their duties. Favorites of the pope secured their appointments to a large number of positions, situated, perhaps, in various lands where it was impossible, in the nature of the case, that they should discharge their duties with earnestness. On the other hand, it sometimes occurred that the same place was given to several different persons, who entered into the benefits of the same, according to a designated order, each succeeding one being obliged to wait for the death of his predecessor in office. This arrangement sometimes led to the most vexatious legal proceedings to determine to whom the benefice was due. But it was at all times clear that it was not the office, but the income, which was intended for him to whom it was given. The Church fell into the hands of mercenaries. The congregations or the authorities of a place were not always pleased with the appointee of the pope. It was necessary that the papal appointee be accompanied, not only by the proper papal documents, but also by papal executives, who installed him by force. The king of England, with his Parliament, decided in 1350 to tolerate no more such papal executives upon English soil. This papal right of filling ecclesiastical offices with his favorites, was felt to be a sort of placing of the country in favor of the political power of the papacy, and at the same time in favor of the Italians and French, who more immediately surrounded the pope; and hence the determination to reserve the English benefices for England and the English. Already, national interest began to assert itself against this universal papal claim of the Middle Ages.

Not alone the nations, but also the bishops and lower clergy, felt themselves injured in their interests by such an exercise of papal power. By the interference of the pope in the filling of the places, the bishops were really weakened in their relation to their dioceses. But the great matter here was the appearance and power of the Mendicant Orders. On account of their many privileges, they were withdrawn from the jurisdiction of episcopal and priestly authority. The bishop had no right to interfere with them; they were subject only and immediately to the pope. The minister could not forbid them his pulpit. The Mendicant monk came and exercised pastoral care of the members of the congregation. He came and preached; he came and heard confession. He even came and exercised the right of excommunication. On account of his papal privileges, he had more wide-reaching

powers of absolution and of chastisement than the
simple pastor, and even than the bishop. What
wonder that the Mendicant monk won the preference over the pastor in the confessor's chair, and in
the pastoral care of the people! The pastor was
not able to prevent the Mendicant monk from becoming more the pastor and preacher of his congregation than he was himself. The ordinary rules
of Church government fell before these papal privileges. The weight of the papal power crushed the
ecclesiastical organization which rested upon bishops
and priests to the earth.

Whatever of episcopal authority yet remained
was destroyed by the right of appeal to the pope.
From the time of Gregory VII forward, appeal to
Rome was systematically encouraged by the popes;
not alone whenever a decision was desired, but in all
affairs of ecclesiastical administration. Soon there
was no act of ecclesiastical administration which
could not be brought to the pope by way of appeal.
As the entire right to fill places, so the entire ecclesiastical administration was fundamentally united
in the papacy. The whole Church was to be governed directly from Rome. As the surplus of
papal power in the right of filling ecclesiastical positions, so the surplus of papal administrative rights,
and of privileges bestowed upon the Mendicant
monks, must be considered as a hindrance to the
healthy development of the Church. The papacy,
until then the leading and organizing element of the

Church, now that its power was transformed into universal power, became an element of dissolution and disorganization.

All the more decidedly, since more and more secular and financial considerations pressed to the front in the exercise of papal authority. Gregory VII had founded the world-rulership of a purely spiritual power. His successors of the fourteenth century prepared themselves to use the power of the "vicar of God upon earth" as the means of an unworthy procuring of money. The gifts which flowed together to the papal court from all Christendom were immense. There were, however, three kinds of taxes, or gifts, to the pope, which were felt to be especially oppressive. The *first* was the regular payment (called annates) of the half of the yearly income by every one upon whom a benefice was bestowed by the papal court. The *second* was the very considerable amount which every archbishop had to pay to the pope for the bestowal of the pallium. If the position changed hands often, the result was debt. As a general thing, the money had to be paid by the whole province, since the archbishops were seldom able to pay the required sums out of their own means. The *third* consisted of sums which had to be paid by those to whom the pope granted dispensations. Since the pope had in many cases himself made the laws from whose observance he "dispensed," the accusation was freely made that many laws were only enacted in order to get money in exchange for dispensations from them. But worst of all was the fact that simony was openly practiced at the papal court. The granting of a ministerial office was dependent upon the use of money. Only those could get on at the court of the pope, in the prosecution of a cause, in urging a plea, or in securing an appointment to a desired position, who were able to scatter gold with liberal hand. The whole horde of those who surrounded the pope, from door-keeper to cardinal, demanded, in some measure, tribute from the one who preferred a request. What a disgraceful exhibition! In the very place from which Christendom expected the incentives to a moral and religious life corruption prevailed.

§ 32. The Babylonian Exile—Schism.

A sign of the inner weakness of the papacy was the severe blow which it received in the fourteenth century. It was during this century that the so-called Babylonian exile in Avignon occurred. After the fall of the house of Hohenstaufen, France, striving after national unity, made rapid progress, while Germany fell into a number of sovereign territories. Boniface VIII (1294–1303), who undertook to exercise the papal claims to authority in all their strength, fell thereby into a severe conflict with Philip the Fair, of France. It was against that monarch that the celebrated bull, *Unam Sanctam*,[35] was directed by Boniface VIII (1302), in which he claimed for the Church, with defiant energy, the right also to wield the secular sword, to set up and depose kings at will. Here, however, the result for the papacy was defeat. Pope Clement V (1305–1314) was compelled, at the instance of Philip the Fair, formally to declare (1306) that France and the power of the French king were not touched by the bull *Unam Sanctam.* Indeed, Philip secured the transfer of the papal seat by Clement V (1309) from Rome to Avignon. Avignon was the property of the pope, but it lay in the immediate neighborhood of the French dominions.[36] What the proud race of Hohenstaufen could not do was here accomplished in a few years by the rising French royalty, filled with the modern ideas of the right of the State. In the same period in which the papacy proclaimed the principle of its unlimited might, it became, in point of fact, a vassal and an instrument for the increase of the might of the French royalty. It was the excessive claims to power which brought about the conflict with the State, which was becoming conscious of its power, and which also brought on the defeat. The Babylonian exile continued from 1305 to 1377, from Clement V to Gregory XI,—that is, almost the entire fourteenth century. It was felt throughout the entire Church to be, in a sense, not only the disenthronement and imprisonment of the papacy, but also of the Church itself. Hence the ceaseless efforts to set it aside. After 1378 a pope established himself in Rome, in opposition to the pope in Avignon. Christendom divided itself into two opposing camps. The papacy, so long the pillar of the unity of the Western Church, had now become the cause of a schism. The two chief heads of Christendom fought each other with ban and interdict. For the first time the nations of the West saw that even the lightning of a papal ban could fall without effect. Inasmuch as the papacy fought the papacy, it destroyed, by the exercise of its own means of power, the impressiveness of its authority. The division continued more than thirty years (1378–1409). In the year 1409 a Council assembled at Pisa, which was to have done away with the schism. It deposed the two rival popes, and set up a third; but it lacked the power to carry its decision into effect. The two rival popes remained. To them was now added the third, chosen by the Council of Pisa. The double-headed schism had been increased to one with three heads (1409–1417). The boasted and coveted rulership of the pope ended at the beginning of the fifteenth century with a tremendous defeat. The bitter fruit of the rulership of the world, when accomplished, was inner and outer decay.*

§ 33. Degeneration of Monasticism.

As the papacy, so also monasticism prepared its own decay by too great success. The thirteenth

---
* See, in this connection, § 35.

and fourteenth centuries, as we have seen, are the period in which the monasteries and nunneries won the
upper hand by means of their influence upon the Third
Order. This very movement among the masses, however, which filled the monasteries of the Mendicant
Orders, could only prove their ruin. How many took
the vows without the necessary consciousness of an inner call! How many entered the monasteries, not to
abjure the world and sin, but to escape toil! Thus,
many a monastery became rather a community of
idlers than of ascetics, and deserving of criticism
rather than reverence. Involuntarily the increasing numbers of those whose existence depended
upon begging, pressed home the question upon the
inhabitants of city and country, whether it was
then really more pleasing in God's sight to do
nothing and live upon the labors of others, than
to discharge faithfully the duties of an earthly
calling. It now became clear, beyond a doubt,
that the principle of monasticism was incapable of
being extended to all Christendom. But could
that be in reality the ideal of a Christian life which
could only be put into practice when the majority of
mankind, remaining in their earthly vocations, contented themselves with a lower form of Christianity?
Still more. It soon appeared that even the increase
of ascetic practices was not able to maintain the
severity of the true monastic spirit. Even in the
Mendicant Orders immorality and impurity found
its way. The fourteenth and fifteenth centuries

echoed with the complaints of immorality made against monks, nuns, and the clergy. It would be unjust to overlook the fact that the mentally and morally better educated elements of society were numerously represented at this time. But the average morality of the masses of the monks, nuns, and clergy, sank below the normal level. While the Mendicant Orders were preparing to conquer the then existing world, it was made plain that even the most severe ascetic rules were not able to overpower the sinful impulses of human nature. It went, as it had gone, with all the monastic Orders. Upon a time of success followed a period of decay,—a decay all the deeper and more fateful, the greater the demands had been, and especially the greater the movement of the masses involved in their rise and fall.

§ 34. Reformatory Agencies.

The Church of the Middle Ages had arrived at the end of the development of her mightiest productions, the papacy and monasticism. The papacy, the victim of its own assertions of power, had become the source of countless abuses, and even a cause of schism. Monasticism, overreaching in its ascetic demands, ended with moral bankruptcy. Both the Church and the world longed after a new source of life. The time for the reformation of the Church had come. There was no one who did not unite in this desire. The perception of the needed reform was deep and universal. Indeed, the agencies already began to appear which betokened the light of the coming day. The fourteenth and fifteenth centuries were not merely the period of decay. This was also the same period which carried the reformation in its bosom. The great work which was to be accomplished was preceded by an intellectual movement which was to bear the chosen of God to his goal.

Wyclif (died 1389), under the influence of the great schism, and the general ruin which proceeded from the papacy and clergy, had declared the pope to be Antichrist, rejected the claim of the Church to power over the State, proclaimed war against the Mendicant monks, and placed upon his shield the Bible as the only pure source of God's Word and the criterion of all Christian doctrine. John Huss, stirred by the writings of Wyclif, had attacked the infallibility of the papal decisions and the value of the indulgences. As the English nation stood by Wyclif, so the Bohemians stood by Huss, who remained true even to death. Huss was burned at the stake in 1415, according to the sentence of the Council of Constance; but the fire which consumed him kindled the hearts of the Bohemians, and led to an uprising at once against their king, Sigismund, who had allowed Huss to be burned, and against the Roman Church. This mighty upheaval came to an end in 1433, in the peace measures adopted by the Council of Basle and the Hussites.

12

In Germany a piety which turned away from the externalities of the Church, and longingly sought an inner communion with God, had been spread abroad by the efforts of the mystic, Eckart (1312–17 in Strasburg, died in Cologne 1328), and of Tauler (died 1361 in Strasburg). The "Friends of God" (after the middle of the fourteenth century, especially in upper Germany and in Switzerland), and the "Brethren of the Common Life" (after the end of the fourteenth century, in Holland and Germany) had produced and spread among a wide circle of the laity a Christianity which looked toward the Bible, sought earnestly for salvation, and expressed itself in deeds of self-denying love. Thomas à Kempis, the celebrated author of the "Imitation of Christ," and John Wessel,* the forerunner of Luther in Scriptural theology, sprang from the "Brethren of the Common Life."

In the same period of the fourteenth and fifteenth centuries, which witnessed the decay of the papacy and clergy, and the downfall of the mental and moral forces of the Church of the Middle Ages, there arose, especially in Germany, an almost impassioned longing for a purified, genuine, and reformed Christianity. Just at this time Germany covered its soil with those magnificent church edifices which to-day adorn her cities, and at the same time with those countless pious foundations which bear witness to the spiritual life of the

German citizens. It was at this time also, and the more as we approach the nearer to the close of the fifteenth century, that the Bible was translated into the mother tongue of the Germans, and an edifying literature, which was intended to reach the masses of the people, arose. The masses awoke, and strove to make themselves inwardly possessors of Christianity. Hence the sympathy of the masses with the Mendicant Orders, and at the same time the stress upon a popular treatment of spiritual things, rendering them accessible to the masses, and suitable to the entire population, high and low. The same great longing after the ideal, which, with the vigor of proud youth, caused one university after another to spring from the soil of the Germany of the fourteenth and fifteenth centuries, found expression not only in the church edifices and foundations just mentioned, but equally in the spiritual literature which answered to the not yet wholly conscious desire of every individual for the highest things. And was it not at the same time that, in the *Renaissance* in Italy, the art and science of the ancients was born again, and entered into the vision of the humanity of the day, breaking with giant power the chains of the traditions of the Middle Ages? The world experienced the downfall of the spirit of the Middle Ages. Hence its hunger after a new spirit; and in this mighty longing after the intellectual and the spiritual which filled such wide circles, lay the upward-tending movement which prefaced that which was to come. As a sign that the time had come, the desire for reformation preceded the Reformation itself. The West rose up to the work of reformation as one man, led at first by the clergy, and then by its secular princes.

§ 35. THE REFORM COUNCILS.

It was the bishops who first entered upon the great task of reform. The Council of Pisa (1409), previously mentioned (page 172), was a first, although vain attempt of this sort. Three popes now stood in opposition to each other. (Page 172.) What a reproach to Christendom! Out of the strength of this feeling proceeded the power of the agitation which resulted in the Council of Constance (1414–1418). The bishops from every part of Western Christendom were here assembled, with numerous representatives of the universities and of theological science. Even the Emperor Sigismund participated. The splendor of the assemblage corresponded to its power, which rested upon the accordant desire of the West for the reformation of the Church by the Council. First of all, the Council asserted its own authority to execute the work. Since the question was one of the reformation even of the papacy and the healing of the schism, the Council was obliged to claim superiority to the papacy. And so it did. The assembly decided that the highest authority did not lie in the pope, but in the General Council. The general

assembly of bishops is superior to the pope. In
the exercise of this highest authority the three
rival popes were deposed, or compelled to abdicate,
and a new pope, Martin V, was set up. The
authority of the Council was seen in the fact that
its choice for the papacy found universal recognition. The schism was thus set aside. At the same
time the entire episcopacy had made itself superior
to the papacy. A retrograde movement which was
to do away with the ecclesiastical monarchy of
Gregory VII, and re-establish the old aristocratic
government of the Church, was thus introduced.
With this, however, the power of the Council was
exhausted. The establishment of the work of the
reformation was reserved for a newly-to-be-called
Ecumenical Council. The Council of Basle (1431–
1443), called by Pope Martin V, shortly before his
death, became the heir and continuer of the
Council of Constance. But the opposition of Pope
Eugenius IV and his party hindered every deep
reaching proposition. The annates (see page 169)
were abolished, appeals to the pope were limited,
conclusions were reached against the papal reservations and concubinage among the clergy. That
was all. When the Council proposed to go further,
it was transferred, by the machinations of the pope,
to Ferrara, and thus divided (1437). A Rump
Council remained in Basle, which, after a vain
struggle with the pope, ended, in 1443, in defeat.
The power of the Synodal movement was broken;

the work of reformation which the bishops had taken in hand had been wrecked. It was only a short time until Pope Pius II (1458–1464), who at the Council of Basle had been one of the leaders in the reform party, could condemn as heresy every calling of an Ecumenical Council (1459). The papacy grasped once more for the reins of ecclesiastical power. The episcopal assertions of Synodal authority were a mere episode.

§ 36. THE AUTHORITY OF THE STATE.

Nevertheless the old, unlimited papal power was no longer active. Already a national power was rising, and becoming daily more and more conscious of itself. The universal ideas of the Middle Ages, upon which the authority of popes and emperors had rested, retreated before the growing feeling of nationality; and with the modern national consciousness, the national power became more and more clear as to its task. In France and England a royalty grew up, rooted in the depths of the national life. In Spain the last remains of Moorish power were annihilated after a long struggle, and the authority of Ferdinand the Catholic[38] was extended over the entire peninsula. The period of the great monarchies was approaching. In Germany the movement benefited the territorial States of individual sovereigns, rather than the kingdom; but in this form of government the German State of the future was preparing. The Synodal movement (see preceding section) could be suppressed, because the pope conferred the right of ecclesiastical rule, and especially the right to fill vacancies in the offices of the Church, to the secular princes, and thereby won them for himself. The State desired authority even in the Church, and the papacy did not decline the demand. The government of the Spanish Church passed over to the king under Ferdinand the Catholic.

Similarly in England, in the beginning of the sixteenth century, under Henry VIII, the government of the Cardinal-legate Wolsey,[39] upon whom the pope had conferred great authority, in fact signified the government of the English Church by the English king. The right to fill the episcopal chairs of his own land was granted to the king of France in 1517. The German sovereigns received similar rights. The time of the rulership of the Church was past, and the time approached when Luther could arouse the Christian nobles of the German nation to the work of reformation. The secular princes took possession of the Church, and sought, by the manner of filling the positions of the Church, and by governmental oversight, to contribute to the needed reform.

But was the State able to infuse new life into the Church? Was the Church of England better because it was controlled by the king? By the rise of the national authority the Western Church broke into sections. A Spanish, a French (Gallican), and an English Church arose. When Henry VIII was refused the sought-for divorce* by the pope, it only required the royal word, even without any inner reform, to separate the Church of England from the Church at large. The consequence of the government of the Church by the State was her dissolution, but not her improvement.[40]

.   .   .   .   .   .

The work of the bishops at their Councils, the work of the State in ruling the Church, was merely that of altering the governmental forms. The garment of the Church was simply given another form. What was needed, however, was not a change of government, but of spirit. It was necessary that the forces of a new life should press upward from the depths of the religious and Churchly being, from the inexhaustible spring of the gospel, which, in her innermost heart, the Church had ever carried. And that was a work which neither princes nor kings, neither bishops nor popes could execute, but God only. The angel of God must come and trouble the waters of the life of the Church, in order to lend them new health-giving power.

§ 37. Scholasticism.

The Scholastic theology spent its chief strength in attempting to solve the relation between faith and knowledge. The great question then, as to-day, was, " What is reality?" The *Nominalists*, following

* See the section on the History of the Church in England.

the Stoics, affirmed that the universal ideas (*univer-salia*), which correspond to our conception of species, are mere abstractions (*nomina*) from individual objects, and have no existence or reality outside of the human mind (*universalia post res*). The *Realists*, on the other hand, asserted the reality of these universal concepts.[41] They were real, without regard to the human mind. But of the *Realists* there were two classes : First, those who, believing in the Platonic *idea*, taught the existence of the universal concept prior to the origin of the individual thing (*universalia ante res*) ; and second, those who, according to Aristotle, taught that the universal idea was in the thing, and reached the human mind only by experience (*universalia in rebus*). Platonic realism depended upon pure thought to learn the nature of the *thing* from the idea. Aristotelian realism depended upon thought and experience to learn the nature of the *thing* from the thing itself. These philosophic distinctions determined the form in which the Scholastics developed their theological systems. Upon one thing, however, all were agreed, viz. : That the doctrines of the Church were true, and could be best explained and defended by the methods of Scholasticism.

Anselm of Canterbury (born at Aosta, Italy, 1033, died as archbishop of Canterbury, 1109) was the first of the Scholastics to recognize and apply the central principle of Scholasticism. He proceeded upon the theory that faith is the condition of true knowledge, but regarded it as a sacred duty to elevate faith to knowledge.   On the basis of Platonic realism he undertook to prove the existence of God by the ontological method, as follows: The idea of an absolutely perfect being exists in the human reason; but his existence is necessary to his perfection, hence he must exist.   Even when the fool says in his heart, "There is no God" (Psa. xiv, 1), he testifies to the existence of the being whose existence he denies.   Roscelinus, as a Nominalist, had declared the conception of the Godhead to be a mere abstraction, and asserted that the three Persons of the Godhead could not be one in essence, since in that case they must all have been incarnated in Christ.   Anselm answered him in his *De Fide Trinitatis*, exhibited the perversity of Roscelinus's argument, and substantiated the doctrine of the Trinity.   This was the blow which deprived Nominalism of its power for more than two hundred years.

Another of the Scholastics was Abelard (1079–1142).   He asserted that no doctrine of the Church should be accepted until it had been tested by reason.   As a consequence he did not affirm at the outset the dogmas of the Church, but raised the question of their trustworthiness, and then proceeded to establish it by proof.   In carrying out this method he seemed to belittle the faith to a mere credulous acceptance of traditionary teachings.   He was also led into the statement of opinions entirely antagonistic to those previously held, and, largely by the efforts of Bernard of Clairvaux, his writings were condemned as heretical. Holding himself in high esteem, he was at the same time exceedingly ambitious; and while he was no doubt honest in his convictions, these qualities of heart probably robbed him of the caution becoming in a theologian.

Peter Lombard (died 1164) is another great name among the Scholastics. He, too, employed reason in the study of theology, but, unlike Abelard, rather to show the harmony of the doctrines with each other and with reason, than to raise doubts concerning them. On the same principle he proceeded with the Bible, stating frankly the difficulties which appeared to him, but endeavoring to reconcile them. Under the title of *Sententiarum*, he issued a text-book of Christian doctrine, which, while not characterized by especial originality, was so marked by other excellences that it became the standard book of theology for two centuries following. He compared it to the widow's mite, but its importance to theology it would be hard to overestimate. His book became the subject of many commentaries, verbal and written. Yet he followed the old trend, and held theological research in the channels marked out for it by the ages.

But while Lombard's work determined the course of theological thought for the majority, it was not blindly accepted by all. Alanus of Ryssel (died 1202), as well as many others, refused to follow implicitly the path thus marked out for them. Alanus asserted that heretics and infidels could not be convinced except by rational arguments, which he therefore attempted to supply.   He undertook to derive the doctrines of the Church from each other by a series of logical processes, deeming this the better method.   Others, as Walter St. Victor,[12] accused Lombard of employing the philosophy of Aristotle to sustain the doctrines of the Church, although he was equally opposed to the doctrines and methods of Abelard.   John of Salisbury (died 1180) opposed the entire Scholastic system, and declared that the contents of theology would finally be lost in the attempt to give it such exact form.   Yet he did not oppose what he regarded as a true use of science and philosophy in theology.

Not until the middle of the thirteenth century, however, did the Scholastic theology reach its highest point of development.   The causes of the rapid growth of Scholasticism during this century were principally two: First, the increasing knowledge of the Aristotelian philosophy, at first through the Arabian and Jewish translators and commentators of Aristotle, and then through direct study of his works in Greek.   Second, the fact that this philosophy, with its rich fullness of ideas, became the possession of a number of enthusiastic and able men who knew how to employ it in the interest of the Church.   Every phase of Christian doctrine was made the subject of a fresh examination in the light of this philosophy. Alexander Hales (died 1245) was one of the most celebrated of these theologians of the thirteenth century. He belonged to the Order of Franciscans. Another, and perhaps still abler, was Albertus Magnus (died 1280), a Dominican. Both employed Aristotle extensively. Some have even called Albert *Simia Aristotelis,* as though he had merely aped the great philosopher. Bonaventura (died 1274), a pupil of Alexander Hales, and a contemporary of Thomas Aquinas (also died 1274), was celebrated rather for his eloquence than his learning, although exceedingly gifted as a scholar also. A Franciscan, he was appointed by his Order as teacher of theology in Paris. Of great purity of character, his teacher, Alexander, called him an Israelite indeed, in whom there was no guile; while his later contemporaries called him *Doctor Seraphicus,* on account of his supposed angelic purity. He combined the doctrinal and mystical elements of theology, but gave decided preference to the latter. He believed, however, that every part of the doctrine of the Roman Catholic Church of his day corresponded to reason, and undertook to prove it in one of his works.

But not until we come to Thomas Aquinas do we meet the most powerful of all Scholastics. He vindicated the truly scientific character of theology. He it was who first introduced into the system of doctrine, and defended, the entire papal and hierarchal system of Gregory VII and Innocent III.

He divided religious truths into two classes,—those which the human reason can discover for itself, and those which, because they are above, not contrary to reason, must be revealed to the human mind.   In his principal work (*Summa Philosophiæ contra Gentiles*), consisting of four volumes, he designated and developed the former in the first three volumes, and the latter in the fourth.   Aquinas was a Dominican, and his Order made not only the contents, but the form of his doctrine obligatory upon all its members.   They regarded every variation from it as treason to the Order, the Church, and Christianity. The other Orders did the same, with the exception of the Franciscans, who were probably actuated by jealousy rather than by conviction.   At length, however, the Franciscans produced a man who was the worthy competitor of Aquinas in theological ability.   It was Duns Scotus (died 1308).   He it was who not only developed Scholasticism to its highest point, but who, in so doing, prepared its fall.   While Aquinas had been a Platonic realist, Scotus was an Aristotelian.   He took a far more lively interest in the proofs of the doctrines than in the doctrines themselves.   He regarded philosophy as theoretical, theology as practical.   He protested against the blending of these two departments of thought by Aquinas.   He taught that things are good because God chooses them, not that God chooses them because they are good.   He affirmed that the merit of Christ in the atonement was sufficient, simply because God had freely declared it to be so. As the Dominicans had adopted the teachings of Aquinas, so the Franciscans adopted that of Scotus, although he had attacked the positions of Bonaventura and other Franciscans with little less severity than those of Aquinas. The result was a long-continued strife between the two Orders, concerning both philosophy and theology.

From this time on, Scholasticism waned; and as Realism had failed to unify thought, Nominalism won the field and held it until the Scholastics died out. The principal names worthy of mention after Scotus, are Durand of St. Purçain (died 1333), Occam (died 1347), and Gabriel Biel (died 1495). But the effects of the Scholastic theology and methods are still apparent in the doctrines of the Church. This is unavoidable; and we need not hope for the coming of a time when the human mind shall ever shake itself free from the influences of the past.

§ 38. CHRISTIAN LIFE AND MORALS.

To the Protestant Christian, accustomed to think of Christianity as determined by Scriptural and rational ideas, the study of the life of the Church in the Middle Ages is, in many respects, a painful disappointment. Heathenism, in its conversion to Christianity, did not undergo that complete inner and outer transformation which we now look for in the conversion of the individual. The heathen converted to Christianity brought with them to the

new faith their life-long views of religion, in many
cases but slightly altered by contact with Christian
truth.　Under Christian names objects and forms of
worship peculiar to heathenism were maintained in
the Christian Church without any consciousness of
inconsistency.[43]　Heathen superstitions were trans-
muted by a slight admixture of Christianity into
Christian superstitions.　An example is the belief
in witches—a belief which had not died out, even
among educated people, at the beginning of the
present century.　These results were due especially
to two causes: First, the methods employed in conversion.　These were almost wholly external.　A
nominal and formal adherence to the Church was
regarded as satisfactory.　Men were no longer
brought to Christ, but to the Church.　Conversion
was not the result of personal conviction, but of
compulsion, or other external means, and proceeded
en masse rather than individually.　One great means
of conversion was the suppression of heathenism by
the Emperor Theodosius.　In 381 he forbade Christians to apostatize to heathenism; in 390 he pro-
hibited attendance upon heathen temples; and
in 392 he forbade all kinds of idolatry.　The steps
are clearly marked.　Christianity had become the
authorized religion of the State; every other must
be suppressed.　The people could be called Christian because they were not externally and formally
heathen; but the spirit of heathenism lived on in
the characters of the so-called Christians, and no

adequate effort was made to produce either the form
or the power of Christian godliness. An instance
drawn from a later period, and fairly illustrating
the wholesale methods of conversion, is the conversion of Clovis and the Franks to Christianity.
Clovis was king of the Franks, and a firm believer in
the heathen religion of his people. His wife, Clotilde,
was a Christian; but he had refused all her efforts
to bring him to her views. In battle with the Allemanians,* in 496, the gods in whom he had trusted
seemed to offer no assistance. In his desperation
he determined to call upon Clotilde's God. He did
so, pledging his allegiance to Christianity if, in answer, the battle should turn in his favor. The God
who was most helpful in battle was the God whom
Clovis would serve. He was baptized soon after,
and with him several thousand of his warriors. He
had, indeed, some conception of Christianity, which
he must of necessity learn from his Christian wife;
but his soldiers, who were baptized, had no other
motive than to follow their leader. They would
have followed him as readily into any other fold.
From that time forward the Franks passed for a
Christian people. By such methods great masses
were, indeed, made accessible to Christianity. But,
unfortunately, the means for infusing them with
Christian ideas, and replacing their heathen conceptions with those of the Gospel, were wholly insufficient. Religious instruction was confined to the

* See Note 13 to page 118.

learning of the Lord's Prayer, the Creed, and the baptismal formula. Throughout the Middle Ages Bibles were practically unknown to the masses of the people, although in this respect some improvement is visible toward the end of the period. The chief sources of Scriptural knowledge were passion plays and others of a similar character, together with the pictures, mosaics, and reliefs with which the Churches were adorned. Preaching was not common prior to the rise of the Mendicant Orders.

The second cause for the perpetuity of heathen ideas has thus been hinted at. The inner nature of Christianity was not made known to the people at large. The monks were drawn from the circles of the nobility. Monastic asceticism passed for Christianity, and was, therefore, inaccessible to the masses. When preaching became common, the content of it was not Christianity as taught in the Scripture, but rather the Church and its authority, or the value of the worship of saints and relics, or the dry, innutritious formulas of Scholasticism. In fact, the prevailing feature of worship in the Middle Ages was that of saints and relics. The rudeness and credulity of the period added to the evils thus introduced. Men altogether unworthy, living and dead, were discovered to be saints, and were revered as such. In proportion as the masses felt that they were excluded from the higher grades of piety, did they revere those who were supposed to be, or to have been, specially holy. Deceit on the part of those interested, and simplicity in the people, worked together to produce the belief in miracles wrought at graves of saints and by their bones or garments. Piety meant submission to these superstitions and obedience to the Church. Great value was attached to external, and even physical, manifestations of divine favor. It was believed that Francis of Assisi had received upon his body marks similar to the wounds of Christ upon the cross. Stigmatization, as it was called, became a mark of peculiar sanctity, and nearly a hundred persons, male and female, were credited during this period with having been thus distinguished. The power to weep almost incessantly was another distinguished evidence of peculiar piety. With such views of Christianity, it is not a matter of wonder that heathenism continued its existence under the name of Christianity. It was during this period that most of the great abuses of the Church and of doctrine arose or were developed. The reverence and respect paid to the Virgin Mary by the early Christians, as the mother of our Lord, "blessed among women," and as a woman of evident depth of piety and excellence of character, was transformed into Mariolatry, or the adoration of the Virgin. All manner of powers were attributed to her. Although our Lord in several instances took occasion, not, indeed, to rebuke Mary, but to teach the world that he was, by virtue of his nature and office, lifted above the obligations and limitations of earthly relationships, she was declared to be able to command her Son to do anything she would for those who called upon her, and he would obey.

So, too, the doctrine of purgatory was fixed during this period. All sins deserved punishment, but there were some which did not merit eternal punishment. Such must be atoned for either in this life or in the next. Souls unfit for heaven at death were to be purified in the fires of purgatory. The atonement in Christ did not secure our release from the penalty of guilt in case of such sins. The Holy Spirit was not expected to sanctify and purify the soul. But the Church had to its credit with God a vast store of merit upon which it could draw. This merit flowed from the works of Christ and the works of supererogation" performed by the saints. What the soul must otherwise suffer in purgatory in penalty for its sins on earth could be commuted by the authority of the Church by the application of a portion of this store of merit to the dead. Hence masses for the dead, and all the superstitious proceedings by which the priests extracted money from the friends of the deceased. In this same connection arose one of the greatest abuses of the false doctrine of indulgences. (See chap. iii, §§ 40–42.)

It was Peter Lombard (see § 37), who fixed the number of sacraments at seven. Prior to him the conception of the number had varied. Some reckoned only two, others an indefinite number. These latter divided the sacraments into three classes: First, such as are necessary to salvation; as baptism, confirmation, and the Lord's Supper. Second, such as, though not necessary, are helpful to salvation; as sprinkling with holy water, confession, etc. Third, such as are necessary to make the other sacraments possible; as consecration. Peter Lombard named, as the seven sacraments of the Church, baptism, confirmation, the eucharist, penance, extreme unction, matrimony, and orders. These sacraments were supposed to differ from the ceremonies of the Old Testament in that they confer grace upon the receiver, without reference to his faith or the character of the administrator; while those of the Old Testament required faith in the coming Redeemer to render them efficacious. In connection with the Lord's Supper the doctrine of transubstantiation received its final power at the fourth Lateran[45] Council in 1215. According to this doctrine, the bread and wine of the eucharistic feast are miraculously transformed under the hand of the consecrating priest into the veritable body and blood of Christ. The whole body of Christ was in every minutest portion of consecrated bread, and the blood of Christ was in every drop of consecrated wine. Christ was in heaven bodily; but he was at the same time in the consecrated elements, and that in however many places bread and wine might be simultaneously consecrated. At the same time the bread and wine retained their natural properties of taste, etc.   So fully was all this believed, and so completely did it take hold of the imaginations of the people that the child Jesus was even seen upon the plate where the consecrated bread had been; and the host was often seen to bear the color of blood.   Under such circumstances it is easily explicable that the cup was no longer given to the laity, lest in its administration a drop might remain upon the lips or beard and be profaned; and also that unbroken wafers were substituted for broken bread, that no crumb might fall and be desecrated.

From the ninth century forward, the terrors of excommunication also increased.   There were two kinds, the greater and the lesser.   The lesser excluded only from the sacraments; the greater from all Churchly fellowship and from a Christian burial. When it is remembered that any who held intercourse, even in business, with an excommunicated person, rendered himself liable to the same penalty, the terrors of the institution became evident.   The "Interdict" was another weapon in the hands of the pope for the strengthening of his power during this period.   If a ruler offended the "vicar of Christ upon earth" his whole land was made responsible.   Bells could no longer be rung; liturgical worship could only be conducted in private; the sacraments of penance and the eucharist were withheld from all but the dying; Christian burial was refused to all except ministers, beggars, foreigners, and children under two years of age, and no one was allowed to marry. Thus a powerful motive was given to the whole people of a section or country to interest themselves in bringing their rulers to make terms with the pope. It was during this period also that the Inquisition, that iniquitous institution which has occasioned so much hypocrisy, treachery, misery, and ignorance, was developed to its perfection. Punishment of offending Church members by excommunication and by lesser penalties was practiced very early. The Emperor Theodosius, who suppressed heathenism by force, appointed judges (inquisitores) to search out and punish heretics. But when, in the Middle Ages, certain heretical sects, such as the Cathari, Albigenses, and Waldenses,[46] began to cause anxiety by their strength and energy, vigorous measures were taken to exterminate all heresy. In 1184, at the Synod of Verona, directions were given concerning the methods of handling heretics. But it was Pope Innocent III who determined to make the Inquisition a permanent institution. The Lateran Council in 1215 made it the business of the bishops to visit personally or by representative every parish in which heresy was suspected to exist. He must put two or three of the best citizens, and if necessary all inhabitants, under oath to reveal the names of those who adhered to heretical doctrines. Refusal to take such an oath confirmed the suspicion of heresy. Friend must testify against friend; relatives against those dearest to them. The accused was cast into

prison, and tortured, to compel confession, and the
more persistent his denial the more severe the
torture applied. The accused and the accuser were
not brought face to face, but the name of the
accuser was withheld. Conviction followed, not as
a result of an impartial sifting of evidence, but
most unjustly as the result of mere suspicion supported by wholly inadequate testimony. A specimen of the method of proof is that two persons
who gave hearsay evidence against the accused were
regarded as equivalent to one eye or ear witness.
If the convicted did not confess and recant he was
cruelly put to death at the stake amidst pomp and
festivity. The distance to which the Roman Catholic Church, which is essentially to-day what it was
in the Middle Ages, has drifted from the gospel
of Jesus Christ, is seen in the institutions just
described.

But with all the darkness that had fallen upon
the Church, there were occasional gleams of light.
The times were rude, ignorant, and immoral.
There was little in the life of the Church adapted
to improve the morals of the people. Yet the
spirit of the gospel had entered the world, and all
the unfaithfulness of those to whom it had been
committed could not prevent its operation. The
duel, which was originally intended as an appeal to
Heaven to confirm the righteousness of one's cause,
and from which the personal element was excluded,
since it was substituted for a battle, was from that

stand-point preferable to a bloodier contest. Yet, while it has a certain warrant in such cases as that of David and Goliath, the spirit of Christianity is opposed to it. Ordeals, such as carrying balls of hot iron in the bare hand without injury, and plunging the bare arm into boiling water and receiving no damage thereby, were instituted to assist in determining innocence or guilt. At first, rejected by the spirit of the gospel, they were afterwards adopted by the Church; but later Christianity abolished them. The feuds and bloodshed so common in those warlike times were checked by the "peace of God," which forbade military strife during certain portions of the week or year. But the false ideas of virtue and godliness of the Middle Ages sapped so much of the moral energy of the period that little was left for the practice of the virtues which God required. Not until the Reformation broke the power of the Church and superstition, and self-imposed and useless efforts at moral self-restraint, did the true idea of Christian morality emerge from the shadow of the great cloud cast upon it by the papal and hierarchical system of the Roman Catholic Church. Never until Protestantism set the example did Romanism systematically undertake to instruct her people in the principles of religion and morals as taught in the Word of God. And even now, Romanism fears to let the light shine in its purity directly from the Scriptures into the mind. The truth must first pass through the

hands of the priesthood and be modified to suit
the tastes of human thought before the Romanists
will allow it to be given to the people. Under
the pretext of a desire for unity, they conceal their
fear to let the light of the gospel shine either upon
their history or the present condition of the Roman
Church.

§ 39. Benevolent Activity.

Jesus said: "Ye have the poor always with
you." The words are true for all generations.
The application of Christian principles to human
society would reduce poverty to a minimum. But
as long as evil and sin exist in the world, poverty
will continue to exist. The unsettled condition of
social and national life throughout the Middle Ages
made poverty very common and increased the
demands upon Christian benevolence. To poverty
must be added the other numerous and ever present
misfortunes of mankind. There always have been
blind, deaf, dumb, cripples, and paralytics to appeal
to the sympathies of those who, like the Master,
would go about doing good. An imperfect knowledge of the conditions of health rendered the
Middle Ages liable to pestilence and disease. Not
only was money needed to care for all the suffering,
but institutions and helpers were needed also. A
special cause of distress was the spread of leprosy introduced into the West as a result of the Crusades.
The number of houses especially established for

lepers throughout Christendom was estimated at nineteen thousand, most of them indeed small, containing not over a dozen inmates. Thus the occasions for the exercise of charity were numerous and urgent.

In many respects the brightest and most Christ-like aspect of Christianity during the Middle Ages is that of its benevolent activities. Not in every case, indeed, were the motives which impelled to benevolence those of Christianity. Even where they were sincerely believed to be drawn from the spirit of the gospel, they were often mixed with false conceptions of the truth. But, all in all, this benevolent side of the Christian life of the Middle Ages is that which most nearly represents the true Christian spirit. We may have little sympathy with monastic ideas in general. We may read, without any pleasing emotions, of the severities to which the monks and nuns subjected themselves, under the mistaken impression that they could thereby please God and purify their souls. But when we see these same monasteries providing hospitals and attention, not only for the sick of their own number, but also for the sick of the neighborhood, and care and refuge for the poor, the stranger, the benighted traveler, and the unfortunate of all kinds, we feel that we are again, at least in a measure, in the presence of the same spirit of human compassion and helpfulness which breathed in Jesus Christ. The hospitals and refuges connected with monasteries not only

relieved much distress, but incited others to emulate
the zeal of the monks. The cities established hospitals at the cost of the citizens; while individual
or corporative beneficence added to the number.
All these institutions were supported, in a considerable degree, by the alms of the people. Begging
became a kind of calling. It was not a vice, but
rather a virtue, since the beggar evoked the charity
of the Christian. It was as benevolent to arouse
such a sentiment as it was to act upon it. Hence
the giver and the receiver of alms were upon the
same level. Here we see the outgrowth of the
false ideas which prevailed. Yet the fact remains
that there was an earnest effort to alleviate the distress of the afflicted.

The prevalence of the idea of beneficence is nowhere more evident than in the large number of
organizations which devoted themselves, either
wholly or in part, to the alleviation of human suffering. Among the most distinguished is the "Order
of Knights of St. John," sometimes called "Knights'
Hospitallers," and afterwards "Knights of Rhodes"
and "Knights of Malta." The necessity for the
Order arose in connection with the vast numbers of
pilgrims to the grave of our Lord. Many became
sick, and in a foreign land needed care. They afterwards devoted themselves more especially to arms,
but their origin was purely benevolent. So great
was their love for the sick that they looked upon
them as masters and brethren, and gave them the

preference in all things. Another Order, known as the "Hospitallers of St. Anthony," was organized in connection with an epidemic called St. Anthony's fire. The "Teutonic Order," or "Knights of St. Mary," was established by wealthy German knights for the support of poor pilgrims, without regard to nationality. The "Beguines" originated in the "Low Countries" (Netherlands), and were probably founded by the priest Lambert le Begue, about 1175. The Order was composed of women, who took vows of chastity and obedience to the rules of the Society. They were active in the care of the sick, not only in hospitals, but also in private houses. The "Beghards" or "Beguards" were societies of men and women, with regulations similar to those of the "Beguines," and established for similar objects, although they never attained such prominence. The "Brothers and Sisters of the Common Life," to whom Thomas à Kempis adhered, were also semi-monastic; but they rejected begging, engaged in labor, and to care for the bodies added care for the souls of men. The "Alexians" subjected themselves both to the parish authorities and to those of the city, and rendered implicit obedience as to their regulations, their toil, and their care of the sick.

Besides these more religious organizations for purposes of benevolence, there were also many of a more secular kind which assisted in caring for the sick and poor. These were the guilds of the various tradesmen and artisans. Besides the furtherance of their special objects, they practiced certain spiritual exercises, and had a treasury for the support of the needy.

Among the individual workers in the cause of Christian benevolence must be named St. Severinus of Noricum, who, although he lived prior to the Middle Ages, his activities falling in the latter part of the fifth century, yet belongs to our period in the spirit and methods, as well as in the field, of his labors. The troublous times in which he lived demanded just such a soul. A layman, never holding any secular or ecclesiastical office—and refusing them when offered—he was, notwithstanding, very active in works of humanity. He always went barefoot, and would eat nothing before sundown; yet he was always cheerful. He once received a present of some prisoners of war. These he released and, feeding them and giving them drink, sent them away with the exhortation to abstain from further violence. When exhorted to care for and nourish his own body, he replied: "I hunger and thirst only with the wretched and sick whom I see hungry and thirsty. That which you see me do is no merit of mine, but an example for you." When asked who he was and whence he came, he replied: "If you take me for a runaway, collect money to purchase my release, if I am demanded back." In this spirit he spent his life of self-denial for the relief of others.

Charlemagne (768–814) united most intimately Church and State under his rule. He himself set a most excellent example in almsgiving. He allowed such a mass of beggars to assemble at his court that both the palace and the empire were burdened with them. But he took care that there should be no deceivers among them. He restored to the Churches the property of which they had been robbed, and made numerous gifts to monasteries. He gave a tenth to the Church, and urged the same practice impressively upon others. The money thus received was to be divided into three parts, for the support, respectively, of public worship, the clergy personally, and the poor and strangers. He provided that as far as possible each landlord should care for the poor upon his own estates. Begging was forbidden. In an address to his people in 802, he exhorted them to love their neighbors as themselves, and according to their ability to give to the poor, to entertain strangers, to visit the sick, and show mercy to the prisoners. He desired the clergy to set the example by public quarterly distributions of alms. Unfortunately the excellent measures which he planned were not carried forward after his death. He did not succeed in permanently impressing upon the people the evils of beggary and the true methods of caring for the poor.

Francis of Assisi personally set an example of benevolence, and was at the same time an influential factor in the general beneficence of his own and succeeding periods. In the cold of winter he gave his cloak to one who was in need; and, when reminded of his own physical weakness, replied that he would regard it as a theft from the Great Almsgiver to withhold any of his possessions from the needy. Upon one occasion he passed a disgusting leper. Involuntarily he turned away; but his conscience smote him, and, springing from his horse, he went to the opposite extreme and embraced the wretched sufferer. But while he was thus personally a pattern of benevolence, he also molded the conditions from which sprang, in subsequent times, innumerable institutions for the relief of the distressed.

In the Church of Assisi is a picture by Giotto, which portrays the one great thought of St. Francis. It represents his marriage to Poverty. Christ himself unites the pair. Faith bestows the wedding-ring, while Love stands close at hand. In this love of poverty for its own sake is included love for the poor. And so a truth was impressed upon the thought of the Christian world by the Mendicant Orders which brought forth abundant fruit in works of charity.

But the most beautiful figure in the charitable efforts of the Middle Ages, although not so broadly influential in determining the modes and degrees of benevolence in others, is Elizabeth, Landgravine of Thuringia, wife of Ludwig, Landgrave of Thuringia. In later years, and after her husband's sudden death in one of the Crusades, she was led, under the influence of Conrad, her spiritual guide, to a most unworthy mode of life, even hardening herself in her supposed Christianity to such a degree that her own children were no longer dearer to her than any other human beings. But while she was mistress of the Wartburg (where later Luther was a prisoner among his friends), she preserved all the most beautiful instincts of humanity sanctified by the spirit of Christ. The beggar, the poor, the sick, and dependent children were her constant care. For the benefit of the sick who could not ascend the mountain to her, she erected a hospital in Eisenach, where she visited the inmates daily. Another house was provided for the care of needy children, toward whom she exhibited the love and faithfulness of a mother, giving most attention to the most miserable. Patiently, even joyfully, she endured the heavy odors of the sick-room. When her means were exhausted in the relief of wretchedness, she disposed of her silken garments, that the proceeds might be devoted to the extension of her labors of love.

The individuals now described are but more illustrious examples of the spirit displayed by thousands in a smaller way and in a narrower sphere. The doctrines of Jesus might be in many respects changed beyond the possibility of recognition; the Church of Jesus might fall into the hands of ambitious and wicked men who used it for their own

14

selfish ends; even the religious life might become perverted into a mere show of voluntary humility and service; but the spirit of love, which was the spirit of Christ, lived on, almost as pure as at its birth, and its blessed and holy influence never once failed in the hearts of men.

Third Chapter.

Period of the Reformation.

FIRST DIVISION.

THE REFORMATION.

§ 40. New Tendencies.

As we enter upon the year 1500 in Germany, we read, in golden letters, over the doorway through which we pass, the inscription, *Renaissance*. A shout of gladness ran through the entire educated world: Rejoice, rejoice! The classic world of the ancients, glorified anew, is born again in youthful beauty. Here is the genuine Aristotle, here the divine Plato, here the masterpieces of art and science filled with marvelous beauty and immortal thought; and the sun of Homer, behold! it shines upon us also.

It was the time of Raphael and Michael Angelo.[1] It was the time in which an uprising, passionful, ambitious, enthusiastic generation, conscious of the soul's needs, and longing after all that was great, kindled its fires at the shrine of antique literature and science. It was the time in which the national consciousness fed and grew upon the heroic figures and political ideals of the ancients, repressing the universalistic ideas* of the Middle Ages; in which

---

* See ¿ 28.

the "Third Order" entered with vigor into the foreground of the world's history, greeting and laying hold of the new scientific spirit as a suitable civilizing agency with which to free itself from the guardianship of the Church; which lifted the citizen to the possibilities of a scholarly education, and made the city, once for all, the center of the national mental life. Life assumed a wholly different form. The spirit of the ancients came into conflict with monastic asceticism, spreading abroad a delight in life and beauty, and an appreciation of a tasteful form of existence and enthusiasm for State and Nation, lending rich color to the entire world.

A new evangel of education, starting from Italy, filled the Occident. The ideas and views of the Middle Ages yielded to the spirit of a resurrected antiquity. A new period approached, fresh as the morning, carrying in its bosom a future full of inexhaustible promise.

And yet, was this the regeneration which the fifteenth century so ardently desired? Was this the fountain of youth after which the Middle Ages panted? No. What the world, during the fifteenth century, longed for, in its deepest heart, was not *renaissance*, but reformation; not the regeneration of art and science, but the regeneration of the Church, throughout its whole being; not the message of the rediscovery of the antique world, but that message which had once been preached to the poor, by which sinners were saved and men were born again. A moral *renaissance*, brought about by the renovation of the life of the Church, was the greatest and highest concern, and which repeatedly set the forces of the fifteenth century into universal motion. In the abuses of the Church, in the degeneracy of the clergy, in the obscuration and obstruction of the sources from which the masses can alone be morally nourished and sustained, the instinct of the period recognized, with striking certainty, the causes of the wide-spread ruin. The Church had lost itself in the world. The salt had lost its savor. The requirements of Christianity were most openly trampled under foot by those who were called to be the vessels of the faith, the preachers of the divine truth, and the examples of the flock. The decay of spiritual life cried to heaven, and it was all the more sensibly felt the wider the circles became which were seized with the longing after spiritual things. Hence, amidst all the gladness and joy which broke forth from the *renaissance* of science and art, resounded ever anew, ever louder swelling, through the whole of the fifteenth century, the mighty cry: Reformation of the Church in all its parts—reformation, not alone of the scientific and artistic, but, what is far more precious, of the religious life.

We have seen the great Reform Councils of Constance and Basle, which occupied the entire first half of the fifteenth century. What flood-tides of desire for the reformation of the Church, carrying the

entire Occident with them, and almost flooding out
the papacy itself with its abuses! What magnificent plans and hopes, and yet what slight results!
We have seen the energies of the State, which, in
the second half of the century, took the work of
reformation in hand. By the assistance of the
State, in the exercise of its rights of appoinment
to vacancies in the Churches, and of oversight, new
energy was*to be restored to all ranks of the clergy,
and the Churchly spirit re-established in the Church.
But of how little promise was this labor directed
toward the outworks of the Church! And instead
of inner regeneration, the Western Church was dissolved into a series of National Churches, each striving for independence.

But perhaps the culture of the period, the courageous, mighty, and oncoming *renaissance* movement, would be able to secure the longed-for improvement in the Church. Alas! this very culture
carried heathenism in its heart. It did not think of
reformation. Rather, it was ready to subject itself
externally, and without much struggle, to the power
of the Church, with all her ceremonies and requirements; for in its deepest heart lived indifference
toward everything Christian, and a sole interest in the
purely human. The *renaissance* of art and science
was not the new birth of morality. It was, however, just this *renaissance* which, in awakening anew
the heroic ideals of antiquity, filled the cities and
States of Italy with those violent, selfish, overbear-

ing, and over-ambitious tyrants, whose exhibitions of genius were only reached by the disregard of all laws of morality. Never has there been a society so brilliantly educated, so rich in varied interests and gifts, so mightily creative in immortal master-pieces, and yet, at the same time, so deeply immoral, so profoundly ruined, so egotistically bestial, as that very society of Italy in the second half of the fifteenth century. This was the time which produced a Cæsar Borgia,[2] who was the type, the ideal, and, at the same time, the terror, of his age. This was the period in which Machiavelli[3] wrote his "Prince," a text-book, and, at the same time, a glorifying of the coolest, most selfish, calculating, and cruel princely egoism. Even when we look at the pictures of Madonnas and saints, prior to the marvelous creations of Raphael, the impression of a beautiful, glorious, and glorified humanity preponderates. It was but seldom that the mysteries of Christianity, as in the eyes of the Sistine Madonna, beamed with entrancing power upon the beholder.

And the papacy of the *renaissance!* In the person of an Innocent VIII (1484–1492), and an Alexander VI* (1492–1503) the profound immorality of the *renaissance,* defiling itself with murder, treachery, and unchastity, ascended the papal throne. They were followed by Julius II (1503–

---

* His son was, as is known, Cæsar Borgia, and his daughter Lucretia Borgia.

1513), a general, rather than a minister, whose life-work was war and violence, in the interest of the increase and political unity of the papal territory. Then followed Leo X (1513–1521), the excellent art connoisseur, the highly cultured man, the patron of Raphael and Michael Angelo. What were the impulses which these men gave to the Church? How great was the papacy of Leo X for the history of culture, and how insignificant for the history of the Church! It was exactly the *renaissance* which produced these popes, which gave them their secular and worldly tendencies, which caused the pope, with light heart, to yield the interests of the whole Church, the rights of appointment to vacancies and of government, to the secular princes; to place the papal territory in the foreground of his interests, and to transform himself from a chief of a spiritual, universal monarchy into a voluptuous, cruel, or even violent and warlike, or artistic and scientific, Italian tyrant.

The interests of the *renaissance* were, in their final analysis, opposed to the interests of the Church; and the high-tide of intellectual life which, about the year 1500, carried the Occident with it, appeared rather to hasten the final ruin than to bring salvation.

In Germany, indeed, the intellectual development took a somewhat different direction. Here was, in particular, the house of that great reform movement of the fifteenth century which, in the

Councils of Constance and Basle, had shaken the whole world, Here, also, at the beginning of the sixteenth century, spiritual interests were still in the preponderance. All classes of the nation, in equal degree, felt themselves to be participants in these. It was these which lent to the German *renaissance* movement, Humanism,[4] such a decidedly Churchly direction. Too deep, and living in the heart of the nation, lay the great concerns which could find their satisfaction alone in Christianity; too mighty was the energy with which the people longed for the certainty of their salvation, for them to forget, in their interest for anything else, this, their greatest desire. And so it occurred that Humanism delivered anew into the hands of the educated the Old and New Testaments in the original tongues, the former by means of Reuchlin, the latter by means of Erasmus of Rotterdam;[5] that philology was valued just in order to help theology to a perfect knowledge of its original sources; and that it was even hoped, by means of the philological investigation of Scripture, to bring about the revival of the Church. Such was the conviction of Erasmus. But this literary movement which, in Germany, pointed with uplifted finger to the New Testament, was far from able to control the masses of the people, and to set a limit to the ruin of the Church. It took possession only of the educated, and of them only through the requirements of investigation, not by fixed, living, vigorous, and

accomplished results.   Assuredly, the Humanists of
Germany were not equally indifferent toward the
Church with their associates in culture in Italy.
But their culture lacked the heat and energy of
great positive convictions.   Hence it occurred that
the fullness of intellect and knowledge which dwelt
in these men, detonated, for the domain of the
Church, in a rocket-like bustle of ridicule and satire
(Praise of Folly, by Erasmus, 1509), with which
they covered the abuses of the Church.   It was a
movement which, like every purely scientific movement, was strong in denial, but weak in affirmation;
which, indeed, saw the need which was to be met,
but which lacked that essential natural vigor which
alone produces great, creative, world-historical facts.

When, in the year 1517, the great Lateran
Council came to an end, having busied itself with
the reformation of the Church, but having contented itself with defining the power of the pope
and the immortality of the human soul (this had
already become necessary, in opposition to the Rationalism of Italy), the bishop of Isernia, in the
closing address, which had been assigned to him,
uttered the words: "The gospel is the source of
all wisdom, of all virtue, of everything divine and
worthy of admiration; the gospel, I say, the gospel."
He was nearer right, perhaps, than he thought.
And already the youthful hero had arisen, the sent
of God, to announce everywhere the already forgotten but true and perfect gospel.

§ 41. LUTHER.

The help came from the circles of monasticism, from whence no one had expected it. Monasticism had once, through the Clugny movement, produced the Church of the Middle Ages; and again, through monasticism, the Church of the Middle Ages was to be destroyed.

Monasticism had become the most despised part of the Church. Purposing to flee from the world and to leave all behind it, it had in its own heart the world, sinful lust, and selfishness. Invisibly, inevitably, these things were carried along into the desert, the hermitage, or the cloister. Even out of the heart of the monk proceeded evil thoughts, fleshly and worldly lusts. Monasticism was consumed by the world from which it desired to flee; and it was exactly this monasticism which had become the sore spot at which the Humanists directed their arrows of ridicule when they wished to scourge the abuses of the Church. Nevertheless, there lived in monasticism, although overclouded and misdirected, and often scarcely perceptible, the product of a genuine Christian purpose, which sought, with fear and trembling, the righteousness pleasing in God's sight. And these religious impulses were to show themselves mightier in release and reformation of the then world than all the culture and all the great discoveries of that period. Monasticism, seeking its salvation in flight from the world and in

works of asceticism, involved in itself, for all earnest
seekers, the necessary final conclusion, that by the
works of the law no flesh shall be justified before
God; that all human effort to flee the wrath of that
just and holy God who hates sin, and visits it even
upon the fourth generation of them that hate him,
and monasticism, with its self-mortifications and ab-
juration of the world for the purpose of meriting
salvation, were alike vain. The development of
monasticism had been a growth of the ascetic principle. This growth necessarily led to self-destruc-
tion. This was the process of the development
which Luther, with all the energy of a fiery and
capacious nature, had passed through. He had
borne the whole weight of the divine law in the
depths of his innermost conscience. He had experienced hours in which his faith in God became a
more than martyr's faith to body and soul, in which
God, "like a lion," crushed the bones of the monk, as
he wrestled with him mightily for the salvation of
his soul. These were the hours in which God was
preparing the monk for his mighty instrument of
reformation. What anxiety, what struggles, and
then, what a victory! "The just shall live by
faith." This was the melody which, sinking ever
deeper and more forcibly into his soul, filled it with
heavenly delight. Man must be justified, not by
his own works, nor by his self-mortifications, nor by
flight from the world, but alone by faith through
grace--free, all-merciful, inexhaustible grace. The

grace and truth which appeared in Jesus Christ
now lighted Luther, brightly, peacefully, joyously,
along the path of his ever stormier life. The
newly discovered gospel, so long misunderstood and
so long painfully desired, became to him a "wide
open door into Paradise," notwithstanding all the
inner struggles which he experienced later in life.
How he had hungered and thirsted after righteousness! Truly, he was now to be filled. How, above
all things, he had longed for the kingdom of God;
and behold! now he had obtained all—the blessed-
ness of the children of God, able to transform
every new day into a day of gladness, the freedom of a Christian man, by his faith "a lord of all
things."

And he was compelled to make known, in
trumpet-tones, to all the land that which had become
to him a blessed certainty. It was his opposers who
forced him ever further out upon the great high-
way, until suddenly he perceived that between himself and the pure gospel of Jesus Christ lay, like a
mighty obstruction, the Churchly organization, with
all its traditions, sacred places and objects, priest-
hoods, and powers, upon which his soul had so
heartily depended. And in this moment—in this
consisted the grandeur of his deed—he did not hesitate a single moment to cast away all that theretofore had appeared to him great, glorious, holy,
necessary, and irreparable, for the sole sake of
the gospel of Jesus Christ. For the sake of that

gospel he became poor in all which had hitherto made him rich. The whole world, in and by which he had previously lived, crumbled about him. The faith which he had set upon his Church, so warmly loved, he must resign; but it was to exchange it for a full and precious faith in redemption and justification in Jesus Christ. The world of his youth he was to lose, but the world of the future was to be given him in compensation. Against monasticism and its asceticism, the Church and its mighty hierarchy, he courageously hurled the gospel, the gospel of justification by faith alone, an inexhaustible gospel, full of reformatory vigor, capable not only of destroying the old, but in a new period, breaking by its inner fullness the traditionary chains, able also to build up.

Monasticism, in the person of Martin Luther, came to an end in that it rejected asceticism, put away its distinguishing garment, its fastings and mendicancy, turned back to the world in order to sanctify, not to escape from it. The regenerated gospel meant the reformation of the Church, and with the reformation of the Church the reformation of the whole world.

To the Middle Ages the world was a world of sin. Hence the piety of the Middle Ages consisted in the renunciation of this world, with all its gifts. With this view, the monk fled marriage, possessions, the whole world, with its art, science, joys, and duties, in order to crucify his flesh with the affections and lusts. What a magnificent sacrifice of self and the world! And yet woe unto him! For with the world of sin he fled also the world of morals. He fled from temptation; but he fled, at the same time, from the duties which God had made incumbent upon every individual in this world, from the duties of family and civil life, with all their requirements of self-renunciation and self-sacrifice, of genuine, real, effective morality. Egoistically the monk withdrew from the world into his monastic cell, to live no longer for his neighbor, but for himself alone. In his retreat the door had been closed behind him. He no longer sees the world, with its obligations; he sees only himself. He has withdrawn himself, in flight, from the storms of life. From the sea of trouble, labor, and the daily vocation, he has turned into a haven of rest, leaving all others without. Let them see to it how they may best help themselves. He has escaped the battle of life. But woe unto him!—for his flight is cowardly desertion of the flag.

How the whole aspect of the world has been changed by the Reformation doctrine of justification by faith alone! "Believe on the Lord Jesus Christ, and thou shalt be saved, and thy house." This is the complete, perfect, divine gospel, which tolerates neither addition nor decrease. Receive its precious contents, and find spiritual quickening thereby. Thou thyself hast nothing to contribute thereto. Away with the self-made morality, piety,

and holiness of a life of asceticism and flight from
the world.   Monasticism will not trust the grace of
God offered in Christ, but must add to the grace of
God a self-acquired righteousness.   Hence, away
with monasticism.   Man is placed in this world, not
to flee from it, but to serve God in it.   Entrance
into the world, into all the pleasures and pains of
the daily vocation, of the family life, of a life with
and for our neighbors, in order to find, by faith in
God, the true satisfaction, and at the same time
fresh power for new victories, and to find in all un-
rest rest, in all things secular the divine and eternal
which leads to higher things,—this is true Christian
morality.   The fulfillment of duty is the true service of God.   Thus faith leads directly into the
world, in the service of our fellow-men.   Thus
faith produces the power of love, which seeks not its
own, but that which is another's, good.   As faith
sets the Christian man free, and makes him lord
over all things, the servant of none but Christ, so,
by love, its effect is to make the Christian man the
servant of all.   That is the true Christian perfection, to be a true Christian in the stress of human
life, to fight in the labor of the day the good fight
to which the promise of victory has been given.

The stamp of unholiness had been taken from
the world and from life in the midst of the world.
Life in a worldly calling, in the State, the community, or the family no longer appeared as an unavoidable evil, admissible because of our weakness,

as a beautiful shell with death-dealing contents, but
as an activity of the true and perfect Christian
morality. All these relations of man to man bear
in themselves a God-given duty, their own moral
worth, a power of true release from temptations to
selfishness. Marriage now appears as the true, sacred, spiritual order of human affairs. It is an institution founded by God himself, an educational
institution even for the adult, giving him not only
wife, children, refuge from the hardships of life,
constantly new sources of joy, and a protecting atmosphere of living love, but also, in the duties of
domestic life, daily exercising, nourishing, strengthening, and correcting him; transforming existence
into a life devoted to others, daily calling forth
anew into light from the hidden sources of the domestic life the ideals which preach to those who
train and teach, as well as to those who are being
trained and taught. The State appears no longer
as of necessity a work of the devil or of sin or of
unrighteousness. Like the family, so the State is
an institution of God, carrying in itself its own independent moral task, destined to render possible
and to secure the constitutional freedom which is
the first step to moral freedom. The entire civil
life, labor in agriculture or commerce, in mechanics
and industries, in science and art, in commanding
and obeying, the work of man and maid, of the
judge, the soldier, the civil officer, and of the
prince,—all these, as God-given callings, consti-

tute a service well-pleasing in God's sight.   The
whole world has been sanctified.   Its profaneness
has passed away.   The world, with all its tasks, has
been transformed into a vineyard of the Lord, into
a temple of God, in which we are to worship God
in spirit and in truth.

These reformatory ideas filled the Western world,
especially Germany, with their stormy roar.   They
founded the world of to-day.   They produced the
present moral ideals of life.   Over against the ascetic ideals of life of the Middle Ages which fled
from the world, appeared a new ideal of life, directed toward the world, understanding and using
the world, and in so far related to the *renaissance;*
but its purpose was not to fill the world with the
ideas of Humanism, but with those of Christianity.

A vast mass of moral energy was set free by this
change of views and directed toward family, political, and the entire civil life.   Now first began the
full and true estimation of the civil callings, of the
State, and of civil freedom.   The State of the present day stands erect;   the moral ideals which exist
in this terrestrial world take their place along-side
of Churchly endeavor.   The terrestrial world has
become free.   It has been rescued from the curse
which the Church of the Middle Ages laid upon it.
The terrestrial world is reformed.   The reformation
of the world was a result of the reformation of the
Church.

The fifteenth century had undertaken the Reformation by means of constitutional experiments and disciplinary precepts. But it was a vain effort. In grasping the doctrine of the Church, the gospel which it preached, and changing its form and filling it with new life and a new spirit, Luther struck, without himself being aware of it, the only point from which the whole being and life of the Church could be set in motion and transformed. The heart of the Church is her faith. As her faith, so is the Church. And the life of faith of the Church received, through the Reformation, new depth and unexpected energy. Of the Church it is also true that it lives not by bread alone, but by every word that proceedeth out of the mouth of God. And the word of God was once more in motion. It ran through the whole land, calling the peoples with iron tongue, awakening life, lifting up hearts, and bringing forth fruit unto eternal life. In ever-widening waves the spiritual agitation spread throughout the entire sixteenth century. It was so strong that it thrust even humanism itself into the background. The heart of the Church beat once more, and thereby it became healthy. Not as though the Protestant Church alone was reformed. In the struggle concerning the great questions of faith, the opposing doctrine, which it was the object of the Middle Ages to sustain and to develop, but not to set aside, attained to new religious energy and clearness and to great reformatory and moral impulses. The fruit of the sixteenth century was schism, the division between the Protestant and the Roman Churches; but not schism alone. It produced, as well, the long-desired, ardently sought Reformation, which came like the rush of a mighty wind. Through the reformatory agitation, which from Germany was enkindled in all Christian lands, by the law of action and counteraction, not only the Protestant Church, but the whole Church, was reformed.

§ 42. The Protestant Reformation.

The "indulgences" of the Church of the Middle Ages offered the external occasion for the appearance of Luther upon the scene of action. The indulgence was originally the remission of an ecclesiastical penalty. Then the effect of the indulgence was extended to temporal punishments for sin in general, even to the punishment which, according to the teaching of the Middle Ages, must be borne after death in purgatory. The indulgence was procured by the performance of some good work. The pope had the right to grant a general indulgence in reward for certain definite good works. Thus an indulgence could be granted for the payment of money for any Churchly object. The idea was that the Church, in granting indulgences in place of the punishment for sin which the receiver of the indulgence would have had to suffer, offered God satisfaction out of the treasury of superfluous good works (*thesaurus supererogationis*) which the Church possessed in the merit of Christ and the saints.

In the year 1517, Pope Leo X had proclaimed a general indulgence in all Christendom. The money paid was to be applied to the completion of St. Peter's,[6] in Rome. Archbishop Albert of Mayence and Magdeburg was the commissioner of the pope for the proclamation of the indulgences in one part of Germany. Half of the indulgence money which was gathered in his diocese was to be given to him, in order that he might repay to the house of Fugger[7] the debt of thirty thousand gold florins, which he was obliged to assume in paying for his pallium. Accordingly the preachers of indulgences sent out by the archbishop were accompanied by agents of the Fuggers, who immediately took possession of the half of all money received. The consequence was that the traffic in indulgences won a still more mercenary character. And it was so felt by the contemporaries. Elector Frederick the Wise, of Saxony, forbade the preaching of indulgences in his dominions, in order that his land might not be burdened with contributions in payment for the pallium of Mayence. But the Elector was not able to prevent one of the most zealous, and, in respect of the money obtained, one of the most effective of preachers of indulgences, the Dominican monk Tetzel, from activity in the vicinity of the Electoral territory, on Magdeburg soil. According to the theory, the indulgence was to be granted only on the ground of sincere repentance. But it was not difficult for the merchant of indulgences to treat this demand

lightly, and allow the payment of the money to become the first consideration. So Luther, then Augustinian monk, professor of theology, and pastor in
Wittenberg, found that when he would demand true
repentance from those who came to him to confession,
they merely exhibited their purchased certificate of
indulgence. Luther felt himself immediately attacked in his pastoral office by the preacher of indulgences. Indeed, he felt himself injured in his
most sacred relations. He had already reached
the conviction, under the influence of like-minded
brothers of his Order, and especially of the general
of his Order, John von Staupitz, that, according to
the testimony of the Holy Scripture, the inner
change of heart, produced by a living faith, was the
only and complete righteousness satisfactory to God
and required by him. His entire religious being
rose up in opposition to this disgrace of holy things
which he saw in the conduct of Tetzel, the Dominican monk. He saw that grace was being sold for
money. In the heat of his zeal he nailed, on the
31st of October, 1517, his celebrated ninety-five
theses concerning indulgences on the door of the
castle church in Wittenberg. They were composed
in Latin. According to the custom of the time,
they signified a challenge to the opponent to a
public disputation. They addressed themselves, first
of all, to the learned, and not to the masses. And
yet with one blow they excited the entire German
people. They developed the proposition that the

indulgence, which, as such, was good and praiseworthy, could only remit the ecclesiastical penalty,
but not future punishment, and that before God
only true repentance was sufficient and required.
"To every Christian who is truly repentant belongs
complete remission of penalty and guilt, even without letters of indulgence." The forgiveness of the
pope and his impartation of the benefits of Christ
signify only a " declaration of the divine forgiveness." (Theses 36, 38.) In opposition to the shame-
ful abuses which were apparent to every eye in the
conduct of the seller of indulgences, appeared a
manly and public witness, and a clear announce-
ment of the gospel of the grace of God. In one
week the theses were scattered all over Germany.
The monk and professor had been transformed into
a mouth-piece of the nation. It was far from
Luther's purpose to make an attack upon the pope,
or even upon the entire ecclesiastical system. He
was rather of the opinion that "if the pope knew
the oppression of the preacher of indulgences, he
would rather have St. Peter's Church go to ashes
than to have it built with the skin and bones of his
sheep." (Thesis 50.) He supposed that he was defending the opinion of the pope against the seller of
indulgences. But the struggle for his convictions
pressed him constantly, from step to step, and at
last he was compelled to recognize that in his faith,
which he drew from the Holy Scripture, and which
had become to him the source and strength of his

life, was contained the contradiction of the whole system of doctrine derived from the Middle Ages; yes, and of the whole Church as it then existed. In January, 1519, Luther, at the request of the papal legate, Miltitz, promised to keep silence in case his opponents would do the same. Even then he did not think that he was called to be the Reformer of the Church. The Ingoldstadt professor, Dr. Eck, had, in a disputation at Leipzig with Carlstadt, Luther's colleague at Wittenberg, attacked propositions announced by Luther. On this account, Luther felt himself released from his promise. On the 4th of July, 1519, he met his opponent at Leipzig. Here the discussion began at once with a dispute concerning the authority of the pope. Luther denied that the authority of the pope was of divine origin. He held it to be solely a product of the development of human history, similar to the authority of the German emperor, and that faith in the authority of the pope was not necessary to salvation. Therewith the fateful step was taken. His enemy reminded him that Wyclif and John Huss had taught exactly so, and that their doctrine had been condemned by the Great Council of Constance as pestilential error. The authority of the Church hurled itself against the convictions of Luther. He stood out thus against the testimony, not only of a papal decision, but also of a General Council. And so he did. He declared that among the propositions of Huss many were quite Christian and evangelical, and that even an Ecumenical Council is to be corrected by the Scripture in matters of faith, that therefore even an Ecumenical Council could err. Thereby he broke down the bridge between himself and the Church of the Middle Ages. In this instant it became impossible for him to turn back. It became clearer and clearer to him that, supported alone by the sacred Scriptures, he must take up the contest against the formal authority of the Church which he had hitherto unconditionally honored. In him the conscience, the faith, the conviction of the individual, lifted itself up against the hierarchical organization. Even before him had some undertaken this unequal struggle. Huss fell before it in the death at the stake (1415). By Luther it was carried out to a victorious result. The hour of the present had struck. The individual entered upon the plan, ready, in his innermost, holiest convictions, to bow himself before no external authority, neither emperor nor pope, neither bishop nor Council, but to the self-recognized divine truth alone. The inner freedom of the individual desired a free course, and it was secured, not by the classical education of the *renaissance*, but alone by the strength of the Christian faith in the truth of the gospel. Founded upon the Holy Scripture and its eternal and divine contents, the individual found, in the person of Luther, the moral energy and the strength for the attack, by which he was enabled to take up the contest against a world,—"even though the

world were full of devils." As early as the year
following the Leipzig disputation, Luther had appeared upon the scene of conflict with a full understanding of his responsibility. The whole great
circle of reformatory thought had now appeared to
him. In the summer of 1520 appeared those two
powerful works from his pen, "To the Christian
Nobles of the German Nation, of the Bettering of
the Christian State," and "Of the Babylonish Cap-
tivity of the Church." He not only answered the
pope's bull of excommunication (of June 16, 1520)
by burning it before the Elster gate at Wittenberg
(December 10, 1520), but, above all, in the book
which he addressed to the pope on "The Freedom
of a Christian Man." The universal priesthood of
all believers, the immediate relation of every Christian to God, the freedom of the Christian by faith
from all sin and from all external servitude of
works,—these were the thoughts, comprehensive
and effective, with which he attacked and shook
the foundations of the system which had theretofore
prevailed.

In the year 1521, Luther went to Worms,[8] there
to confess and explain his faith in the presence of
the emperor and the assembled princes of the empire, and to affirm that he would yield only before
reasons produced from the Holy Scripture (April
17th, 18th). Neither the ban of the pope nor of the
empire was able to check the work begun by him.
The time of the involuntary leisure upon the

Wartburg[9] (from the fourth of May, 1521, to the third of March, 1522), he employed in beginning the German translation of the Bible. During the year 1522 he completed the translation of the New Testament; but the Old Testament was not completely translated until 1534. Even the revolutionary agitations of the knighthood of the empire under Francis of Sickingen (1523), and of the Peasants' War[10] (1525), which made the gospel an excuse for attempts at secular changes, and even the iconoclastic, tumultuous, and destructive undertakings of the eccentric fanatics Carlstadt[11] and his associates, were not able to hinder the progress of the work of reformation.

Luther, in his address to the Christian nobility of the German nation, had made plain to the princes their right and duty as founded in the universal priesthood of all believers themselves to take in hand the reformation of the Church, in case the regular organs of Church authority, the pope and the bishops, refused to do it. Upon how well prepared a soil his words fell, the Diet at Nuremberg of 1522 showed, where the assembled States brought forward one hundred complaints against the Roman See, its exactions of money and its ordinances, and declared that they would help themselves if no alternative was otherwise brought about. The Diet of Spire (1526), gave the States, the sovereigns, and the free Imperial cities, the legal freedom to act according to their consciences in carrying out the edict of the Diet at Worms concerning the ban against Luther and his followers. Thereby the right of reformation by the sovereigns, in the exercise of which they determined for themselves as to the furtherance of the reformation in their own lands, received its legal and Imperial support. But the Diet at Spire, in 1529, making a retrograde movement, withdrew this authority from the Imperial States, and demanded the unconditional execution of the Edict of Worms against the heretics, but under protest of those Imperial States which were inclined toward reformation, a protest from which the evangelical States have received their title of Protestant. At the same time two parties sprang up, the one in favor of carrying the renovation of the Church still further, the other favoring a cessation of reforms. The Lutheran party, at the Diet of Augsburg (1530), handed in a confession of faith (the "Augsburg Confession," *Confessio Augustana*), which became the doctrinal symbol under which the Lutheran movement was afterward carried on. The Schmalcald League[12] (1531) gave military unity to the evangelical States. The "Schmalcald Articles" (1537) were the final declaration of war against Rome and of the independence of the Protestant Church. In the year 1546 the emperor responded with the Schmalcald War, which led first to the subjection of Protestantism, but also to the legal recognition of Protestantism by Maurice, duke of Saxony.

(Treaty of Passau; 1552, Augsburg Religious Peace,[13] 1555.) The empire transformed itself into a state which rested upon the equal right of both Confessions, the Roman Catholic and the, Evangelical—a result which was finally confirmed after the severe contests and fearful sufferings of the Thirty Years' War[14] by the Peace of Westphalia (1648). Thus the Protestant Church fought for its existence with severest struggles. Her doctrine is founded on the one side upon the formal principle that the Holy Scripture alone is obligatory as the rule of faith. According to this principle, the doctrinal authority of the Church is overthrown, since, according to the Protestant view, the doctrine of the Church, merely *as* the doctrine of the Church, has no power to bind the consciences of men. The last appeal must always be to the Word of God, although each denomination has, of course, the right to state its own doctrinal position, and to exclude all who teach contrary thereto. On the other side, the doctrine of Protestantism is based upon the material principle of the justification of every man by faith alone. According to this principle, the special priesthood of the ministry, and monasticism, with all that is connected with it, was overturned.

§ 43. The Protestant View of Church Government.

The purpose of the Reformation was not originally directed toward a new organization, nor in general toward the establishment of a new Church. The reformers did not propose to develop and purify the government of the Church, but solely the doctrine; and if they did not succeed in winning the entire Church to their convictions, they nevertheless proposed to remain with their followers in the old Church, recognize the authority of pope and bishop as an external human governmental arrangement, if they were only granted the right to preach the pure gospel and to administer the sacraments according to a true understanding of their meaning. This was still the stand-point of the Augsburg Confession of the year 1530. For example, Article VII, Part Second: "Now, our meaning is not to have rule taken from the bishops; but this one thing only is requested at their hands, that they would suffer the gospel to be purely taught, and that they would relax a few observances which can not be held without sin." But it turned out otherwise. The Schmalcald Articles of 1537 saw the necessity of a separation of the Churches, and refused further obedience to pope and bishops. "Because the bishops are so devoted to the pope, defend godless teaching and false forms of worship, and will not ordain pious preachers, but help the pope to murder them, the Churches have sufficient and necessary reason no longer to recognize such as bishops. To the new Church must be given a new constitution."

But what shall the constitution be? "Wherefore the ecclesiastical and civil powers are not to be confounded." That was the fundamental thought. To the Church belongs the spiritual, and only the spiritual; to the State the secular, and only the secular, authority. The secular authority is the external compulsory power ("protects, not souls, but life and property against external force with the sword and corporal penalties"). The spiritual authority ("the power of the keys or of the bishops")—that is, the authority of the Church— is not an external compulsory power, but "a power or commandment from God, of preaching the gospel, of remitting or retaining sins, and of administering the sacraments. Such power of the Churches or bishops bestows not corporal but eternal things (by the administration of the Word and the sacraments), and is exercised alone by the preaching office. This preaching office is the fundamental right of every bishop and pastor alike; since, according to divine law, there is no difference between bishops and pastors." (Schmalcald Articles: "Of the Power of the Pope.") "The Roman Catholic distinction between bishops and pastors is derived alone from human authority." "Neither Peter, nor any other servant of the Word, may attribute to them any power or supremacy in the Church," since "Paul teaches that the Church is more than the servant," and "the keys" (the spiritual power) "are not given to one man alone, but to the entire Church," and Christ's is "the highest and best judgment of the Churches." Hence, "because the regularly constituted bishops persecute the gospel, and decline to ordain suitable persons, a Church of the present day has a right to ordain ministers for itself." (Schmalcald Articles: "Of the Power of the Pope.") Thus the spiritual power belongs to the Churches; that is, to the entire body of believers whether it be large or small ("where two or three are gathered together in my name, there am I in the midst of them"), assembled for the sake of the Word and the sacraments. But the power of the Church is ordinarily exercised by means of the ministry. Only in case of necessity, when the ministry fails to perform its duty (for "nothing dare receive more power or respect than the Word of God") is the power of the keys (the spiritual authority) exercised by the Churches themselves, "as, in case of necessity, even a sinful layman may absolve another and become his pastor." The preaching office is at the same time the ruling office in the Church, although in obedience to the Church. But the content of this governing power is of a spiritual nature only,— the authority to preach the gospel, to administer the sacraments, to employ the ban of the Church (lesser excommunication) as a penalty, and to ordain the servants of the Church; and all this "by means of the Word, and without bodily force." External compulsory authority—that is, a formal, legal authority to compel subjection—is not contained in the authority of the Church. Thereby the secular authority would be given to the Church.. Secular authority is compulsory and legal. It should be its care to aid the Church in unfolding her spiritual authority. "But above all, should kings and princes, as the principal members of the Church, lend their aid, and see that all kinds of error are done away and that consciences are properly instructed, even as God exhorts kings and lords to such an office." "For this should be the chief care of kings and princes, that they diligently advance the honor of God." (Schmalcald Articles: "Of the Power of the Pope.") The sovereign, "as the chief member of the Church," should place his secular authority at the service of the Church. In what sense? In the sense that he himself should rule the Church? By no means. The sovereign can only exercise the ecclesiastical authority in cases of necessity, when the regularly ordained authorities of the Church decline to do their duty; since the sovereign is not, as such, either bishop or pastor. In this respect he stands upon a perfect equality with the other members of the Church. But he must exercise his secular authority (for such alone he has) in such a way as to protect the true doctrine, and that "such abominable idolatry and other unnumbered wickednesses" should no longer be maintained. To the sovereign belongs the police power, which we to-day would call supremacy in the Church; that is, the police power, which (so the sovereign's right of supremacy was then thought

16

of) includes oversight over the proclamation of correct doctrine, and its protection. The reason why this police power of the sovereign won such a profound significance, even in the inner life of the Church, is, that according to the convictions of the Reformers, the Church, as such, lacked all compulsory authority. Whatever of legal compulsory authority existed in the Church belonged not to the Church, but solely to the secular power. It was the time in which (even as early as the fifteenth century) the sovereign's right of reformation—that is, that wide-reaching authority of oversight over doctrine and worship—formed an object of universal conviction of justice. It was in view of this conviction that Luther, in 1520, addressed the Christian nobility of the German nation, in order to arouse them to the work of reformation; and the sovereign's right of reformation (*jus reformandi*), which, in the Augsburg Religious Peace, and in the Peace of Westphalia, found a final legal recognition, is the secular authority with which the sovereign, as above stated, was expected to serve the Church. It is not in and of itself ecclesiastical authority, but only a power which prepares the way for the Church; but it is a power which, because the boundaries between oversight and government are very narrow, is liable at any instant to be transformed into the authority of government. The power of reformation belonged equally to the Roman Catholic sovereign in Roman Catholic territories. Did the

ecclesiastical authority belong to him therefore?
Far from it. Exactly so in Protestant lands. The
Protestant sovereign no longer had the authority of
reformation. Even the Protestant Church was,
according to reformation ideas, ideally a self-govern-
ing organization through the bishops—that is, the
pastors—or in case of necessity through the congregation.

From this beginning grew, in fact, the Churchly
rule of the sovereign. The sovereign at first exercised his authority of oversight (his right of reformation), by means of commissions which arose in connection with each case; afterwards by means of
permanent colleges (consistories), to whom the su-
perintendents (as the officers of the sovereign) were
subordinate; and this organism, for the purpose of
superintendence, has become the organism of government in the Protestant Church in monarchical
countries. It has asserted for itself also the right
to fill vacancies and to exercise the right of excommunication (both according to the doctrine of
the Reformation belonging to the spiritual authority); so that the employment of the Word in ordination and in excommunication has been taken
from the pastors, and only the preaching of the
Word and the administration of the sacraments—the
ministerial office, in the narrower sense of the term—
is left. But why? Because the congregation fell
below the ideal of the Reformation; because the
purely spiritual power (in the sense of the Reforma-

tion as above developed) was not, in fact, sufficient to maintain Christian order in the congregations; because sin, lukewarmness, and lack of discipline demanded external compulsion. Hence it is that the secular authority rules supreme in the Evangelical Church (in Germany), and that its right of oversight has been transformed into the right of rulership; for external, legal, compulsory authority, according to the teaching of the Reformation, belongs only to the State. Because the Church was incapable of spiritual self-government through the Word of God alone, the government of the Church has become the duty of the sovereign as a last resort.

Thus the rulership of the sovereign in the Church is at once in harmony and in contradiction to the fundamental ideas of the Reformation. In contradiction so far that, according to the Reformation idea, the secular authority should aid but not rule, the Church. In harmony so far that, according to the principles of the Reformation, legal authority is never employed by the Church, but only by the State, even when exercised in, and with reference to, the Church. So soon, and so far, as the authority of the Church is legal authority, it must transform itself from spiritual authority, which rightly belongs to the Church, into the authority of the State.

§ 44. Lutheran and Reformed Protestants.

Luther was the first great herald of the Reformation; but he was not the only one who determined the method of its execution. Along-side of him stood Melanchthon, the finely educated Humanist and theologian, who smoothed out many of the severities of Luther, the creator of Protestant instruction (*præceptor Germaniæ*) and of scientific Protestant theology. In opposition to Luther stood the great men who carried out the Reformation, according to what is called the reformed, in distinction from the Lutheran idea.

In Switzerland, Ulrich Zwingli appeared as a reformer almost simultaneously with Luther. The study of the Holy Scripture had set him, as it had Luther, in opposition to a series of the doctrines of the Church. In 1518 he preached in the Hermitage of St. Mary, a celebrated place of pilgrimage, against pilgrimages and indulgences. Called, in 1519, as pastor of the Cathedral Church in Zurich, he soon controlled city and government by his preaching, and in a few years secured the complete introduction of the Reformation. His point of departure was not, as with Luther, the needs of the religious life, but a knowledge of religion in which the understanding should preponderate, and which was determined by a Humanistic education. Hence the aversion of the Zwinglian Reformation to the mystical. The external form of public worship was simplified as much as possible; all images and pictures were removed from Churches; only the pure Word of God was allowed to remain. In the doctrine of the Lord's Supper, Zwingli not only came into opposition to the Roman Catholic doctrine of transubstantiation, but also to the Lutheran doctrine of consubstantiation; that is, that the true body and the true blood of Christ are received by the partakers of the eucharistic feast " in, with, and under the bread and wine." In this doctrine the opposition between Luther and Zwingli became irreconcilable. In all other respects a reconciliation appeared possible. Luther and Zwingli came together at Marburg, in October, 1529; but the discussion of the questions in dispute ended with the establishment, not the reconciliation, of their differences. After that the division ran through the entire Reformation. Even at the Diet of Augsburg, 1530, the opposition appeared. The four upper German cities of Strasburg, Constance, Memmingen, and Linden, refused to subscribe to the Augustana (Augsburg Confession), on account of its doctrine of the Eucharist, and handed in a separate Confession of Faith, the so-called Tetrapolitana, which, however, the emperor refused to receive. Zwingli met his death in the year 1531, on the battle-field of Cappel,[15] in the defense of his faith against the Roman Catholic cantons. His work was carried on, and lifted to world-historical significance, by John Calvin. He gave the French reformed idea fixed form in Geneva, and, by means of his numerous pupils, gave it to France, the Netherlands, and above all, through John Knox, to Scotland, from whence it sent forth mighty religious impulses into the Church of England and into America. The characteristic features of the Calvinistic Reform were the doctrine of predestination and the puritanic severity of Church discipline. In the doctrine of the Eucharist he found a middle way between the stand-points of Luther and Zwingli. According to Calvin, only bread and wine are taken into the mouth, but spiritually the glorified Christ is received by the believing guests at the table of the Lord.

Even in Germany the Reformed doctrine was widely diffused, especially in Hesse and in the Palatinates. The " Heidelberg Catechism" (1563), is one of the most important confessions of the Reformation. But the full severity, especially of Calvinistic Church discipline, never took root in Germany.

The division of the Protestants into Reformed and Lutheran, was a misfortune for the Reformation which can never be sufficiently regretted. It broke the power of the Reform movement, produced unending, and, in part, extremely bitter, disputes, and gave the enemies of the gospel courage and strength for opposition. Nevertheless, it is not only the natural and necessary expression of the individualism which is a part of the character of Protestantism; but it has been, at the same time, a source of richest blessing. The struggle after the truth of the gospel found expression in two distinct forms, and upon the soil of the Reformation two great Church tendencies exhibited themselves, which, however different, are in their last analysis one, and each of which is furnished with its peculiar capabilities and gifts. The historical task and result of Lutheran Protestantism has been, above all, to sound the depths of divine teaching and the secrets of the person of Christ and his work; while it was given to the Reformed Church to spread the gospel far and wide over the Romanic, English, and American world, and to lay hold of the practical life of the individual Christian and of the Church with organizing power. What warmth of religious life, what world-historical capacity for effectiveness operated in the stern Puritanism of the Scotch Church, which, in such a form, was only possible upon the soil of the Reformed faith! And in the Reformed Churches those great forms of Church government, the modified Episcopal, the Presbyterial, or the Synodal characteristics appear in various combinations, which have given to the congregations an orderly form of participation in the general government of the Church. Ruinous as the contests of the two forms of the Protestant Confession with each other have been, their action and reaction upon one another in the mutual impartation of their advantages have been equally blessed.

SECOND DIVISION.

COUNTER-REFORMATION.

§ 45. The Roman Catholic Reformation.

The mental energies which the Church of the Middle Ages had produced and carried forward, were by no means destroyed in the sixteenth century. They had only been repressed by the appearance of the new reformatory movements. Indeed, by means of the new spirit which the Protestant Church had produced, they were able to satiate and revive themselves anew. In the demand for a thorough reformation of the Church, all lovers of the Church during the fifteenth and sixteenth centuries were agreed. The difference of opinion pertained only to the extent of the reformation and the features of ecclesiastical life which it should comprehend. The reformation of doctrine upon which Luther, Zwingli, and Calvin proceeded, was rejected in Roman Catholic circles, and a mere reformation of the discipline, life, and organization of the Church was all that was demanded. But the storm of fresh intellectual agitation, which was excited by the Protestant reformation of doctrine, and by the great struggle of religious convictions thereby brought about, furnished just the force by which a reformation, in this narrower sense, was now made possible. Indeed, the agitation excited by Protestantism must, of necessity, produce, as a countereffect in the domain of Church doctrine, a sharper, clearer, more complete configuration, even of the opposition doctrine; so that even on the side of the opposition a series of newly formulated dogmatical statements (and in this sense even here a reform of dogma) appeared, which, by reason of their intellectual contents, prepared the way for the development of new religious energies.

Thus the Roman Catholic Reformation, the so-called counter-reformation, appeared in opposition to Protestantism. While the Protestant reform movement filled and controlled the first half of the sixteenth century, the Roman Catholic counter-reformation took its rise about the middle of the sixteenth century, gathering around it the forces of the traditionary Church of the Middle Ages, and ever lending them more vigorous life, and in the struggle, and at the same time in involuntary co-operation with Protestantism, producing the Roman Catholic Church of the present day. The two powers by which the Roman Catholic Reformation was brought about were, on the one side, the Order of Jesuits, and, on the other, the Council of Trent.

§ 46. THE ORDER OF JESUITS.

The Order of Jesuits is a product of Spanish Roman Catholicism. In Spain, in the heated contest with the Moors, the national enthusiasm coalesced with the religious during the whole of the Middle Ages. There the Roman Catholicism of the

Middle Ages had maintained a measure of heat and religious energy which had been lost in the other sections of the Church. At the same time Spain had become, as it were in a night, the ruling power in the Old and New World. As the Spanish kingdom undertook the guidance and development of the absolute monarchy, so Spanish Roman Catholicism undertook the guidance of the re-erection of the authorized, unlimited authority of the Church in matters of doctrine. A Spanish noble, Ignatius Loyola, had founded the Order of Jesuits (1534, confirmed by Pope Paul III, 1540), in the idea that thereby a multitude of unconditionally devoted champions might be placed at the disposal of Jesus Christ, the head of the Church, and the pope, his visible representative, for the purpose of winning the victory over the unbelievers in heathenism, and unbelief in the bosom of the Church. To the three usual monastic oaths of poverty, chastity, and obedience, a fourth was added, the oath of perfect obedience to the pope. The duty of obedience, which in the old Orders was a means to an end, was here given the first place, in order to reach the highest object of the Order, the unfolding of a power in the service of the papacy and of a Roman Catholicism which knew no forbearance. The idea of the Order of Jesuits, "the Company of Jesus," is that of an unconditional military subordination, even in the domain of the spiritual life. This is attained by the isolation of the individual. The

Jesuit may know no friendship and no relationship, all narrower relationships, even of the individual members of the Order, among each other being excluded, in order that the superior alone might have influence and authority over the individual. It is further attained by the perpetual oversight of the individual, which was accomplished by an intricate system of espionage and delation, and, by a rule of the Order, to confess to the superior everything, even the most secret feelings and emotions. Finally it is attained by a system of spiritual exercises (*exercitia spiritualia*), which, wrought out in a masterly manner by the founder of the Order himself, ever anew unveils before the eyes of the leader of the exercises the condition of the souls of those under his care, and is intended to give them, in the excitation and overcoming of the spiritual sensibilities, that perfect mastery over themselves which capacitates them at once to rule others, and, on the other hand, to subject themselves unconditionally and without reserve to another. The principle of subjection reaches its climax in the statement that every adherent of the Order is under obligation to see in those set over him Christ himself. The crown of moral personality, freedom to form one's own moral judgments, is here discarded. True perfection here appears as subjection to the convictions of another. What a dishonoring, overpowering, and mortification of the most precious gift bestowed upon man! The last consequences of monasticism have become visible.

Perfect asceticism demands even the emptying of the will. The Order of Jesuits is the manifestation of the principle which stands most completely in opposition to the spirit of Protestantism and, indeed, to the common moral convictions of the present. But as the Protestant principle of the freedom of the conscience of every man from every human authority has its believers, so has also the opposite principle of the subjection of the individual being, even of the conscience, to a visible authority. But in this enormous and, its extreme consequences, this immoral extension of the principle of authority, lies the chief force to which the Order of Jesuits, and with it modern Roman Catholicism, owes its achievements.

Protestantism must, of necessity, appear to the Jesuits as their born foe, to whose destruction they were first of all called. The first thing to be accomplished was the production of an intellectual movement in opposition to that of the Reformation. This German Catholicism was unable to do. Almost without opposition the Protestant doctrine spread throughout all Germany, even into Bavaria and Austria. The universities, the schools, the clergymen, and the monks who yet remained true to the old faith, nevertheless lacked the power of effective opposition to the gospel which was preached, as it were, with new tongues. They were themselves inwardly affected by the true doctrine, more in doubt and uncertainty than filled with the living power of an opposite conviction. The situation only changed when, in the second half of the sixteenth century, the Jesuits entered Germany. The "Spanish priests," as the Jesuits were called by the people, gave the Roman Catholic faith new impressiveness in the pulpit and in the professor's chair. Their object was to fight Protestantism with its own means. The science of the Dominicans, the Scholasticism of the Middle Ages, had given way before Humanism, which now made common cause with Protestantism. The Order of Jesuits had made themselves master of the scholarly, humanistic culture, in order to place it in the service of the Church. In opposition to the scholarship of Protestantism was set the scholarship of the Jesuits; in opposition to the science of Protestantism stood the science of the Jesuits, provided with all necessary implements; in opposition to Protestant preaching the preaching of the Jesuits, also delivered in the language of the people, connecting with the Scripture, but adapted to the spread of Roman Catholicism. A great quantity of mental and moral forces were brought to bear for the purpose of destroying Protestantism with its own weapons.

But the literary and purely intellectual method of operation did not lead the Jesuits rapidly enough to the desired end. The means of external force must also be employed in the service of the Church. In the second half of the sixteenth century, therefore, and at the behest of the Jesuits, began the

so-called counter-reformation in the narrower sense,
the counter-reformation carried on by violence.
In Germany the Augsburg Religious Peace (1555),
which referred to each sovereign the decision as to
the Confession of Faith in his own territory, afforded
the Jesuits the necessary legal foundation. In Bavaria, where the Jesuits had been established in
Ingoldstadt since 1556, this form of the counter-
reformation took its start at their instigation. In
the year 1563 the evangelical preachers and laity
were expelled from Bavaria, and the evangelical
nobility excluded from the Diet. The spiritual
princes followed the example thus given. In
Treves, Würzburg, Bamberg, Salzburg, the Protestant preachers were replaced by the pupils
of the Jesuits, so that the preaching of the Reformation doctrine was silenced. And what was
begun in Germany was also begun elsewhere.
The bloody reign of the Roman Catholic Mary of
England* (1553–1558), of the Spanish duke of
Alva [16] in the Netherlands (1567), St. Bartholomew's [17] night in France (1572), were so many terrible monuments of the counter-reformation, filled
and led by the Spirit of Jesuitism. In Germany,
also, the counter-reformation finally led, in the beginning of the seventeenth century, to the insuffer-
able tension which ended in the Thirty Years' War,
with so much blood and misery. The conclusion
was that in the Peace of Westphalia (1648), Prot-

---

*See § 54.

estantism secured its final legal recognition. But, as a result of the counter-reformation, Protestantism suffered irreparable losses in the territories of Roman Catholic sovereigns, especially in Bavaria and Austria. Whereas, about the middle of the sixteenth century Protestantism bade fair to conquer all Germany, it was driven back and limited to definite limits. However, even in Germany its existence was secured, and even to this day Protestantism stands as the opponent of the Order of Jesuits, restraining the absolute rule of the Order even within the Roman Catholic Church. The pope raised his voice in opposition to the Peace of Westphalia, and declared it, as previously the Augsburg Religious Peace, as invalid. But his words fell unheeded. It was the first time, in a long while, that a great political action took place without the co-operation, and even against the opposition, of the pope. The times had changed, the Middle Ages were past. The secular sword of the pope was broken. In spite of the Jesuits, Protestantism had accomplished two things. It had asserted itself, and, by the destruction of the world-rulership of the papacy, it had changed the face of the entire political world.

§ 47. The Council of Trent.

The Roman Catholic Reformation found its formal expression and termination in the Tridentine Council, which, with numerous interruptions, was assembled in Trent during the years 1545–1563. Here, with the aid of the Scholasticism of the Middle Ages, were fixed, in a sense entirely anti-Protestant, the dogmas of tradition (the binding force of the teachings of the Church), of original sin, of the seven sacraments, of transubstantiation, of penance and extreme unction, of the sacrificial character of the mass, of priestly ordination, and the hierarchy, of the sacrament of marriage, of purgatory, of the adoration of saints and relics, of monastic oaths, of indulgences, etc. What had previously been merely scientific (Scholastic), and although ruling, yet, properly speaking, not obligatory, doctrinal opinions, were now established as strictly obligatory Churchly doctrinal law. In opposition to the doctrinal agitation of Protestantism arose the Roman Catholic dogma of the new period then given its first exact expression. In opposition to the Protestant principle of the sole authority of Holy Scripture as the rule of faith appeared, in clearest self-consciousness, the Roman Catholic principle of the authority of the Church, and precisely, the authority of her dogmatic conclusions. To the Roman Catholic his Church is an object and a source of his doctrinal faith. To believe in this visible Church, her holiness and infallibility; to believe that which the Church teaches, is what it means to be a Roman Catholic. The principle of authority, of making the authority of the Church superior to the conscience and belief of the individ-

17

ual, found clear expression as the true character of the Roman Catholic faith as fixed anew in the Council of Trent. With this principle given, all other doctrinal decisions followed as a consequence. With the re-establishment of the dogma was united also a reformation of the constitution and discipline of the Church. A series of the most crying abuses was abolished, the employment of indulgences as a source of gain was forbidden (since then the sale of indulgences has disappeared), the clergy were obligated to the personal administration of their offices, etc. The principal thing was that the papacy and clergy were filled with a new spirit. As by a miracle disappeared the corrupt, worldly-minded papacy which had flourished in the fifteenth and in the beginning of the sixteenth centuries. Since the Reformation movement began to get the upper hand, the papacy has more and more taken the lead of the severely Churchly disposed party. In the struggle with Protestantism, the papacy came to itself again. And as it was with the papacy, so was it with the clergy. The reformatory movement of the sixteenth century was general. Over against the reformed Protestant Church appeared a reformed Roman Catholic Church.

THIRD DIVISION.

PIETISM AND RATIONALISM.

§ 48. Pietism.

The great struggle of the period of the Reformation for the re-establishment of the gospel of justification by faith produced two powerful movements, which, partly co-operating, partly in antagonism to one another, controlled the next succeeding period, from the close of the sixteenth into the first half of the eighteenth century.

The one movement was directed toward the working out of a doctrinal system which should give perfect self-consciousness to the newly recognized evangelical truth in its scientific form, and thereby to the Church. This tendency was especially controlling in the Lutheran Church. It connected itself with the work which Melanchthon had already begun. Its result was the Lutheran dogmatics of the seventeenth century, the creation of a Lutheran theology which found its most important expression in the writings of John Gerhard (after 1616 professor of theology in Jura; died 1637), and the influence of which extended over the entire domain of Protestantism. With this development of the systematic theological teachings of the Church was connected the danger of pushing the truly life-giving truths of salvation into the background in the interest of the in part exceedingly subtle questions of

dogmatics, and also of laying as a law upon the neck
of the Church the yoke of a theological doctrine ex-
tending into the smallest minutiæ. But the Church
is able to live only by the true, pure word of God,
not the disputed or disputable products of human
theological science. And it is clear that the Lutheran Church has not escaped this danger. The
Formula of Concord, of 1577, which, however, has
found acceptance in but a part of the Lutheran
countries, took very decidedly the direction just designated. While in the Augsburg Confession of
1530, and likewise in the Schmalcald Articles of 1537,
only those truths were uttered with emphasis upon
which the evangelical faith depended, the Formula
of Concord proceeds in such a way as to bring theology, with its disputed questions, to the front, in
order, by means of statements conformable to reason,
to rule not only the science, but also the life of the
Church. And the Lutheran theology of the seventeenth century entered upon the path marked out
by the Formula of Concord, and it was in this way
that it exercised such a powerful influence upon the
Church. The fruit of a socially dogmatically subtle
movement was, as the Lutheran theologians of that
period themselves testified (*c. g.*, John Arndt, celebrated even to-day for his devotional writings; died
at Celle, 1621), a new Scholasticism, an external
Churchmanship, which denied the inner power
of Christianity. This movement found its special
impulse in the opposition to the Reformed doctrine;

and thoroughly as Lutheran theology was in the
right in defending the Lutheran confession, it fell
equally into error as soon as it yielded to the temptation to exaggerate the opposition, and, in the interest of its own teaching, to set up the contents of
its own confessional documents before the contents
of the Holy Scripture. By means of a Church
doctrine which had been transformed into Scholasticism, the one-sided dogmatism of the Lutheran
theology of the time came very near darkening,
after the manner of the Roman Catholics, the
power and clearness of the Scriptural Word for the
congregations. But the Lutheran Church had
within itself the capability of freeing itself from
such excrescences; and, along with the dogmatic
movement, she gave life and impressiveness also to
those energies which were destined to serve as a
counterpoise to the danger of dogmatism.

The second movement which went forth from
the Reformation had for its object, first of all, not
doctrine, but the practical configuration and production of the Christian life. This movement attained its first influence in the Reformed Church,
and especially through the influence of Calvin. It
produced the Puritanic vigor and severity of the
French and Scotch-English (Presbyterian) Reformed
Church. By means of its Presbyterial organization
and Synods it was able to give the congregations a
part in the life of the Church, which protected
them from the deadness and formality into which

the Lutheran congregations had so generally fallen
under the Churchly rule of the sovereigns and the
orthodox theologians.　But the Calvinistic-Puritanic
form of Christianity included in itself, at the same
time, a legality, a rule of external authority which
destroyed the freedom of the Christian man, and
struck a direct blow at the spirit of the gospel.
And here also grew up (recall the Church history
of Scotland, England, and the Netherlands) a dogmatism, and insistance upon particular articles of
faith set forth alone in the doctrine of the Church,
which, in respect of malignity against every least
variation and of self-righteous consciousness of superiority, in no particular fell behind the dogmatism
of the contemporary Lutheran theologians.　It appeared as though both the spirit of monasticism
and the spirit of Scholasticism were about to renew
their power in the realm of Protestantism.

　　But the true spirit of the gospel remained still
more powerful, both in Evangelical Lutheran and
in the Evangelical Reformed Churches.　A reaction entered, which inwardly freed the Protestant
Church from the dangers of a one-sided development.　This movement, which we are accustomed
to designate by the term *Pietism*, took its point of
departure from Reformed circles.　In the Reformed
Church of Holland (at first under the leadership of
Labadie, about 1660), and then in other Reformed
domains, societies of the "Regenerate" formed
themselves, which, indifferent to questions of doc-

trine, as such, strove to attain a practical Christianity in the form of an ascetic life and a mystical consecration to Christ as the Bridegroom of the saints. The dogmatism of Puritanism was rejected, and to the peculiar endeavors of the Reformed Church after the production of the Christian ideal of life, a new expression was given. Nevertheless the palm belongs to the Lutheran Church in this new development. This it was which constituted the significance of Lutheran Pietism, which, through Spener and Francke, rose up in opposition to dogmatism at the close of the seventeenth century. Spener (born at Rappolsweiler, in Alsace, 1635), who had spent considerable time as a student at Geneva, united in his own personality the effects which both the Reformed tendency toward a severe Christian, and even ascetic life, and the Lutheran tendency to a Scriptural doctrine of the Word of God, had exercised upon him. It was the time in which, especially through Spener's teacher, Professor Sebastian Schmidt, of Strasburg, the thorough exegetical study of the text of Scripture awakened to new life in the Lutheran Church. It was also the time in which the sufferings of the Thirty Years' War had made the hearts of the people tender, and prepared them for the consolations revealed in salvation through Christ; in which Paul Gerhardt lifted his voice, strong and sweet, in order, in genuine poetic expression, to press home to the heart the precious, living experiences possible to Chris-

tian faith; in which a series of Lutheran theologians, like Grossgebauer (died in Rostock in 1661)
and others, had already appeared, to prepare the
way by decided testimony for the as yet unlost truly
evangelical Lutheran idea, the desire for the inner
reproduction of an effective life of faith in the
power of the Spirit.

Upon this whole movement, Spener set the crown,
and led it to victory by demanding, with searching
earnestness, in his *Pia Desideria* (1675), a general
study of the Bible in private assemblages, and
participation of the laity in the life of the Church,
and the exhibition of the Christian faith by a life
of love; and especially by means of " Hours for Devotion and Bible Study" (1670), in which he prepared the way for a treatment of the Scripture
which regarded the Word of God, not as a fountain
of Scholastic dispute and discussion, but as a
power for the impartation of life. The Bible took
its place of priority once more before the Confessions
of Faith of the Church; the requirement of regeneration ran like a mighty cry of warning and awakening through the Protestant world; and Francke's
magnificent foundation in Halle (the corner-stone of
his Orphanage was laid in 1695) formed an imperishable witness to the practical energy of genuine
Christian love, which united with an equally genuine Christian and unconditional trust in God.
From Pietism went out the decisive impulses which
led to the establishment of the independent, free,

Christian Society at Herrnhut (1727); and from these Moravians went forth influences which helped to mold Methodism, which in England, but especially in America, represents a newly enlivened form of the Reformed Church life, distinguished by its emphasis upon personal sanctification (the first formation of a Methodist Society in London by John Wesley took place 1739). But aside from this indirect influence upon Methodism, the greatest work of Pietism was its production of the Lutheran missionary spirit. The first Lutheran missionaries (Ziegenbalg, and others) went out from the Orphanage of Francke, at Halle. The seal of manhood was given to the spirit of Protestantism when it moved its messengers to go forth into the world to conquer it for the gospel of Christ.

The weakness of Pietism lay chiefly in the fact that, while it inclined toward the formation of separate societies within the congregations composed of those who were truly awakened, and thus in a measure robbed itself of influence upon the great masses in the Church, it did not go far enough to form a separate Church organization, and thus provide itself a vehicle for its own perpetuation. The German conception of Christianity, including and emphasizing the doctrine of justification by faith, has always failed to see how what its representatives denominate a righteousness of works—such as abstinence from dancing, games, theater-going, etc.— can be harmonized with the spirit of the gospel.

Emphasizing the doctrine of justification by faith, German Christianity has almost gone to the extreme of admitting everything into the Christian life except actual sin. It fears the earnestness and profound spirit of self-denial which genuine conversion introduces into the heart. And hence, while Pietism failed to organize for the continuance of its own existence, on the other hand it was not adopted by the German Church at large. And thus its work was dissipated and prevented from exercising its true power.

Nevertheless, the effect of Pietism is imperishable. It remained the power which, throughout the whole reign of Rationalism in Germany, and even into the nineteenth century, preserved true and unharmed, although in narrow and limited circles, the life of evangelical Christianity to the hour when, in the beginning of our century, the hour struck for the rejuvenation of the Evangelical Church. It represents in Germany, even in our day, a form of Protestantism which is the necessary complement of the Confessional tendency for the life of the Protestant Church. While in Confessionalism the first place is given to doctrine, here it is the life in accordance with the gospel which forms the goal of the effective spiritual energies employed. Neither movement can unfold its effects healthfully without the other. In the nature of the case, individuals will favor one or the other. But the Church must have both; and in the union of correct doctrine with conscientious Christian living is the hope of the Church in the midst of its foes.

Pietism, from the end of the seventeenth century and the beginning of the eighteenth was the last great wave of the ecclesiastical movement upon the Continent of Europe, which began with the Reformation. The time came when a far different intellectual power seized the hearts of men.

§ 49. Rationalism.

Up to the close of the seventeenth century the Church and its development, culminating in the Reformation and counter-reformation, occupied the foreground in all Western Europe. From that time forward a new spirit began to make itself manifest.

The discoveries in natural science during the sixteenth and seventeenth centuries, and a philosophy incited by them and taking its rise especially in England, introduced a new view of the world which sought its standing-place, not in the faith or creed of the Church; but in the cognitions of the human reason. Freedom from the power of tradition was courageously coveted in order to subject the historically customary to a criticism by means of which the historical, positive, and accidental might be distinguished from the eternal, reasonable results deduced from the nature of man and things. A natural right, a natural state, a natural national economy, a natural religion appeared as great ideals upon the horizon of humanity, stirring the world of the eighteenth century to agitated and passionate endeavor. In the midst of these conflicts the origin of modern humanity was prepared.

The traditional Christian religion was also criticized from the stand-point of its reasonableness and harmony with nature; and neither the Protestant nor the Roman form of Christianity was able to furnish to philosophic thought a content wholly equal to the demands of reason. And naturally, since religion arises from the relation of man to God, whose nature, according to the necessity of the very idea of his being, lies outside the forms of thought of the human understanding. Religion must end in the incomprehensible, and its peculiarly religious power, by which the heart is satisfied and released from the burden of the earthly, and the life of the individual as of nations made complete, is found only in those features of religion which are incomprehensible and above human thought and understanding, not in those which are comprehensible. In the mystery by which it leads to God, the incomprehensible, lies the power of religion.

The eighteenth century sought for a religion which should harmonize the contradictory, which should satisfy at once the understanding and the desire of the heart for the eternal and incomprehensible. The result of this movement was a creed which knew only the three great objects of faith — God, virtue, and immortality. The positive features

of the Christian faith were done away, and yet a
reasonable, final, provable chain of truths not attained. Only so much was accomplished, that the
firm staff of the Christian faith upon which one
could safely lean in the journey through life was
transformed into a bending reed and so represented as
to produce uncertainty and awaken doubt. In the
second half of the eighteenth century, Rationalism
was victorious at all points along the line of battle.
It was controlling both in the Protestant and
the Roman Church. Defended by Voltaire and
Lessing[18] with the weapons of irony and profound ingenuity, it unfolded its highest products in
Kant's philosophy, in which he exhibited the limits
of the pure human reason and declared the existence
of God and the immortality of the soul to be
indemonstrable demands of the practical, moral
reason. The philosophy of Kant signified the completion and the self-overthrow of Rationalism, the
reaching of a summit of development which suddenly opened visions of a wholly new and un-
thought-of country. The limits of the understanding had been pointed out, and philosophy itself
had recognized that religion was not designed as
a kind of philosophical teaching to satisfy the need
of the understanding for knowledge, but rather as
a might which fulfills immediately the need of the
human heart for freedom from the world and sin,
the need of God felt by every human soul. Kant,
however, remained in the camp of Rationalism,

since he gave to religion a purely moral purpose, "the recognition of our duties as divine commandments;" and the superlative energy which Kant attributed to the moral law as the unconditional, obligatory commandment ("categorical imperative"), alone because of its contents and without any reference to its purpose, could but imperfectly compensate for his transformation of God into the Lawgiver of Sinai, and the omission from his system of the "Word of God," who had revealed himself to the world "full of grace and truth."

The great practical results of Rationalism were the overthrow of the Order of Jesuits, the founding of the supreme power of the State, and the idea of tolerance.

§ 50. The Overthrow of the Order of Jesuits.

The Order of Jesuits had prepared its fall by its own development. The morals which it proclaimed had been transformed into a casuistry in which the instances were sought in which one might do evil and yet preserve a clear conscience. Such cases were, for example, when one inwardly directs the purpose not toward the sin as such, but toward something else, perhaps even praiseworthy (*methodus dirigendæ intentionis*). Or when one, for a good purpose, inwardly gives to his promise a limited sense or a secret condition (mental reservation) or makes use of an expression capable of a double meaning (amphiboly). In these cases the doctrine that "the end justifies (or sanctifies) the means" was not directly expressed, but it was applied. Indeed, the moral-theological Jesuit authors transformed the demands of morality into mere opinions concerning moral conduct, and developed the doctrine that one may even act contrary to his own conscience whenever one has but a "probable opinion," that is the favorable testimony of an author of recognized authority in favor of an opinion. This so-called "Probabilism"[19] was first systematically developed in 1577 by a Spanish Dominican, Bartholomew of Medina, and afterward brought to its highest development by Jesuit authors; as, for example, the Spaniard Escobar (died 1633). By this "probabilism" the door was thrown wide open for every kind of immorality. Even the papacy, much as it desired to protect the Jesuits as its most faithful adherents, was compelled to make front against the morals of the Jesuits. Alexander VII disapproved of probabilism and the doctrines connected with it (1665); Innocent XI, by a solemn bull, condemned sixty-five of the lax moral propositions of the Jesuits (1679). The Order was compelled (1687), by a formal declaration, to renounce its solidarity with probabilism. It simply did not prevent the teaching of the anti-probabilistic doctrine. Nevertheless, Gonzalez, the general of the Order (1687 to 1705), whose election Pope Innocent XI had brought about on account of his anti-probabilistic sentiments, met with decided opposition within the Order, which never heeded the immense power over his inferiors which he applied to the suppression of the probabilistic doctrines of morality so especially defended by Jesuit authors.

A mighty opponent of Jesuitism arose in Jansenism, a movement which proceeded from the University of Louvain, where Jansen was professor (1630–1636), and which was especially wide-spread in France. While the Jesuits represented the doctrine accepted by the Roman Catholic Church, that man, by reason of the freedom to good which remained to him, notwithstanding the fall, co-operated in securing his own salvation, Jansenism, similarly to the Protestant reformers, defended the Augustinian doctrine that the gracious predestination of God, according to which one is saved and another lost, is the sole cause of the salvation of the elect. Jansenism, in the nature of things, was repeatedly condemned by the popes. It was an attempt at reformation within the Church in opposition to Jesuitism. Its popularity was due to its moral earnestness, which rose even to ascetic severity, and which distinguished its adherents, whose local center soon was found in the Cistercian nunnery of Port Royal, in the vicinity of Versailles.

The world-historical significance of Jansenism consists less in its dogmatic statements of doctrine than in the criticism which it exercised upon the morals of the Jesuits. Jansenism meant the exact opposite of the Jesuitic moral principles. Besides,

Jansenism engaged in a life-and-death struggle with Jesuitism concerning doctrine. Hence it is that the most powerful counteracting agencies against the morals of the Jesuits proceeded from the circles of Jansenism. To the Jansenists belonged Blaise Pascal,[20] the celebrated mathematician and naturalist, who, in his *Lettres Provinciales* (1656–57), most fully, intellectually, and forcibly gave expression to the righteous wrath of the more honorable classes at the Jesuitic morals. Jansenism yielded before Jesuitism. Upon the soil of the Roman Catholic Church the Order of Jesuits, which defended the official dogma of the Church, was naturally the more powerful. Nevertheless, Pascal's attack, which sparkled with wit, intellect, and scorn, was never weakened by the Jesuits. The *Lettres Provinciales* were scattered abroad in more than sixty editions. They gave the mighty Order the first great blow which subsequently shook its position. In its morals the Achilles-heel[21] of Jesuitism was struck.

In addition, the Order became ever more deeply involved in the interests of secular might and riches; great commercial undertakings and moneyed transactions quenched all its spiritual-mindedness; the doctrine of the Order which, under certain conditions, especially the supposed interests of the Church, approved even of the murder of princes; a doctrine which, for example, placed the steel in the hands of the murderers of Henry III and Henry

18

IV of France,—this doctrine naturally attracted to itself a large measure of hate. But the decisive factor, to which the Order finally yielded, was the spread of Rationalism in the eighteenth century. The Jesuitic Order appeared to the eighteenth century, which was filled with the spirit of philosophy and free investigation, as an anachronism of the most vexatious kind. A spirit of darkness, bearing with it the Scholasticism and intellectual barbarism of the Middle Ages,—such appeared the spirit of the Order of Jesuits to the eighteenth century. Even the Church, the Roman as well the Protestant, began to imbibe the ideas of Rationalism, which renounced the positively Christian, and held fast only to the universal human religious conceptions as the real germ of Christianity. Only the Order of Jesuits maintained its position, paying homage to the extremest Romanism, a monument of past tendencies of the human mind. The whole culture of the eighteenth century stood in opposition to Jesuitism.

Thus the hour of its fall had come. To the desire of the king of France that the general of the Jesuits should introduce a reform of the Order, he gave this celebrated reply: *Sint ut sunt, aut non sint* ("They shall remain as they are, or they shall not exist"). Conflicts with the State, which saw in the Order of Jesuits a State within a State, gave the decision. In 1759 the Order was abolished in Portugal, in 1764 in France, in 1767 in Spain and

Naples. Finally Clement XVI (1773), yielding
to the united pressure of the governments and the
tendencies of the times, abolished the Order of
Jesuits, for the Church, "forever."* Rationalism
had triumphed over the Order of Jesuits.

§ 51. THE OMNIPOTENT STATE.

If the ideas of the Middle Ages contributed to
the benefit of the power of the Church, those of
Rationalism signified an equally decided counter-
movement in favor of the power of the State.

The movement favoring the State had taken its
rise as early as the fourteenth century, when the
National State, and a royalty founded upon it, announced itself. It became visible in the monarchy
of Philip the Fair, and in the rights of oversight
and government which, during the course of the
fifteenth century, were attained in all parts of Europe, and in an ever-increasing degree, by the authority of the State. In the Reformation it had
gained a new and powerful grip. The Reformers
(with the exception of Calvin and his successors)
taught that no kind of external rule is to be exercised by the Church, but solely the preaching of the
divine Word and the administration of the sacraments. The entire domain of civil life, and even
the government of the Church, so far as it includes
the application of external authority (such as legislation, the filling of vacancies, and Church dis-

* See ? 52, p. 282.

cipline, belonged to the State. The State prepared
itself to govern the Church, not in Protestant lands
alone, but equally so in Roman Catholic. The
idea was one which was not peculiar to the Reformation ; but, so far as it had to do with the supremacy of the State over the Church, had been
inherited from the fifteenth century, and which,
after the sixteenth century, had become perfectly
clear and reached its full influence in the entire
West, in Spain and France, in Bavaria and Austria,
as well as in the Protestant North. Gallicanism,
ruling the Church of France from the sixteenth to
the eighteenth century, and Febronianism, defended in Germany by Justinus Febronius (suffragan bishop of Hontheim, in Treves), with breadth
of learning in a book on Church government and
the power of the pope, signified the same great and
growing tendency, even in the Church, to ascribe
to the State the highest supervisory authority in
spiritual things, and, under certain circumstances,
even the power to interfere in the same. The secular authority discovered its inborn power, and, in
the growing feeling of the might which it possessed,
demanded the life of the whole civilized world for
itself.

Even here Rationalism introduced the finally
decisive turning point. The result of philosophical
thinking concerning the origin and nature of the
authority of the State, was that it arose from a
social contract (*contrat social*). This idea went back

to Aristotle. It had been familiar even to the Middle Ages. But it now first unfolded its full indwelling natural power. According to this doctrine, the social contract is concluded solely in the interest of the authority of the State, and of none other whatever (as, for example, not even in the interest of the authority of the Church). In favor of the State, and of the State alone, the individual divests himself of his natural freedom. It follows from this that all public authority belongs to the State, that all exercise of power within the State can rest alone upon the commission or delegation of the authority of the State. This authority is omnipotent. Even the authority of the Church is an efflux from that of the State.

Up to this time this whole line of thought had appeared as a mere theoretical reflection, and such it had remained through long centuries. But Rationalism contained that which acted like a spark to the powder; the idea, namely, that the present is free from the past. According to rationalistic convictions, the results of historical development are, as such, without binding force. This they lose the instant their unreasonableness, their incompatibility with the results and conclusions of philosophical thinking, are made clear. The authority of the State is pefectly justified in transforming natural, reasonable right into reality. Indeed, it is not only the highest right, but also the highest duty, of the authority of the State to advance this ideal into practical right by the overthrow of current conditions; for it is all powerful, even in opposition to traditionary legal order, and the present demands of it, first of all, that it empower the rights of reason in place of the rights developed in the course of history.

How the power of the State and legislation took wing! The eighteenth century believed in the power of the State to make an end of all the hardships and imperfections of the order of human society by means of legislation, and thereby to give a perfect law, completely just, and according to reason, which should secure freedom and happiness. A deep-reaching movement of reformatory legislation went through the world, sweeping away much which was already inwardly dead. The French Revolution arose as the most splendid attempt to renew the world according to the eternal and reasonable principles of Freedom, Equality, and Brotherhood, and to restore the long-forgotten human rights. By what high hopes was it borne along! With what deep and noble enthusiasm was it met! The State, legislation, the reason of man,—these were declared to be the rulers of the world. It was believed that in this Revolution alone lay the power to regenerate the whole legal and social being, to empty out, upon a humanity delivered from the fetters of the past, the cornucopiæ of happiness. The revolution ended in the Reign of Terror. The dreamed-of fortune gave way to horror. Freedom passed over into the despotism of a military dictatorship. It turned out that even the power or the State is not almighty; that, in general, law can not be treated according to human pleasure; that sudden freedom from the past does not lead society to the heights of heaven, but rather into the abyss of hell. Like a refining fire went the Revolution, with its effects, through the world, only to hand over, at last, the continuation of the work to forces originating in the past.

In this energetic reform movement the old State, with its privileges of families and distinctions of class, perished, thus making way for the modern State, whose fundamental principle is the equal public rights and duties of all. The old style Church was also swallowed up by this movement. The Church appeared to be like wax in the hand of the omnipotent State of the second half of the eighteenth century, which felt itself called and qualified to define the position, and even the inner life, of the Church according to its ideas of reason. It was under the control of this thought that Joseph II began his reform legislation in the domain of the Church. He reformed the religious Orders by abolishing all which did not serve the purposes of instruction and pastoral care (1782), and united their property into a "religious fund" administered by the State. He reformed the education and training of the clergy by putting in place of the ecclesiastical educational institutions State "general

seminaries," designed to introduce the spirit of Rationalism into the ranks of the pastors of the people.
He regulated the forms of public worship, the style
and contents of preaching, the hymns of the monks,
and the decoration of the Churches, large and
small.   The whole domain of Churchly life was to be
formed, all at once and with a firm hand, according
to his ideas wisely and reasonably.   But the result
was the Belgian Revolution (1787), which cost
Austria one of its most beautiful provinces, and the
necessity of retreat from a number of the proposed
reforms.

The legislation of Frederick the Great, which
has determined the contents of Prussian national
justice (1794), was conducted in a similar spirit.
Prussian national law knows no Church whatever,
neither a Protestant nor a Roman Catholic, but
only the congregation (the so-called Church society);
several congregations ("Church societies") which,
according to Prussian national law, happen to
have the same faith, form—not a Church, but a
"religious party," similar to the parties of the
evangelical or the Roman Catholic powers of Europe.   No common organization whatever is therein
included.   The Church societies of the Roman
Catholics have the peculiarity that several of them
(the congregations of a diocese) have the same general officer (the bishop), as with the Protestants
several Church societies (those of a province) are
subject to the same consistory.   But in the eyes of

Prussian national law this arrangement is purely accidental, and rests, not upon the constitution of the Church, but upon the constitution of the individual local congregations (Church societies). The Church is atomized. It is dissolved, the Roman Catholic Church included, by law, into a series of local congregations. All power which is above that of the congregations is fundamentally the power of the State. The king of Prussia appears as the chief bishop and authority, both in the Protestant and the Roman Catholic Church. Foreign superiors (for example, the pope) can undertake no legislation, no jurisdiction, no administrative acts, in reference to the Church of Prussia, without the consent of the king. If the pope wishes to exercise rights in Prussia, he may appoint a native vicar, a subject of the Prussian king.

Such was the law of the Church of the Prussian monarchy as the lawgiver drew it from his reason, and he believed himself justified and qualified to transform these results of his philosophy by a simple act of legislation of the authority of the omnipotent State into actual, operative law.

The French Revolution proceeded also to legislate, in the domain of the Church, for the realization of a free natural right and justice thought out by reason and by a decree of the State. The reasonable, natural law of the Church, as formed in the Revolution, is contained in the "Civil Constitution of the Clergy," of 1790. The constitution of the

Church corresponds to that of the State. Every canton has its parish priest, every department its bishop. The parish priest is to be chosen by the citizens of the canton, without reference to their confession of faith; the bishop, by the citizens of the department. No pope is recognized in this "civilly constituted" Church. Even the confession of faith no longer plays any part, so far as every citizen is, as such, a member of this Church. The Roman Catholic Church, in the old traditionary sense, had ceased to exist. It was set aside by the law of the State. The State is now also the Church, and the administration of the Church a part of the administration of the State. Hence the same elective bodies which choose the officers of the State, as the district and department Councils, are also justified in choosing the parish priest and the bishop. With rule and compasses, this Church constitution is drawn in exact harmony with the constitution of the State. The living forces of the Church, the papacy and the traditionary faith, were ignored. The State claimed the perfect right to rule over the Church, her law, and her existence as it would. In the days of the Reign of Terror, although only temporarily, Christianity was actually done away, and the worship of "the Reason," and afterward of "the Highest Being" introduced. The power of the State appeared as the unlimited lord, even of the religious life. Napoleon again introduced the papacy and the Roman Catholic Church into the law of France

by the Concordat of 1801 ; but even to-day the Revolutionary idea of the period of Rationalism still
lives in French law, which Napoleon created, that
the Church and her administration is a part of the
general administration of the State.

The authority of the State over the Church
meant also its power over the property of the
Church.   Joseph II formed a State "religious
fund" out of the property of the abolished monasteries.   The French Revolution declared the entire
property of the Church to be national property.
The same procedure was executed also in Germany.
The Peace of Luneville (1801) ceded the left bank
of the Rhine to France.   The German Empire made
the promise that the secular princes who were
thereby deprived of their civil authority should be
remunerated out of the treasury of the empire.
The expense of this indemnification had to be paid
by the Church.   In 1803 the secularization of the
property of the Church (of bishoprics, monasteries,
etc.) was legalized, as well as the abolishment of the
spiritual princedoms.   The death-blow was thus
given to the secular power of the Roman Catholic
Church.

The State took satisfaction for the period of the
Gregorian system.   Armed with the philosophical
ideas of the eighteenth century, it struck down the
Church itself, the Roman Catholic and the Protestant Churches alike, as it had abolished the Order
of Jesuits.

§ 52. The Idea of Tolerance.

The permanent consequences of the intellectual movement which we term Rationalism, however, are found neither in the abolition of the Order of Jesuits, nor in the supremacy which the State attained over the Church. The Order of Jesuits was reinstated in 1814 by Pope Pius VII. The period of the omnipotent State is already past. The lasting fruit of Rationalism—and no great intellectual movement goes by without such lasting fruit—is seen rather in the principle of tolerance which it awakened everywhere, especially in contrast with the Roman Catholic Church.

The Roman Church is fundamentally intolerant. Since, according to the Romanist faith, subjection to pope and bishops (adherence to the Roman Catholic Churchly body) is essential to the soul's salvation of every one, that Church holds itself not only justified, but under obligation, in case of necessity, to secure the return of the heretic by force to the requisite subjection, and even to attach the penalty of death in the most extreme cases of heresy as to the most extreme case of crime. Even the Protestant Church has repeatedly applied principles of intolerance, and has condemned and punished with secular force those who swerved from the faith. The most celebrated case of this kind is the execution of the anti-Trinitarian Spaniard, Michael Servetus,[22] in Geneva (1553), which took place either at the suggestion, or by the consent, of John Calvin.

The idea of toleration kept pace with the progress of Rationalism. In the second half of the eighteenth century it was set in operation in Germany by Frederick the Great, of Prussia, and Joseph II, of Austria, and in France by the French Revolution. The Declaration of Human Rights (1789), which in a certain measure contained the political program of Rationalism, proclaimed at once freedom of religious worship, and thereby gave to the Protestants of France the so long wished-for toleration which had been refused them since the revocation of the Edict of Nantes[23] (1685).

The Roman Catholic Church has repeatedly given expression to her principle of intolerance in the nineteenth century in condemning, by the mouth of Pope Gregory XVI (1832) and Pope Pius IX (1864), freedom of faith and of conscience. Nevertheless the demand for freedom of faith and conscience, by reason of which every kind of external compulsion is excluded from doctrinal convictions of the individual rules to-day, without exception, the law of our civilized States, and alike the convictions of educated Roman Catholic and Protestant humanity. In this fact we see the great outcome of the intellectual movement of the preceding century, the final victory which Rationalism bore away over the external might, especially of the Roman Catholic Church.

§ 53. Benevolent Activity.

With the reformation of doctrine came, of necessity, a reformation of the motives and methods
of Christian benevolence. When salvation was no
longer believed to be dependent upon Mendicancy
(as with the Mendicant monks), nor upon any other
such externalities, unnecessary beggary must consistently be discouraged. When a life of faithfulness in a chosen vocation came to be regarded as
more pleasing in God's sight than a life of fruitless dependence upon others, the demands for almsgiving were greatly reduced. When men no longer
expected to purchase salvation by gifts to the poor,
or by sacrifices for the sick and suffering, but solely
by faith in Jesus Christ, the motives, as well as the
methods, of administering benevolence were entirely altered. When the Scripture came to be
taken as the rule of faith and practice, Scriptural
principles and precepts must be applied to the
whole domain of beneficence. These changes of
principle at once did away with a vast number of
abuses. Giving was no longer, in and of itself,
meritorious; hence, it must be discriminating, that
the unworthy might not receive what was due only
to those in actual need. Those who gave alms
under the influence of Reformation principles did
so, not for their own benefit, but for the benefit of
the needy and suffering. Benevolence had become
selfishness. The spirit of the Reformation restored it

to its Christ-like character. It was no longer a merit
to be poor, or to deprive one's self of property in the
interest of the poor, but it was held as a duty to
administer the earthly goods, which God had bestowed, in the spirit of Christ. The Christian and
all he possessed belonged to God, and it was only
left to the individual to determine the mode and
extent to which he was obligated to make his general consecration specific in acts, and in gifts to the
suffering. In addition to the spirit of human pity,
Christ-like sympathy, and the responsibility of
Christian stewardship, the motive of gratitude for
spiritual blessings received from the Giver of every
good and perfect gift, and the desire to imitate
Christ, who, though he was rich, yet for our sakes
became poor that we, through his poverty, might
be made rich, acted as powerful stimulants to the
activity of benevolence in the period of the Reformation.

It would appear as though such motives should
prove even more effective than those in vogue prior
to the Reformation, and that, with industry where
there had been beggary, there should have been no
lack of food and clothing for the hungry and naked,
and that personal help should have been abundant.
But while the motives and views of the Reformation were true and right in themselves, it was
not possible in every case to make them effective in
the individual where alone they can find practical expression indeed. A generation which had inherited

the traditions of centuries, together with the fallen nature of humanity, could not so easily and quickly be elevated to the full conception and purpose of the spirit of the Gospel. This was reserved only for the finest spirits and most active laborers in the Reformation period. From these the grades shaded downward to the masses, both rich and poor, who are always more intent upon receiving the benefits of salvation than upon bestowing them on others. Many who had alms to give when it was supposed that they could merit salvation thereby, lost all interest in charity when it was taught that salvation was by faith alone. Yet with many others these motives were effective, and especially all the leaders in the Reformation are bright examples of what a true and unselfish exercise of charity means. Besides, the return of the monks and nuns to their daily callings withdrew from the work of benevolence an immense number of voluntary and trained workers, whose places it was impossible to fill with paid helpers. Not until recent years has it fairly dawned upon the Protestant Church that, in order to the systematic exercise of benevolence and the best possible response to the constant demands for the relief of suffering, individual effort is insufficient, and organization necessary; and that vast numbers of voluntary workers in this cause can be supported and employed without the re-establishment of the monasteries and nunneries of the olden time. To all these hin-

drances to the effective care of the needy and sick
there must be added, besides the usual causes of
suffering, the counteracting effect of a slow adjust-
ment to new relations; a place had to be made in
society for these one-time monks and nuns; the
many who were impoverished by the persecutions
which drove them from their homes on account of
their faith, and especially the wars—as the Peasants'
War, the Schmalcald War, and the Thirty Years'
War—which were the almost direct result of the attempt at reformation in the Church,—these causes
tended to increase, rather than diminish, the number of those needing help in comparison with the
days when Mendicancy was a divine service and
almsgiving a means of purchasing salvation. And
noble were the efforts to meet the necessities thus
so unjustly thrust upon the Protestant Church.
And these efforts shine all the brighter because they
sprang from the motives of genuine brotherly helpfulness and Christian love.

Pietism added very little which was really new
to the principles which had actuated the Reformers
in their benevolent work, although some of the best
results of Christian work in all departments, and
some of the best existing benevolent institutions,
especially in Germany, were either founded by the
Pietists, or can be traced to their influence. They
made an advance upon the principles of the Reformation period—not by the introduction of new
elements, but by the peculiar emphasis which they

placed, in word and deed, upon some features of the
Christian life.   Men were indeed to be justified by
faith, but faith must be proved by love.   And this
love was not to be a mere sentiment, but an active
exhibition of loving helpfulness to both friend and
foe, but especially to such as were of the household
of faith.   But the most striking feature of their
benevolent work was the combination of the spiritual with the temporal relief of those in distress.
It was not sufficient to feed the body, and allow the
soul to starve.

As Luther, in visiting his congregations, discovered their fearful ignorance of divine things,
and was led thereby to prepare his smaller and
larger catechisms as vehicles of religious instruction to the people, so Francke (1663–1727), one
of the most celebrated and benevolent of the
Pietists, when he catechized the children of the poor,
who assembled at his door once a week in Halle for
alms, discovered the ignorance of both young and
old, and undertook measures for its relief.   He was
himself without means, and his salary as pastor and
professor at Halle was small.   Placing in his living-
room a box into which money was to be dropped for
carrying forward his efforts at instructing the poor
in religious truth, he waited until there had been
gathered the sum of about three dollars and sixty
cents, which he deemed a capital large enough to
justify the commencement of the work.   He bought
books, and employed **a poor** student to give instruc-

tion. Thus he began (1698) what is now the cele-brated Orphanage of Halle, which, at the time of Francke's death, had grown to such proportions that it employed the services of one hundred and seventy-five teachers, male and female, and had under instruction two thousand two hundred children. The effort was to train the children to piety. They were taught to be diligent, truthful, and obedient; to examine themselves with rigor as to their moral and spiritual condition, and to utter the prayers of their hearts to God publicly, in the presence of the classes.

Very little regard seems to have been had for the exuberant and joyful nature of childhood. The hours of recreation were few, and these were chiefly occupied with prayer and Scripture reading, and with the distribution, at the close, of bread and fruit. But if the government was ill-suited to the child nature, it at least illustrated the emphasis placed upon the value of instruction and training in religion. The ideal was more true to the spirit of Christ than that which relieves the wants of the body alone, even though the methods employed for its attainment were defective. The influences for good which have gone forth from the Orphanage at Halle, the friends it has ever found, and its permanent success, are the best vindication of the fundamental truthfulness of the principles upon which it was conducted.

The roots of the benevolent methods and institutions of the present day are all found in those of the past. The Church of to-day has profited by the efforts of those who in every age have undertaken the relief of suffering. Great as is the emphasis upon the relief of bodily distress the effort to evangelize the masses is in almost all cases combined with it so far as the activity of the Church is concerned. A characteristic feature in the benevolent work of to-day is found in the number and variety as well as in the strength and completeness of the organizations which devote themselves to charitable objects. These afford scope for the participation of all who have either time and strength or money to bestow. The whole field has been surveyed and studied with minutest care, and the entire resources of medical science, as well as the principles of political and social economy as modified by those of Christianity, are employed in the execution of the task. The ripe fruit of past efforts is seen in the fact that in Christian lands all classes, without regard to creed, and even those who reject religion as a personal concern, combine to perpetuate the spirit of the Master who went about doing good. In nothing has the leaven of the gospel been so successful as in humanizing the hearts of men. It has proved itself to be indeed a gospel of love. Even when passion has not yielded to its pervasive influence a spirit of gentleness and brotherliness has entered in, which can be traced directly to the power of the gospel of Christ. It is well. For nothing is clearer in the light of history than the fact that the causes which produce want and suffering are constant in their operation, and will never afford a respite to the cry for sympathy, mercy, and help. To say nothing of the active workers of our generation and the immediate past, mankind will never cease to honor as personal illustrations of the power of Christian love the names of Martin Luther, Philip Melanchthon, John Bugenhagen, August Hermann Francke, John Frederick Oberlin, John Henry Pestalozzi, John Fletcher, John Wesley, Thomas Chalmers, Elizabeth Fry, and scores of others who, in the midst of a multitude of duties, found time to give free play to the spirit of charity which is the spirit of Christ in their hearts.

If there is anything really new in the benevolence of the present generation, it is in the strenuous, and in part successful, efforts at the prevention of human suffering. The causes of crime and suffering are being studied as never before, in the hope that the way may be made plain for their prevention. Individual and organized efforts to abolish drunkenness, guide the erring, lift up the fallen, instruct and train the young, and place all in the best conditions for happy living, were never so numerous and energetic as to-day. Without neglecting on the one side the necessity of regeneration in order to a holy life, or on the other attempting to make men Christians by means of law, legislation is being widely and in part effectively employed for the prevention of the conditions from which suffering and crime arise. Almost all the efforts of the past have been directed toward relief. The tendencies of the present are toward prevention. Doubtless a united effort on the part of all who have a heart to sympathize with human woe in the employment of all the agencies and forces which God has placed within human reach would do much to check the tide of sorrow in which mankind is ingulfed. But the one lesson which the history of human misery teaches is that the Old Book which declares that we live in a fallen world, where thorns and thistles grow in place of fruits and flowers, sets forth the unalterable truth, and points every one to the Great Physician, and to heaven, where there is no woe because there is no sin.

FOURTH CHAPTER.

THE CHURCH IN GREAT BRITAIN AND AMERICA.

§ 54. THE CHURCH IN GREAT BRITAIN.

THE introduction of Christianity into the British Islands is involved in obscurity. Not a few believe that Paul is the founder of British Christianity, while tradition variously bestows that honor upon St. James, Simon Zelotes, and Joseph of Arimathea. Eusebius (the "Father of Church History," died 340) says that some of the apostles preached in the British Isles. Tertullian (died 220) says that some places in Great Britain were subject to Christ to which the Romans had not penetrated. The episcopal form of government early took root. British bishops signed the census of the Council of Arles (314). In the Diocletian persecution large numbers of British Christians suffered martyrdom, although the names of but three are preserved. The insular position of Britain prevented Christianity there from being very much influenced for many centuries by Rome, and also from being very much known in the Continental World. Pelagius sprang from British soil. Monachism took early hold. But besides the facts already mentioned, we know little of the state of the Church prior to the

Saxon invasion[24] (449). Except Wales, Cornwall, Scotland, and Ireland,[25] Britain was swept clean of its Christianity under the rule of the heathen Saxons.

But those who had destroyed Christianity were destined to be themselves Christianized. The Scotch and Irish sent missionaries into England for their conversion. But it was especially due to the efforts of Pope Gregory the Great that the Anglo-Saxons were converted. While he was yet abbot of the monastery of St. Andrew he saw in Rome three boys, Anglo-Saxon slaves, whose fair complexions and bright expression of countenance suggested the famous play upon the name Angles.[26] Having inquired concerning their country and religion, he immediately secured permission from the pope to go and preach to the English people. But he only reached the Alps on his way, when he was recalled at the earnest solicitation of the populace. When he became pope (590), the Anglo-Saxons were not forgotten; and in 596 he commissioned Augustine (not to be confused with Augustine, bishop of Hippo) and forty other monks to win England to Christ. Ethelbert, king of Kent, and chief of the Saxon monarchs,[27] was the first convert, and his baptism was followed by that of ten thousand of his people, and gradually by the other kings of England. Augustine became the first archbishop of Canterbury. But he was unable to win over to his Roman ideas the other British bishops, who, after two conferences with him, refused to yield a single one of his demands.[28] Gradually, however, after Augustine's death, the Roman views prevailed, and the British clergy departed to Ireland, leaving but few Christians of the original British type, who were finally merged into the body of Roman Christians.

From this time forward the process of Romanization in the English Church was very rapid, although for several centuries the claims of the popes were not pressed with much success. The first great impulse to the influence of Rome was given by St. Dunstan (925–988), a man of great learning ability, and energy, all of which he exerted in the effort to secure the supremacy of the pope in the affairs of the English Church. As personal adviser of King Edgar, he aided greatly in the improvement of general morals; he strove to reform the lax discipline of existing monasteries; and by the establishment of the Order of Benedictine Monks in England contributed to the rapid spread of monasticism in Great Britain. A little later, King Canute (995–1036), the Dane,[29] enacted laws for the suppression of heathen worship. A pilgrimage to Rome (1026) still further increased his enthusiasm for the Roman form of Christianity. King Edward the Confessor (1004–1066), brought up in Normandy, and imbued from childhood with monastic and Roman principles, carried on the work of Romanization. Under William of Normandy, the Conqueror

(1066–1087), the papacy may be said to have gained its firmest hold upon England, both in State and Church. Personally, William was able to maintain a considerable degree of independence of the pope; but in his contest with Harold II, whom Edward the Confessor had nominated as his successor to the crown, William appealed to Pope Alexander II, who, influenced by Hildebrand, afterwards Pope Gregory VII, favored him as against Harold. This placed the English crown, by precedent, at the disposal of the papacy, which was not slow to assert its recognized prerogative. Prior to William the affairs of Church and State had been interwoven with one another. Under him these jurisdictions were separated. This afforded later the basis of a demand for the complete exemption of the clergy from temporal jurisdiction. The elevation of William to the English throne also brought England into more immediate connection with the Continent, and resulted in many sweeping changes, all in the interest of the Roman see. From Normandy the task of establishing monasteries in England was carried forward; the chief ecclesiastical offices, which hitherto had been filled by Englishmen, were now filled by foreigners; and above all, it was owing to this cause that England participated so enthusiastically in the Crusades. Anselm, archbishop of Canterbury (1033–1109), and his successors, still further fastened the Roman ideas upon the English Church, and especially with reference to the marriage of the clergy, which had hitherto been allowed, but which was now forbidden. With the establishment of the papal claims began, as a matter of course, a struggle between the papacy and the English kings, which lasted till the days of the Reformation, and which, in a large measure, prepared the way for it.

After the fusion of the British and Roman Christians of England, there is little heard of heresy on English soil until the days of John Wyclif, " the morning-star of the Reformation" (died 1384). He attained great popularity, both with the masses of the people and with the authorities of the universities, by his opposition to the Mendicant monks, who wandered about England, as over the Continent, disturbing almost every relation of human society. The monks did not fail to seek revenge. But by his bold and skillful defense of England, as against the papal claims, Wyclif won the favor of the king, who bestowed upon him the rectorship of Lutterworth, where he openly and unmolested proclaimed the principles of the Reformation. The pope, however, was not content to let Wyclif alone, and several attempts were made to silence him. But in vain. He satirized the monastic orders, opposed the granting of benefices to aliens, objected to the doctrine of transubstantiation, and translated the Bible into the English tongue. The longer he strove to correct abuses, the more plainly he saw that they were inseparably connected with the Church of Rome, and the more vigorously did he denounce them. Unable to burn him alive, the authorities of the Church had his bones exhumed in 1428, and burned. His ashes were cast into the river Swift, thence they were carried to the Avon, the Severn, and the sea, and thus scattered over the the whole world, an emblem[30] of the wide dissemination his doctrines were to find in the course of time. Huss, in far Bohemia, caught his inspiration from Wyclif's doctrines, and Huss was burned at the stake (1415), in the same century in which Luther was born. As on the Continent, so in England, there were reformers before the Reformation. The followers of Wyclif, under the name of Lollards, suffered bitter persecution, many burning at the stake for their faith.

The crisis which prepared the way for the English Reformation occurred during the reign of Henry VIII (1509–1547). Henry had married Catharine of Aragon,[31] his brother's widow, and daughter of Ferdinand and Isabella. But there had always been some question as to the validity of the marriage. The pope had declared in favor of its validity; but when it suited the convenience of Henry to divorce her, Wolsey, cardinal and prime minister, undertook to secure the pope's consent. But the king soon began to show his preference for Anne Boleyn, an enemy of Wolsey. The crafty cardinal now strove secretly to prevent the divorce on account of his fear of the elevation of Anne. Cranmer, who afterward perished as a martyr to

the cause of Protestantism, but who was at this time
merely a tool in the hands of Henry, proposed to
refer the question to the universities, which unani-
mously decided against the validity of the marriage
with Catharine. Wolsey's fall now followed; and
upon his elevation to the See of Canterbury,
Cranmer divorced Henry and Catharine, and married
Anne and the king. Because the pope declared
these proceedings illegal and threatened to excom-
municate Henry, Parliament took measures to free
England from papal authority and papal taxations.
This was in 1534. The suppression of the monasteries followed,[32] a few changes in doctrinal statement were made, and the Church of England
with Henry, instead of the pope, as its head, was
established.

But the ecclesiastical system of Henry VIII
lacked much of being a true Reformation. It has
been well described as popery without the pope.
Henry had early written against Luther a treatise
on the Roman Catholic sacraments, for which the
pope rewarded him with the title of "Defender of
the Faith" (1521). And although he renounced
the authority of the pope, he never changed the
essentials of his doctrinal position. His prede-
cessors had for three centuries striven to check the
exercise of the papal power on English soil. Henry
threw it off altogether, and reduced the clergy to
subjection to himself. Those who swerved from the
received doctrines, especially of transubstantiation,

he punished severely, sometimes even with death.
By the masses no theological change was demanded.
The real Reformation was begun in the next reign,
that of the youthful King Edward VI (1547–
1553). The changes under Henry merely prepared
the way. The signal for the beginning of the
strictly religious Reformation was the publication of
a book of homilies in the first year of Edward's
reign. They were prepared by Cranmer, and were
commanded to be read in all Churches occupied by
clergy who were themselves unable to preach. In
order that the people might be instructed in the
truths of the gospel it was ordained that a sermon
should be preached in each church at least once in
every three months. But so great was the in-
capacity of the clergy as a whole that even this
minimum of preaching was with difficulty secured.
A book of common prayer was also published which
was intended to be free from Romanistic errors, and
even this was revised in the interest of Protestant
views in the six years of Edward's short reign.
Confession was no longer required; in communion
the cup was restored to the laity, who were to be
prepared for that sacrament by an exhortation of
the minister on the preceding day. Parliament
repealed the acts according to which those holding
reformed views were persecuted; and in 1552 forty-
two articles of religion were published, forming the
basis of the **Thirty-nine Articles** of Elizabeth,
the **English Church Creed** of the present day.

Under Mary (1553–1558), the daughter of Henry VIII and Catharine of Aragon, the reformatory measures of Henry and Edward were set aside, and the authority of the pope was re-established. So bitterly did she persecute the Protestants that her short reign of five years permanently fastened upon her the designation of "Bloody Mary." Elizabeth (1558–1603), daughter of Henry and Anne Boleyn, favored the Protestant cause, and by the middle of her reign the Reformation of England was well-nigh complete, so far as the permanent establishment of Protestantism was concerned. Much, however, still remained to be done in order to imbue the English mind with the true spirit of the Reformation. This was brought about first by Puritanism and later by Methodism. Elizabeth was a firm Protestant, but she was an equally firm Episcopalian. Puritanism was not originally a movement in the interest of a doctrine. In this respect the Puritans and their Episcopalian opponents were one. If there was any preponderance of ultra Calvinism to be found in either party during Elizabeth's reign, it was in the Episcopal. Whitgift, the deadly foe of the Puritans, wrote the nine Lambeth Articles to check the progress of Arminianism[33] which began to show itself in England between 1590 and 1600. Not until two decades later when the Episcopalians became pronounced Arminians did the Puritans adopt the Lambeth Articles. The real struggle of the

Puritans was for freedom to worship God according to forms of the individual's own choosing; the introduction of the Presbyterian form of Church government; and greater strictness in matters of practical godliness, such as the observance of the Sabbath. The spirit of Puritanism was directly derived from the Calvinists of Zurich and Geneva; the Puritan party was composed of a moderate and a more extreme element. The latter would not yield even in external things, and they were of necessity the real leaders. Elizabeth answered, with an Act of Uniformity, which required under increasingly severe penalties[34] for repeated offenses, the use of uniform prayers, a uniform mode of administering the sacraments (all must kneel in the Lord's Supper), uniform clerical vestments, and other matters which, while they contribute to the feeling of unity, when made compulsory rob the Church of what is far more highly to be prized, the spirit of free and unconstrained worship. For the sake of unity men may be willing to yield to the wishes of others in matters of ceremony. But the very essence of Protestantism is trampled under foot by the attempt to *compel* uniformity in the service of God. It was the natural result, therefore, that a conflict arose between the throne and the Puritans, which never ended until the Act of Toleration of 1689 gave Presbyterians, Baptists, Quakers, and Independents, the free right to perform their religious exercises according to their own con-

sciences. The attempt to coerce the Puritans into
compliance with the oppressive laws against them,
transformed them from an element of purification
into one of dissension. They organized according
to the Presbyterian form of government and adopted
Knox's liturgy. Every effort was made to suppress
the organization, but in vain. It continued to
grow until the time of the Restoration. Both
parties grew more and more intolerant. The
advocates of the episcopacy declared for the
divine right of the bishops; the Presbyterians that
theirs was the only Scriptural form of Church
government.

Under James I (1604–1625) matters grew
rather worse than better for the Puritans. His
motto was, "No bishop, no king." He felt his own
position insecure should Presbyterianism prevail.
Notwithstanding the dastardly "Gunpowder Plot,"[35]
he was more favorable to the Romanists than to
the Puritans. Under his oppressions the "Pilgrim
Fathers" (1620) forsook their native land for the
shores of America. They were followed by many
others, until even this was forbidden, and seven
vessels, in one of which was Oliver Cromwell, were
compelled to discharge their cargo of human souls
in the land from which they desired to flee. This
was under Charles I, who undertook to carry out
all the oppressive measures of his father (James I).
He even undertook to force the English liturgy
upon Presbyterian Scotland, where the bold Knox[36]

had withstood the beautiful but treacherous Mary, Queen of Scots. Rebellion was the result, and the Parliament refused him the means for its suppression. Instead of taking lessons from this experience, he did all he could to exasperate and alienate Parliament and people. Laud, the prime minister, tried to raise the necessary funds, but he was only partially successful. The king became more and more violent in his measures, until, during the "Long Parliament" (1640–1653), the civil war broke out (1642). At first the war went in favor of the king. But Oliver Cromwell, whom Charles had prevented from going to America, collected an army of "Ironsides," in which no oath or obscene word was ever heard, no drunkenness seen, and of which every man fought in the name of the God whom he worshiped. Cromwell's religion was of the Old Testament type, stern, God-fearing, courageous, confident in the God of battles. He and his army were thoroughly invincible. The Scotch and English bound themselves in a "*Solemn League and Covenant*" to extirpate popery and prelacy. They fought under the firm conviction that both their civil and religious liberties were at stake. Thus every motive was supplied which could lend strength to the hand and courage to the heart. But from the ascendency of Cromwell the star of Presbyterianism waned in England and Independency arose. For although Cromwell was a Puritan, he was not a Presbyterian. His task was arduous; and if he manifested severity it must be remembered that his age was one which had not yet learned the spirit of toleration.[37]

With the restoration of Charles II (1660–1685) the episcopal party again gained the supremacy. An Act of Uniformity, more severe than those of Elizabeth and her successors, was passed, and, rather than submit to it, two thousand Puritan clergy forsook their livings. The act had in it inexcusable elements of harshness. It was to go into effect just before the clergy were to receive their incomes for the preceding year. If they refused to subscribe, they lost, not only their places, but the pay due them for their year's labor. Clergymen deposed under Puritan rule had been allowed one-fifth of their regular incomes, to save them from starvation. But these Puritans were robbed of all at a single blow. Little wonder that the Sunday preceding was called "Black Sunday," and that the refusal to conform, under such circumstances, is regarded as one of the most heroic deeds in the annals of history. One act of oppression followed another in rapid succession under Charles II and James II (1685–1688). The former tolerated Romanism, although he was compelled by Parliament to withdraw his decree. The latter re-established the Court of High Commission, which, with the Star Chamber,[38] had been abolished by the Long Parliament. He forbade preaching against Romanist errors, renewed the toleration of Romanism, and even required this decree to be published in the Churches.

Such high-handed measures were sure to meet resistance. Seven bishops were sent to the Tower. After trial they were acquitted, and the news was hailed by the people with unbounded enthusiasm. Soon after, in 1688, William, Prince of Orange, landed in England, and the career of James II and the struggles of Puritanism for religious liberty were ended. In 1689 the Act of Toleration was passed, and the battle of nearly one hundred and fifty years was over.

§ 55. The Church in the United States.

The Christianity of the United States is the Christianity of Europe developed under peculiar social and political conditions. Prior to the Revolutionary War there had been colonies in which Christianity was established in the form of particular creeds and theories of Church government. In New York, Maryland (after 1691), and Virginia, Christianity was established in the English Church. The Plymouth Colony and its offshoots were practically ecclesiastico-civil States in which Christianity was only free in the form peculiar to their Puritan founders. On the other hand (prior to 1691), Maryland, where the rulers were Roman Catholics, and Rhode Island, where the ruling beliefs were those of the Baptists, every one was left free to worship God as his conscience might dictate. The same was true also of several of the other Colonies. As a result, the original thirteen States were populated by a great variety of European nationalities, and by people of an equal variety of doctrinal faith. Left free to propagate their special views of Christian doctrine and life (which in nearly all essentials are, however, not peculiar, but identical), the orthodox denominations of the United States, were prepared, after the treaty of peace of 1783, to make rapid advances in numbers and missionary enterprise.

Christianity, as thus represented by the different denominations, enjoys in the United States a position of freedom which it has nowhere else found. On the one hand it is not neglected nor despised, but is a part of the fundamental law of the land. On the other hand it is not interfered with nor surrounded by any unnecessary restrictions. Church property is free from taxation; religious gatherings are protected against disturbance; while the individual is neither compelled to worship, nor to worship in any other way than his judgment and conscience dictate. The Churches, not supported by public taxation, are thrown upon their own resources and energies. All denominations having equal rights before the law, each is left to commend itself to the public favor according to its inherent excellences. No system could be better adapted to develop energy and zeal in action and devotion and brotherly love in sentiment. Error can not support itself, nor truth be robbed of its vigor by dependence upon secular authority. Every religious idea must be able to justify itself before the judgments and consciences of those to whom it appeals, both theoretically and as to practical results. The system is, in the best sense, the application of the principle of the survival of the fittest.

America was discovered twenty-five years before the Reformation began. Of necessity, therefore, the Roman Catholics were the first explorers of America. As early as 1528 the pope appointed a bishop of Florida, and under him the first mission to the Indians was begun. But it failed, and it was not until 1565 that a colony was permanently established at St. Augustine, where, soon after, the first Church was erected. In 1609 a Romanist chapel was erected in Maine, while Romanist missionaries had penetrated to California as early as 1601. The mild and tolerant form of the Roman Catholic faith in Maryland (beginning with 1630) was suppressed first by the Puritans (1644–1646), and afterwards by the Anglicans (from 1704 onward). Many of their missions among the Indians were lost to them by the transfer of the territorial jurisdiction from Roman Catholic countries to England. Notwithstanding, their zeal, especially that of the Jesuits, and the tide of immigration rapidly increased their numbers. Their losses by defection, however, have been very heavy in the atmosphere of American intelligence and freedom. The first bishop after the Revolution was Dr. Carroll, who was appointed to the See of Baltimore in 1790. In 1808, Baltimore was raised to the dignity of a metropolitan See, with the four suffragan bishoprics of New York, Philadelphia, Boston, and Bardstown (afterwards transferred to Louisville, Kentucky). In missions and in works of charity the Romanists of the United States are very active. But the entire spirit of the Roman hierarchy is contrary to the spirit of freedom in the United States. The priests are exceedingly intolerant of any public measure, however necessary for the general welfare, which interferes with their plans and purposes. They prevent, wherever possible, the use of the Bible in the public schools as godless, and do all in their power to prevent the children of Romanist parents from attending them. Even the truths of history, if they reflect upon the Roman Catholic Church, may not be taught without their most bitter opposition. Their adherents, although in a less degree in the United States than elsewhere, are subservient to the will of the hierarchy. Roman Catholicism, controlled by one of the most absolute monarchies the world has ever seen, and permeated by a thoroughly foreign spirit, is one of the dark storm-clouds which threaten the, for the most part, peaceful sky of American civil and religious institutions.

The first successful Protestant colony was settled at Jamestown, Virginia, 1607. Prior to this, numerous attempts at Protestant colonization had been made, but none of them had proved successful. A colony of Huguenots on the St. John's River was

massacred by the Roman Catholics of St. Augustine
under their desperate leader, Melendez, before the
close of the sixteenth century. The colony of
Jamestown was composed of Englishmen, and was
the first from that country permanently established
in America. The charter provided "that the true
word and service of God be preached, planted, and
used, according to the rites and doctrines of the
Church of England." The Rev. R. Hunt, a member of this colony, was diligent and pious in labors
and in life. Each clergyman was allowed by the
Colonial Legislature "fifteen hundred pounds of
tobacco and sixteen barrels of flour annually."
A college was founded, which was to educate
Indians as well as whites; but after the Indian
massacre of 1622 it had to be abandoned. The
Church of England was tolerated and flourished in
the Roman Catholic Colony of Maryland. In 1692
the Church of England was established there by law.
Dr. Thomas Bray was soon after appointed as com-
missary to the bishop of London. He brought
with him a number of clergymen, who assisted in
preaching the gospel in Maryland. He was instru-
mental in founding the "Society for Promoting
Christian Knowledge," and the "Society for the
Propagation of the Gospel in Foreign Parts," both
of which rendered valuable service in spreading the
gospel in America. In New York, as soon as the
English had taken possession of the Colony, the
English Church was established by law, according

to its policy wherever it could be carried out. Only in New England were the services of the English Church forbidden by the Puritans, who had just cause to dread the existence of that Church in their vicinity. Had they been intolerant to none others, history would have judged them mildly in their treatment of the English Church. It was not until 1679 that a church of that denomination was erected in Boston. During the Revolution most of the clergy of this Church were loyal to England, and hence the denomination attracted the suspicion and ill-will of the patriots. But those of the clergy who remained after the war were a determined company. As England for a time refused to send or ordain them a bishop, they contemplated organizing under the Presbyterian form of government. But in June, 1786, after many discouragements, the clergy and laity in convention adopted a constitution. Drs. White and Provorst, who had been sent to England for ordination returned as bishops in 1787 (arriving on Easter Sunday), from which the completion of the Churchly organization dates. The growth of the denomination has not been rapid. But its conservative character, its exclusive claims, persistently advanced; the wealth and ability of its members and clergy give it a wide-spread influence in the country.

The existence of Congregationalism in the United States began with the landing of the "Pilgrim Fathers" at Plymouth Rock, in 1620.

Although they did not exhibit the tolerance for others which they had demanded for themselves, they possessed other sterling qualities which have done much to determine the civil, moral, and religious character of America. Congregationalism took form first in New England; and although the Puritans who came to the shores of America later than the Pilgrim Fathers sincerely professed loyalty to the Church of England, and were anxious only to purify it from all error, yet they gradually and naturally fell into the ideas entertained by their brethren of Plymouth, and forsaking the episcopal adopted the congregational form of government. According to this theory, each separate congregation constitutes a Church. The government is democratic, and is therefore in harmony with the spirit of American institutions. In 1801 the General Congregational Association of Connecticut entered into an agreement (called the Plan of Union) with the Presbyterian General Assembly, to prevent the establishment of Churches of both denominations in the same locality. But it was found prejudicial to the growth of Congregationalism, and in 1852 was abandoned. They lost heavily in the early part of the century on account of the organization of the Unitarian Church.[39] Their influence is specially great among the wealthier and more educated classes. They are orthodox in faith, and active in every benevolent, educational, and missionary enterprise.

The first Lutherans to bring with them a minister to their spiritual wants, were a colony of Swedes which settled where the city of Wilmington, Delaware, now stands (1638). The first German Lutherans came to America in 1644, and in 1669 they were supplied with a minister in the person of John Fabricius. Their first church edifice was erected in 1671. The Lutheran Church in America has reason to be proud of its founders. August Hermann Francke, the Pietist founder of the celebrated Orphan House at Halle, induced the Rev. Henry Melchior Mühlenberg to come to America (1742) and attend to the spiritual wants of the Lutherans who were scattered over the land. He at once proceeded to organize them into a compact body. His measures were wise and his efforts successful. After his death an effort was made to confine the services to the use of the German language, resulting in a large number of defections among the younger element. The General Synod was formed in 1820. The General Council was organized in 1866–7, the division arising from a difference in the interpretation of the Augsburg Confession. The Southern General Synod was formed on the slavery issue, the rock on which so many of the Christian denominations have split. There seems to be no good reason for the separate existence of the Synodical Conference. Owing to their antecedents the Lutherans appeal chiefly to the German elements of American society. On

account of the rationalistic character of much of
the German population, the Lutheran bodies have
a discouraging task. Nevertheless they are constantly advancing in numbers; and their ministry
includes some of the most godly men of the
American pulpit.

The history of the Baptist Churches in America
begins with the expulsion of Roger Williams from
the Plymouth Colony for denying the right of the
civil authorities to interfere in any way whatever
with the religious convictions and practices of the
individual. Originally he had been a clergyman
of the Church of England. When expelled from
Plymouth he settled in Rhode Island. Here he
welcomed all who were oppressed on account of
their faith. He established the first Christian State
in which absolute religious liberty and equality
were incorporated into the fundamental law. Having convinced himself that immersion was the only
true mode of baptism, he was immersed in 1639.
As a people the Baptists were greatly persecuted in
New England, New York, and Virginia. After the
Revolution they grew rapidly, and they now constitute one of the largest of America's religious
bodies. In 1845 the denomination suffered a division on the question of slavery. The majority of
Baptists are Calvinistic in doctrine; but the Free-will
Baptists are Arminian. The majority of them also
adhere to close communion, admitting none to that
sacrament who have not been regularly immersed.

They are very energetic and successful in missionary enterprise, and are increasing with great rapidity.

Prior to the close of the seventeenth century Francis Mackemie, an Irishman, who has the honor of being the founder of the Presbyterian Church in America, began to establish congregations of that denomination in Maryland. As early as 1705 the Presbytery of Philadelphia was organized, and in 1716 the Synod of Philadelphia, with three Presbyteries. In 1729 the Westminster Confession of Faith and the Westminister Catechism, were adopted as the doctrinal basis of the Church. The preaching of Whitefield in America was looked upon with disfavor by many, and in 1741 a division occurred between those favoring and those opposing the revival. This division was, however, happily healed. About one hundred years later, in 1838, the division took place between the Old and New Schools. The former adhered strictly to the old Scotch ideas of doctrine and discipline, and refused to denounce slavery, on the ground that that was not an affair of the Church. The latter were more liberal in theology, and were opposed to slavery. Both bodies claimed the title, "The General Assembly of the Presbyterian Church in the United States." Their pacific spirit was again attested in the reunion in 1871. Besides this large and influential body of Presbyterians, there are the Cumberland Presbyterian Church, the Reformed Presbyterian Synod, the United Presbyterian Church of

North America, and the United Synod of the Presbyterian Church, South.

All these great Christian bodies, as well as others of smaller numbers, have exerted an influence upon the general religious life of America, and upon her institutions, which it would be hard to estimate. The peculiar genius of each brings something to the entire mass of truth and practice, each modifying the other, so that there is a growing spirit of union. An organic union of the religious denominations is hardly to be expected, and certainly not to be desired, unless it should come about as the result of a natural course of development under the influence of the Spirit of God. The true union is the "unity of the Spirit in the bonds of peace."

§ 56. METHODISM.

The real founders of Methodism were but three in number—John and Charles Wesley, and George Whitefield. All these had been members of the "Holy Club"[40] of the University of Oxford. But the ascetic principles of the Holy Club were not the controlling ones in later Methodism, else Methodism would never have exerted so powerful an influence upon the religious world. When the members of the Holy Club became Methodists, they did not cease their careful examinations of self, nor their earnest interest in the temporal and spiritual welfare of men : but these were made subordinate

and tributary to the consciousness of present salvation and the pursuit of holiness as the free gift
of God.   It was while following the light given
them that they came at length and gradually into
possession of the convictions and experiences which
characterized the great religious movement called
Methodism.   They had no purpose to found a
Church.   They had no idea of the wide dissemination which their teachings should obtain.   Full of
zeal they preached to others the gospel as they experienced it in their own souls.   The development
of their work was in the strictest sense providential.
Whitefield, who became the greatest preacher of
the gospel since the days of the apostles, was the
first to be led into the light.   Gifted with great
natural oratorical abilities, he attracted attention
even as a boy.   Employed about an inn kept by
his mother, he found a copy of Thomas à Kempis's
"Imitation of Christ," the reading of which made a
profound impression upon his mind.   Entering the
Oxford University at the age of eighteen, he de-
frayed his expenses chiefly by serving his fellow-
collegians.   Here (1735) he became a member of
the Holy Club.   It is a sad illustration of the state
of religion at the time that these young men should
have been left so long to struggle for salvation by
good works and austerities.   But no one seemed to
know that this hard, severe self-torture was not precisely the way in which to become saints of God.
The conversion of Whitefield was followed soon

after by that of Charles and then of John Wesley. The Wesleys had gone to Georgia to preach to the Indians. Charles soon returned, while John remained some months longer, imposing the greatest self-denials upon himself, and administering the offices of the Church with severity to others. His intercourse with the Moravians, while crossing the ocean, had revealed to him his lack of true spiritual life. A Moravian friend in London instructed him; and in a meeting of Moravians, and during the reading of the preface to Luther's "Commentary on the Epistle to Romans," Wesley felt his "heart strangely warmed," and knew that he, too, was a child of God (May 24, 1738).

It is not a matter of surprise that men of such education and ability, finding the joys of salvation after such struggles, should proclaim the gospel with zeal and effect, and that the power of God's Spirit should attend their ministry. But these supernatural elements were not alone concerned in bringing about the vast results of their labors. Great movements affecting large masses of people are apt to partake of fanatical elements. Methodism, on the contrary, was held in the channels of practical effort by the sound sense of its chief propagators. Yet no religious movement was ever characterized by greater and more numerous innovations upon established ideas of propriety. The movement was saved from degeneration by the fact that these innovations were not premeditated nor invented, but sprang from the necessities of the situation and the evident indications of a Providential hand. The first Methodists, especially the Wesleys, were strict Churchmen. They firmly opposed any unnecessary variation from Church order, and only yielded when the necessity or advantage was unmistakably evident. Whitefield was the first to break over the prescribed bounds. At first the Methodist preachers, as clergymen of the English Church, preached in the pulpits of their brethren. In a few cases they were permitted to preach repeatedly, but generally the first Methodist sermon was the last. One after another the pulpits were closed against them. This was not because they taught false doctrine, for their teachings were strictly orthodox, but because they preached orthodoxy as if it were true and as though it were important for men to act accordingly. Under these circumstances, Whitefield went to Bristol, his native city, where in a short time every church-door was shut against him. Near Bristol is Kingswood, a region of coal-mines, then inhabited by a very degraded and lawless population. There was no church there, and Whitefield determined to preach in the open air (February 17, 1739). The number of his hearers increased until it reached twenty thousand. He next preached to immense throngs on a large bowling-green in Bristol. Wesley hesitated at first to approve the measure, but, after consideration, himself adopted the plan which has resulted in so much blessing.

21

Another means employed was the power of sacred song. Knowing the fondness for music that exists in almost all men, and recognizing its influence for evil or for good, Wesley determined, he says, that the devil should not have exclusive possession of all the good things, and he would turn this love of music to religious account. His directions for congregational singing were arranged under five heads, as follows: 1. Sing all; 2. Sing lustily; 3. Sing modestly; 4. Sing in time; 5. Above all, sing spiritually. His own hymns and translations of hymns would alone have rendered him famous. But Charles Wesley was pre-eminently the poet of Methodism. His hymns set forth the chief doctrines and almost every conceivable shade of religious experience, in language at once simple, Scriptural, and sublime. They found their way into the hearts of the people, and contributed powerfully to win them to Christ. When the rabble, gathered to interrupt the service in the open air, could be controlled in no other way, it often occurred that the preacher, by raising his voice in song, could subdue the tumult, and, the people catching up the strain, the hardest hearts would be melted, and opposition would be disarmed.

Another agency which was very effective in converting men to God in those days was the class-meeting. That institution is indebted to a peculiar circumstance for its origin. A chapel in Bristol was in debt. No one knew how the debt was to be paid. At length some one said, Let each pay a penny a week until the obligation is met. To this it was objected that many of them were too poor to pay so much. The originator of the plan replied: "Put eleven of the poorest with me, and what they can not pay I will give for them." The plan was agreed to, and several such companies were formed. The collectors went about each week to collect the dues. After a time these collectors began to take note of the religious needs and experiences of those whom they visited, and the plan was thus turned to spiritual profit. Finally it was agreed that the eleven should meet the collector at a given place and time, pay what they could, and engage in religious exercises. The collector was thenceforth styled the leader. It was found that these meetings afforded much encouragement and instruction. Preachers were not numerous, and preaching was comparatively infrequent. These gatherings, in part, supplied the deficiency. The leader became a sub-pastor. The members of the classes inspired with zeal, would invite their friends to the meetings, where they often came under conviction and were converted. It was a return to the apostolic and primitive employment of lay talent in the propagation of the gospel.

By a similar good providence lay preaching early began to be employed, and with wondrous effect. Wesley did not design that his lay helpers should do more than exhort, and read and expound

the Scriptures. But Thomas Maxfield, who supplied the Foundry (a Wesleyan chapel) in the
absence of Wesley, did not confine himself to these
functions. When Wesley heard of the innovation
he hastened back to London to check it. But his
mother approved of Maxfield's course and warned
her churchly minded son: "Take care," she said,
"what you do respecting that young man; he is as
surely called of God to preach as you are." Upon
the advice of his mother he inquired into the fruits
of Maxfield's preaching, and heard him himself,
whereupon he exclaimed: "It is the Lord; let him
do what seemeth to him good." Thomas Maxfield
was the first of a great host of men, who toiled in
obscurity often, and in poverty, but with wondrous
success in the vineyard of the Lord. They were
not learned men, although some of them became
well acquainted with theology, and with the sacred
languages of the Bible. But they were men of
sound sense, deep piety, and inexhaustible zeal.
Some of them became powerful orators, swaying
vast multitudes with the spell of their eloquence.
They were not hastily admitted to the itinerant
ranks. Wesley tested them well, and seldom was
he deceived. Their history reads like romance.
They labored faithfully and well, and the fruit of
their labors indicates the wisdom of admitting them
to the ranks of the itinerants.

The results which attended the use of the means
thus described were marvelous. In the Wesleyan

societies alone, **to say** nothing of the Calvinistic Methodists, there were at Wesley's death five hundred and forty traveling preachers, and one hundred and thirty-four thousand five hundred and ninety-nine members. But the numerical results are not the only index to the success which the movement had. The moral and spiritual achievements of Methodism are the best exponent of its significance. Drunkards became sober, the profane reverent, thieves honest, the licentious pure, and the degraded and ignorant were lifted up to aspirations after a nobler life. Nor were these effects confined to the Methodistic societies. Many of the English clergy became infected with the Methodist spirit, and co-operated with Wesley within and without the bounds of their parishes. Especially is this true of the saintly Fletcher.[41] The movement reached many of the nobility. Lady Huntingdon[42] became the leader of the Calvinistic branch of Methodism, to which Whitefield adhered. Thus large numbers not only of the noble, but also of the learned heard the earnest gospel from Methodist lips. The influence of Methodism was perhaps greater outside the specifically Methodist bodies than within.

Such results were not attained without great expense of effort and suffering. Whitefield crossed the Atlantic seven times. In America he preached chiefly among the Presbyterians and Congregationalists, kindling a blaze of revival fire which has never died out. Wesley was equally active, but confined his efforts chiefly to Great Britain. His plan was to organize, not for the purpose of establishing a Church, but for convenience of oversight. He frequently visited and personally examined into the condition of the societies. The record of his labors is almost incredible. To these unceasing efforts were added opposition and persecution. It was no uncommon occurrence for violent mobs to be led by the parish clergyman. Wesley and Whitefield, as well as the lay preachers, made many narrow escapes from death at the hands of the brutal rabble. It is all the more strange since they went about doing good to all within their reach. Wesley lived, however, to be revered in almost every place; and those who had once greeted him with stones and curses learned to rejoice at his approach. It could not be otherwise, he preached a gospel of salvation for all; and those who heeded his word proved its truth by victory over sin and the consciousness of communion with God.

The beginning of Methodist history in America is dated from the first lay sermon in New York by Philip Embury under the promptings of Barbara Heck. When Susanna Wesley trained John and Charles Wesley in the rectory at Epworth, and gave them advice and encouragement in their difficult and delicate work, she influenced Methodism to an extent and in a manner which will ever secure the recognition and admiration of mankind. Barbara

Heck, by a simple act of Christian loyalty and duty, set in motion influences and activities whose results none but God can measure. She was one of a company of Methodists from Ireland, although of German origin, who had immigrated to New York. Philip Embury was also one of them, but he with the rest had forgotten his duty. At the earnest solicitation of Barbara Heck he began once more to exercise his office of lay preacher. His first congregation was his own family, Barbara Heck, and a few others. This was in 1766. Soon a church was built. Captain Webb, of the English army, and a local preacher also joined the little company. He introduced Methodism into Philadelphia, preaching at first in a sail loft. He also introduced Methodism into Long Island, New Jersey, and Delaware. In response to his earnest appeal, Wesley sent to America Joseph Pilmoor and Richard Boardman, two of his most experienced and trusted itinerants. The twenty-seventh Methodist conference was held in London, August 7, 1770. Fifty circuits were reported. The fiftieth was America; and to the "America Circuit" four men were appointed, Joseph Pilmoor, Richard Boardman, Robert Williams, and John King.

Methodism was exactly adapted to the moral and religious wants of the New World. A settled pastorate could not follow the pioneers into new regions. But the itinerant could. By preaching from one to three times each day, he could reach many points in a journey of four weeks. The local preachers labored in his absence in the vicinity of their homes. The class-leaders still further supplied the lack of pastoral care; while the very infrequency of the preacher's visits made them occasions of deep and solemn interest. Nor did a Methodist preacher need a church. A · house, a barn, or the open air, answered for a place of assembly. Such men and such measures could but master the difficult situation of their times. By such methods the little beginning in the house of Philip Embury, in 1766, swelled until, in the eighteen years which elapsed to the year 1784, the number of itinerants had increased to eighty-one, besides some hundreds of local preachers and exhorters; the number of members to eighteen thousand; and the number of hearers to two hundred thousand. There were also more than sixty chapels, although these were but a small part of the preaching places.

This was the situation at the time when the Christmas Conference met in Baltimore, in 1784, and organized the Methodist Episcopal Church. In England, Wesley resisted every move looking toward separation and independent organization, only yielding at the very last so far as to provide a successor for himself. But in America the Methodists were widely scattered, and could not obtain the sacraments. Wesley was appealed to. But he would not consent to have his preachers administer the sacraments without having first received ministerial orders. He could not induce the bishop of London to ordain even a presbyter for America. After waiting four years he determined that the emergency had become so pressing as to make further hesitation dangerous. The Rev. Dr. Coke was a Methodist and a presbyter of the Church of England. Wesley now proceeded, with the aid of Rev. James Creighton, another presbyter, to ordain Dr. Coke bishop[43] or superintendent of the Methodist societies in America. At the same meeting, Richard Whatcoat and Thomas Vasey were ordained—first as deacons, and then presbyters or elders. Coke, Whatcoat, and Vasey were now sent to America to organize the Methodist societies into an independent Church. The Conference met on Christmas-eve, 1784, and remained in session ten days. When their labors came to a close, the Methodist Episcopal Church was an established fact. Francis Asbury had been ordained deacon, then elder, then superintendent or bishop. The plan and polity of the Church, essentially as it is to-day, was fixed. Wesley saw the Minutes of the Conference, and approved its work.

Methodism has suffered several divisions, but never except on questions of government, and on the question of slavery. On that issue the Methodist Episcopal Church, South, was formed in 1844. In doctrine the Methodists are a unit. They have given great attention to education from the begin-

ning, both in England and America. In missionary and benevolent enterprise they keep pace with
the foremost. Methodism has outlived and lived
down most of the opposition which it met at the
beginning. Of the three great movements in the
Protestant Church—Puritanism, Pietism, and Methodism—the last named profited by having followed
the other two. Like them, although perhaps in a
greater degree, it has become a part of the life of
the entire Church of Christ.

APPENDIX I.

Supplementary and Explanatory Notes.

NOTES TO FIRST CHAPTER

Note 1, p. 9.—A Roman legion consisted of about ten thousand effective soldiers. It was composed of six thousand heavily armed infantry, drawn from the citizens (Romans proper), with a body of auxiliaries (soldiers from the provinces). Three hundred cavalrymen belonged to each legion. The only standard was a silver eagle, with outstretched wings. After Hadrian (emperor from 117–138), it was made of gold. The Etruscans (see Note 6) were the first to employ it as an emblem of royal power.

Note 2, p. 9.—Rome was first a monarchy (B. C. ?–509), then a republic (B. C. 509–27), then an empire (B. C. 27–476 A. D.) Augustus Cæsar was the first emperor, and it was during his reign that Christ was born. (Luke ii, 1–7.) The empire was divided into provinces, which were under governors, who were often very tyrannical. Pilate was governor of Judea when Christ was condemned by him to be crucified.

Note 3, p. 9.—The Orient included the Eastern countries of the empire, as Greece, Asia Minor, Syria, and Egypt. After the conquests of Alexander the Great in the East, the Greek language and civilization spread from Greece eastward. The Occident included the western portions of the empire; as Italy, Spain, Gaul

(France). Latin was the most important language employed.

Note 4, p. 10.—JUPITER, a god of the Romans, literally means "the heavenly father." The Romans regarded him as the lord of heaven, and believed that he controlled all its phenomena, as rain, storms, thunder, lightning, etc. On this account he was held as the highest among the gods. It was believed, also, that he determined all events connected with the earth and man. APOLLO was one of the greater gods of the Greeks. He was believed to punish the wicked, protect from evil, and to delight in cities and civil constitutions.

Note 5, p. 10.—OLYMPUS is a mountain of Thessaly, and rises to the height of 6,000 feet. Its summit was higher than the clouds, and in that cloudless region a city was supposed to have been built which was inhabited only by gods and goddesses. The gates of the city were believed to be the gates of heaven. The gods of Homer's great poems—the "Iliad" and the "Odyssey"—resided there.

Note 6, p. 10.—ISIS was one of the principal goddesses of the Egyptians. She was believed to have introduced the cultivation of wheat and barley. Later she was worshiped in the West, although her worship was opposed by the authorities on account of the licentious practices connected with it. SERAPIS was also an Egyptian divinity. His worship became very popular in Italy. The worship of these two divinities was not checked until Christianity became general. The *Etrurians*, or *Etruscans*, were a tribe of Italy. They cultivated divination beyond any other people, and the art is supposed to have originated with them. The *mysteries* were sacred ceremonies of the Greek religion. They were supposed to have a beneficial effect upon those who participated in them, although they were sometimes immoral. To participate in them, *initiation* was necessary. This required time, and was so conducted as to rouse expectation, and produce reverence for what was seen, heard, and handled. CYBELE, in the Greek mythology, was supposed to be the mother of Zeus (identified with the Roman god Jupiter), and those deities of which he was head; hence called "mother of gods." Her festivals were conducted in forests and mountains, and consisted of orgiastic dances by priests, accompanied by drums, cymbals, and horns.

Note 7, p. 11.—*Seneca* was a philosopher, who lived in the early part of the first century. His life was generally upright, although he was guilty of some serious moral errors. His moral doctrines are so lofty that it has been thought he must have drawn them from Christianity. *Marcus Aurelius*, emperor from 161 to 180, was also a philosopher, and one of the noblest characters heathenism ever produced. Both were Stoics (see Note 8), although the former did not follow the Stoic philosophy exclusively.

Note 8, p. 11.—The Stoic philosophy taught a high morality; but it was distinguished especially by the doctrine that we must not enjoy the blessings nor regret the ills of life, but meet both with utter indifference. Plato's was the prevailing philosophy of Greece. Neo-Platonism was an attempt to harmonize the various conflicting philosophical systems. See remarks concerning it in §11. The reader should see Charles Kingsley's "Hypatia" for a popular, yet correct, exhibition of Neo-Platonism in its relation to Christianity.

Note 9, p. 11.—Monotheism, the belief in one, personal God, is opposed to Polytheism, the belief in many gods, and to Pantheism, the belief that everything is god. The heathen were polytheists, having "gods many." But gradually the idea that there is but one God grew up in connection with heathen philosophy, influenced, perhaps, by the Jewish belief in Monotheism. The Jews were found everywhere in the empire.

Note 10, p. 12.—A strong desire for redemption from the ills of life in this world was prevalent in the first Christian centuries in heathenism. It no doubt inclined many earnest souls toward Christianity, which promised true redemption.

Note 11, p. 12.—The ancient Greeks called their country Hellas, and their people Hellenes. Slavery was one of the earliest institutions of Greece. Slaves could be set free, and thus become freedmen, but not freemen, since they could not be citizens.

Note 12, p. 13.—The Roman emperors were not regarded as gods because of their supposed goodness, but because of their power over their subjects, which was far more absolute than any ruler now exercises in civilized lands. The emperor was worshiped ·while still living. His supposed divinity added greatly to his authority. (Cf. Virg., Ec. i.)

Note 13, p. 15.—When the Jews were under subjection to the Syrians, the Maccabean family took the leadership in a temporarily successful effort for the freedom of their nation. Accounts of these wars will be found in the Apocrypha in the larger family Bibles, and in Josephus's works.

Note 14, p. 15.—The Jews were at this time under the authority of the heathen Romans. They hated their oppressors all the more because they were heathen.

Note 15, p. 17.—A large portion of the city of Rome was burned in the year 64 A. D., the fire raging with great fury during six days and seven nights. The follies of the Emperor Nero were so great as to give color to the report that he had set fire to the city for the pleasure of witnessing the conflagration. The Christians were accused, in order to divert the wrath of the people from Nero. He practiced the greatest cruelty toward them. Enveloping them in inflammable material he used them as torches to illuminate his private grounds. The masses of the people were equally pitiless in their hatred of the Christians.

Note 16, p. 18.—Rome was called the " Eternal City." The pride of the Romans in their city and empire was equal to the splendor of their history.

Note 17, p. 19.—*Cæsar* was not in every case a personal name, but was, after Diocletian, the title applied to the ruler second in authority in the empire. The "Cæsar" to whom Paul appealed (Acts xxv, 11) was the emperor himself. The title *Augustus* which Octavianus (Emperor Augustus) gave himself, and which was higher than that of Cæsar, was intended to indicate his sacred character.

Note 18, p. 21.—*Antoninus Pius* (called Pius because of his piety) was one of the best of the Roman emperors. It is remarkable that even under the best of the emperors—as, for example, Marcus Aurelius—the Christians were persecuted. *Polycarp* was a disciple of the apostle John, and had heard him tell of Jesus Christ. He was martyred in extreme old age. *Ignatius* was a pupil of Polycarp.

Note 19, p. 21.—*Septimius Severus* (193–211) and *Alexander Severus* (221–235) were the two principal rulers of the Severan house. Both were able and good emperors.

Note 20, p. 21.—The Cynics were philosophers who felt it their duty to go about the country preaching against the follies and wickedness of men. They were, in fact, critics of the then existing order of things. Our word " cynic " describes them well.

Note 21, p. 22.—That Trajan's measures resulted as here described is true. But there are those who believe

that he meant to deal kindly, and not, as here represented, with cruelty and calculation.

Note 22, p. 27.—Constantine (the Great) in the campaign
which made him emperor of the West, is said to have
seen a flaming cross in the sky bearing the inscription, " *In hoc signo vinces* "—" By this sign thou shalt
conquer "—and to have received on the following
night a direct command from Christ to exchange the
standard of the eagle for that of the cross, which he
accordingly did. The standard was called the *labarum.*
Licinius was the ruler of the East, and hated the
Christians. Constantine defeated him, and became
the sole emperor of East and West (325). There
are many who hold the opinion that Constantine, in
accepting Christianity, was actuated wholly by motives
of policy.

Note 23, p. 38.—The gloomy views of the world and of
life called pessimistic, are opposed to those cheerful
and hopeful ones called optimistic. The latter are
inseparable from a true conception and belief in
Christianity. The word pessimism has only been in
common use for about fifty years.

Note 24, p. 41.—Christendom now includes all so-called
Christian nations. Christianity is only represented
by those individuals who somewhat perfectly reflect
its doctrines and principles.

Note 25, p. 49.—Charismatic gifts were supernatural
abilities bestowed upon the early Christians; for
example, profound knowledge, prophecy, power to
work miracles, power to speak languages not learned
by study (the gift of tongues), etc.

Note 26, p. 51.—The eucharistic feast, or simply the eucharist, is a name for the Lord's Supper. It originally
designated the fact that the Lord's Supper was a
giving of thanks. That meaning is now lost sight of
in the popular use. (See Note 39.)

Note 27, p. 52.—It was the Church which won the victory by such external aids. Christianity, as such, can only win its way according to its own pure and spiritual principles. The distinction between the Church and Christianity must often be made in the study of Church history.

Note 28, p. 56.—Byzantium was the original name of Constantinople. It became the capital of the empire in 303 A. D. When the empire was divided into the Eastern and Western, the former was called the Byzantine Empire. The city received the name Constantinople from Constantine the Great. (See Note 22.)

Note 29, p. 64.—The Hellenes or Greeks (see Note 11) sought to bring everything to the test of reason. To Hellenize means, therefore, to give great prominence to thought and reason, and very little to faith and feeling.

Note 30, p. 65.—The *Logos* (Word) of the Hebrews (see John i, 1: "In the beginning was the Word," or *Logos*) differed from the *logos* of philosophy. In the latter it meant reason. The Greek philosophers assumed that the world was controlled by reason. *Logos* is a word frequently met in Greek philosophical literature.

Note 31, p. 67.—*Homoousia* is the word for which Athanasius and his party contended at the Council of Nice. *Homoiousia* was that proposed and defended by Arius and his party. There is a difference in orthography of only one letter, but the difference in meaning is great. The former means the "*same* substance," the latter, "*like* substance," with the Father. The former makes Christ truly divine, the latter denies his true divinity.

Note 32, p. 74.—The "Roman See" is simply another name for the authority of the pope. The term *see* was originally applied to the authority or "chair" of any bishop, and all "sees" were believed to be apostolical, since it was supposed that every bishop derived his authority in unbroken succession from the apostles.

Note 33, p. 78.—Asceticism, in its original meaning, signifies an exercise. The ascetic exercises self-restraint, and trains (schools) himself to hardship. Every form of self-denial or hardship endured, which really contributes to our usefulness and growth as Christians, is to be commended. But the ascetics denied themselves of perfectly innocent and even useful things; as palatable food, comfortable homes and beds, as well as clothing and the society of their friends and relatives. They endured many useless and harmful things; as excessive fasting, beatings, etc. The doctrine was that these things were pleasing to God, and would secure his favor. One could be an ascetic and live by himself as a hermit, or even without withdrawing altogether from men. Monasticism united these ascetics into companies, and gave regularity in kind, time, place, and degree to ascetic practices.

Note 34, p. 84.—Manicheism (so called from its founder, Mani, Manes, or Manichæus, who lived in the second half of the third century) taught that there are two eternal principles from which everything proceeds. The one is the kingdom of light, under the dominion of God, the other, the kingdom of darkness, under the dominion of the demon. It rejected much, but also retained much, of the New Testament. It was one of the many attempts to explain the existence of evil side by side with good in the world.

Note 35, p. 84.—The following summary of the doctrines of Pelagius is given in McClintock & Strong's Cyclopedia, Vol. VII, pp. 869, 870: "1. That Adam was created mortal, and would have died whether he had sinned or not. 2. That Adam's sin injured himself alone, and not the human race. 3. That new-born infants are in the same condition in which Adam was before his transgression. 4. That since neither by the death nor transgression of Adam the whole human race dies, so neither will the whole human race rise again on account of Christ's resurrection. 5. That the law guides into the kingdom of heaven as well as the gospel. 6. That there were men who lived without sin before the advent of our Lord. 7. That the grace of God is not absolutely necessary to lead men to holiness. 8. That grace is given to men in proportion to their merit." Pelagius was actuated by a desire to secure a more perfect holiness in Christians; hence the stress upon man's ability, in opposition to the doctrine of his inability, to do good.

Note 36, p. 84.—The Donatists (so named from their leader, Donatus) were orthodox in faith, but advocated a severity of Church discipline which the Church refused to execute. As complications arose, the Donatists became a separate party in the Church, or, rather, defied the authority of the Church, and thus became schismatics. Constantine finally granted them the right to an independent ecclesiastical existence. The germ of the difficulty, however, lay in the fact that the Donatists favored a rigorous, the Church a more lax, execution of discipline.

Note 37, p. 89.—There are three things commonly included by Roman Catholics in those which are supposed to be counseled, but not commanded, in the Scripture. First, the unmarried state, and chastity in same; second, voluntary poverty; third, obedience to the monastic superior in office. The third is in no way provided for in the Bible; the second is only a duty in case property becomes the right hand or eye which offends (Matt. v, 29, 30); the first, if changed to chastity whether in or out of the married state, would be right.

Note 38, p. 90.—In the early Church those whose sufferings for the faith ended short of death were called "confessors," in distinction from martyrs, who were put to death for the cause of Christ. The confessors were held in great respect. Later, any one was called a "confessor" who was supposed to have lived a life of eminent piety. King Edward, of England, was made "Confessor" by decree of Pope Alexander III.

Note 39, p. 91.—The Love-feast was a meal eaten in common by the members of a Christian congregation. It was prompted by and gave expression to the brotherly love which existed among them. At first it was celebrated together with the eucharist (see Note 26), and the whole was called the Lord's Supper. Certain irregularities, as the neglect of the poor by the rich at these feasts, caused the institution to fall into disfavor. It is still preserved in a simple and spiritual form in the Methodist bodies in England and America, and by the Moravians.

Note 40, p. 91.—The apostolic age ended with the death of the last of the apostles (John, about 100 A. D.) The so-called "post-apostolic age" reaches far into the second century. The "apostolic fathers," so called because they lived early enough to have conversed with the apostles, or with some of them, are Barnabas, Clement of Rome, Ignatius, Polycarp (see Note 18), and Hermas. Writings still extant are attributed to these men.

Note 41, p. 92.—The catechumens (candidates for baptism) in the early Church were taught the Creed, the Lord's Prayer, and the rudiments of Christian doctrine—but not (always) in the form of question and answer, like the catechisms of the present day. The design was to give those coming from heathenism time to become acquainted with the nature of Christianity before assuming its obligations.

Note 42, p. 92.—The name Sunday, the heathen (Roman) name for the first day of the week, means "Day of the Sun." It was dedicated to the worship of the sun. The Christians adopted the name from the Roman Calendar, since with them the day was dedicated to the worship of Christ, the "Sun of Righteousness." Christ rose from the dead on the first day of the week, instead of the seventh. His reported appearances to the assembled disciples were on the first day of the week, and although they had (doubtless) meetings on other days, he is not reported as meeting with them. The Day of Pentecost occurred on Sunday. The apostles and earliest Christians seem to have observed that day. (Acts xx, 7; 1 Cor. xvi, 2.) All this, together with the almost uniform practice of the early Church, points to a purpose on the part of Christ and the apostles to change the day of worship and rest to Sunday, the day of Christ's resurrection.

Note 43, p. 94.—The power to banish the evil spirit from the heart was believed to be a power bestowed upon the Church. The rite was performed either by clergy or laity, and consisted of the invocation of Christ, and the use of the sign of the Cross. However gross and erroneous their conception of the rite, it indicates that they clearly recognized the need of a change from the rulership of Darkness to that of Light.

Note 44, p. 97.—Tertullian was one of the greatest Fathers of the Church who wrote in Latin. He was born at Carthage, 160 A. D. He wrote much, and we owe a great deal of our knowledge of the early Church to his writings. At first he was a strong Churchman; but in later life he adopted the rigoristic views of the Montanists (see § 10), and opposed the Church.

Note 45, p. 98.—Chrysostom (golden mouth) was so called on account of his eloquence. His proper name is John. Hence he is often called John Chrysostom. His mother, Anthusa, like the mother of Gregory of Nazianzen, and of Augustine, was an excellent Christian woman. Libanius, a heathen rhetorician, exclaimed, referring to Anthusa: "O, gods of Greece! what women there are among the Christians!"

Note 46, p. 103.—The name was probably given to those who voluntarily exposed themselves to death in the care of the sick in times of pestilence. The Greeks employed a similar term for those who hired themselves out to fight with wild beasts for the entertainment of the people. The *Parabolani* were a kind of lower order of clergy, under the supervision of the bishop.

NOTES TO SECOND CHAPTER.

Note 1, p. 105.—Islam is the correct name of the religion commonly called Mohammedan, after Mohammed, its prophet. One great source of its power over men is that it demands perfect submission to its tenets. Another is its promise of sensuous happiness in paradise. It affirms that Islam was the true original religion; adheres to the monotheistic idea, and has for its chief sacred books the Koran.

Note 2, p. 106.—The Moors were the ancient inhabitants of *Mauritania* or *Morocco*, but with the infusion of the manners, language, and religion of the Mohammedan Arabs, by whom they were conquered in the seventh century. They, as all Mohammedan peoples of that period, were exceedingly warlike. They long held their ground in Spain.

Note 3, p. 106.—Charles Martel was a high officer under the weak Merovingian kings (see note 10 to p. 114). He received the title *Martil*, "hammer," in consequence of the blow he dealt the Moors. He ruled with the power though not under the title of king. Upon his death his son Pepin was recognized as king, he being the first king of the Carlovingian line. (See Note 11 to p. 116.)

Note 4, p. 107.—Prometheus is a character in ancient Greek mythology. He is represented as of tremendous energy, and the protector, teacher, and benefactor of the human race. Æschylus's drama, "Prometheus Bound," represents him as chained to Mt. Caucasus.

Note 5, p. 107.—The Jews and Mohammedans held firmly to the unity and spirituality of God, in this respect having a purer faith than the image-worshiping Christians. Leo, the Isaurian, did not hope to win them to Christianity while Christians adhered to so false a practice and one so repuguant to the Jewish and Mohammedan mind. Hence he became the first of the so-called "Iconoclasts"—image-breakers.

Note 6, p. 108.—It is a remarkable fact that, after all visible symbols except of Christ in the eucharist were pronounced blasphemous or heretical, it was a woman, the Empress Irene, as regent, who assembled a Council at Constantinople in 787 (afterward removed to Nice), which "decreed that the cross and images of Christ, the virgin, the angels, and the saints were entitled to reverential worship, but not to divine worship." Also that it was a woman, Theodora (not to be confused with Theodora, wife of Justinian I), who finally, in 842, confirmed by a Council in Constantinople, the decision of the Council of Nice.

Note 7, p. 109.—The Slavonians originally inhabited the country in and about the Carpathian Mountains. They spread over the lands included in the Eastern Empire, especially Turkey and Greece, after the destruction of the kingdom of the Huns. The Rus-

sians, Servians, Bulgarians, and Bohemians are representatives of the Slavs of the present day.

Note 8, p. 110.—The *Goths* were originally located about
the Caucasus Mountains. They assisted in the overthrow of the Roman Empire. "Visigoths" and "Ostrogoths" are respectively West and East Goths. The
Suevians are mentioned by Cæsar as inhabiting the
country between the Rhine and the Weser. The
Vandals are by some regarded as a portion of the
Suevians. The *Alans* were a tribe who united with
the tribes just mentioned, and others, to invade the
Roman Empire. The Burgundians lived between the
Oder and the Vistula. Burgundy, France, is named
after them, they having settled there during the
migration of nations. All these were German tribes.

Note 9, p. 113.—The Franks were a confederacy of Germanic tribes. But they soon crystallized into a
nationality distinct from the other Germans and
became the French of later centuries.

Note 10, p. 114.—Merovingians, the name of the first
Frankish dynasty in Gaul (France). It was so called
from Meroveus, king of the Ripuarian Franks (448–
458). His son was Childeric I (458–481). The next
king of this dynasty was Clovis, the conqueror of
Gaul, and the first Frankish Christian king. (See
p. 175.) The dynasty degenerated, and made way
for that of the Carlovingians. (See Notes 3 to p. 106,
and 11 to p. 116.)

Note 11, p. 116.—The emperors of the Carlovingian
dynasty were Charlemagne (800–814.) He had been
king since 771, but was not crowned emperor until
Christmas (800), Louis the Weak, also called the
Debonnaire (814–840), Lothaire (840 855), Louis II,
Lothaire's son (855–876), Charles the Bald, of France
(876 877), and Charles the Fat of Germany (877–
887). There were, however, successors of the

Carlovingian dynasty who were kings both in Germany and France.

Note 12, p. 116.—The Lombards were a tribe of Suevians, and were first found in the time of the Emperor Augustus, on the River Elbe. The name is derived from *Langobardi*, "long-beards." They gave name to and founded Lombardy, in Upper Italy.

Note 13, p. 118.—The *Allemanians* were German confederated tribes, the name *Allemani* (all men) signifying either their tribal diversity or their valor. The *Bavarians* were another confederation of German tribes for purposes of defense or attack against the Romans. They founded the modern Bavaria. The *Thuringians* were also Germans living south of the Hartz Mountains, and between the rivers Soole and Werra. They were conquered and ruled first by the Franks, and then by the Saxons.

Note 14, p. 118.—The *Celts*, or *Kelts*, came originally from Asia, although their origin and first locality are unknown. They scattered over many parts of Europe. The Irish and Scottish peoples were of Celtic origin.

Note 15, p. 120.—The Anglo-Saxon, or English, missionaries were not sent to Germany until the English Church had been Romanized. Hence the zeal of Boniface and his coadjutors to Romanize the Church of Germany. The Irish and Scottish missionaries had not been Romanized. The early missionary zeal of the Anglo-Saxon people has never forsaken them.

Note 16, p. 121.—The Frisians (of Friesland) lived between the Rhine and the Ems. They were a German tribe. In the fifth century they united with the Saxons in an invasion of Britain.

Note 17, p. 121.—A large oak dedicated to *Jove*. The legends vary. It is said that Boniface ordered the tree cut down, but that after a few strokes a storm of wind blew it over. Another form of the legend is, that it fell at the prayer of Boniface. In any event, it was taken as a proof of the power and truth of the religion which Boniface taught.

Note 18, p. 122.—Looked at from one stand-point, the papacy was a necessity to the Church. God deals with men as he finds them. Ideal means can only be employed where men are perfect. But from the gospel stand-point the papacy was not necessary to the Church, and hence not from God's stand-point. It *was* necessary if the human and perverted institutions substituted for God's Church were to be perpetuated. That God employed these institutions to convey the truth to later generations does not prove their righteousness.

Note 19, p. 125.—The Tridentine Council, or Council of Trent, was occasioned by the progress of the Reformation, and was intended to extirpate heresy, reform discipline, and restore peace; in other words, officially to reform the Church, and make the Protestant Reformation unnecessary. The Council held twenty-five sessions during the years from December 13, 1545, to December 3 and 4, 1563.

Note 20, p. 127.—Hincmar, archbishop of Rheims (born probably in 809, died 882), was one of the most celebrated ecclesiastics of his time. He opposed the temporal power of the popes, and favored the independence of the Gallican (French) Church.

Note 21, p. 128.—The "Magdeburg Centuries" is the title of the first history of the Church from the Protestant stand-point. It treats the history by centuries, but includes only the first thirteen. Each century is treated under sixteen different heads. The work is controversial in tone. It, however, brought to light a good deal of historical matter previously unpublished.

Note 22, p. 130.—The following quotations are from the excellent article, " Fief," in " McClintock and Strong's Cyclopedia:" "Under the feudal system the whole order of society rested directly on the tenure of land by military service. Territorial possessions were granted by the suzerain, or supreme lord, in consideration of prompt and gratuitous service in war, and participation in his deliberative and judicial courts." "The system was strictly military in its nature—a uniform organization from the crown to the lowest landholder." "The vital germ of feudalism is contained in an act of homage. . . . The liege-man knelt down, placed his hands between the hands of his intended chief, and took upon himself the obligation of absolute *fidelity* in certain prescribed relations. . . . The contract was sealed with a kiss, and confirmed with the sanctions of religion." "The principal object of this close correlation of the constituents of society was to maintain the population in a state of constant preparation for war. It also operated to maintain social order and public safety."

Note 23, p. 131.—Investiture signified the granting of property or the income of property by one person to another. It was the custom for the king to send to a clergyman about to be installed in an ecclesiastical office a ring signifying the close union between himself and the king, and a staff as a symbol of his pastoral office. It led to many abuses. There were enough who gladly paid the king for the right to enjoy the benefits of the property of a Church. Hence the popes opposed it as simony, although they did not themselves hesitate to receive pay for investing a clergyman with a benefice.

Note 24, p. 133.—Before there were any popes the bishop of Rome was elected by the clergy and people of Rome. Upon the recognition of Christianity by the

State, the secular authorities claimed a share in the choice of the pope. For many centuries the Church struggled against the interference of the emperor in papal elections. When the Romans themselves fell into dispute, the Church gladly availed itself of the interference of the emperor. Later (in the Lateran Synod of 1059) the right of electing the popes was conferred upon the cardinal-bishops. But later Councils claimed the right to depose and set up popes at will. (See §35.) Popes are now elected by the cardinals in conclave. Counting St. Peter and the early Roman bishops, there have been 263 popes and anti-popes (rival popes), including Leo XIII.

Note 25, p. 136.—The round arch was the distinguishing feature of the Romanesque architecture, as the pointed arch is of the Gothic.

Note 26, p. 136.—Hroswitha was a celebrated nun of the tenth century. She wrote Latin poems of great purity of style. It is a singular fact that the nuns of that period were experts in the Latin language.

Note 27, p. 136.—The Ekkehards were a celebrated family from which sprang a number of learned monks connected with the monastery of St. Gall.

Note 28, p. 143.—The *secular* clergy were those who did not adhere to the monastic mode of life. The *regular* clergy, on the other hand, were monks.

Note 29, p. 147.—The *interregnum* here referred to is that which occurred between the extinction of the house of Hohenstaufen, in the death of Conrad IV (1254), and the election of Rudolph I (1273), during which period Germany was without a king. The principal kings of the Hohenstaufens were the celebrated Frederick Barbarossa and Frederick II. The present ruling house of Germany is the Hohenzollern.

Note 30, p. 148.—The Crusades, or religious wars of the Christians against the Mohammedans for the conquest of the Holy Land, were seven in number, and continued from the close of the eleventh to the close of the thirteenth century. The first Crusade (1096–1099) was occasioned by the impassioned speeches of Peter the Hermit. The Crusades were generally disastrous and unfruitful, but gave vent to the warlike propensities of the period, and satisfied the badly instructed consciences of thousands.

Note 31, p. 152.—The *Carmelites*, or "Order of St. Mary of Mt. Carmel," were founded by an association of hermits on Mt. Carmel, in 1156. They claimed that the prophet Elijah had founded their Order, and that the Virgin Mary had been a member. The *Cistercians* were founded about 1098. They wore a black habit at first, but asserted that they changed to white at the behest of the Virgin Mary. The *Carthusians* were founded about 1086. There are still monks and nuns of this Order, but they live in the spirit of the Middle Ages.

Note 32, p. 153.—Mystics are those who profess an immediate knowledge of God and communion with him, independent of the powers of reason. In all profound religious experience there is an element of Mysticism. The Mystics have, however, committed many errors and excesses, and they do not, therefore, always appear to advantage in Church history.

Note 33, p. 149.—Gregory VII (monk Hildebrand), perhaps the greatest of the popes, was the son of a carpenter. He was a Clugny monk of great austerity. He aimed at the reformation of abuses, but is responsible for the establishment of many others.

Note 34, p. 149.—The Notkers were a celebrated German family, which, like the Ekkehards, furnished several of the most learned of the scholarly monks of St. Gall.

Note 35, p. 157.—The famous papal bull of 1302 is named *Unam Sanctam*, from its first two words which mean, "One holy"—the remainder of the first sentence being, "Catholic and Apostolic Church we must recognize." It claims that outside of the Church of Rome there is no salvation nor forgiveness of sin. This Church has one head—not two, like a monstrosity. The one Shepherd has two swords in his power (Luke xxii, 38), where the Lord did not say "It is too many," but "It is enough." Of course the one head is the pope, and he has under his control the two swords (authority), the ecclesiastical and the secular—the latter of which must always take second rank.

Note 36, p. 158.—The effect of the residence of the popes at Avignon was their protection, since France and the papacy were in alliance. Hence these popes could oppress other lands with the aid of France. But the papacy thus became dependent upon France, and so lost in moral power. The effect was, further, to increase the political power of France, since it had the aid of the pope.

Note 37, p. 176.—*Eckart* (or Eckhardt, often with the title *Master*) was a Dominican and a profound thinker. *Tauler* was greatly influenced by his master, Eckart, and, like him, was a Mystic. After a severe struggle, he experienced the power of conversion, and preached with such effect that numbers fell down as dead under his words. He was also very benevolent and self-sacrificing. *Wessel* was born some two centuries later than Eckart and Tauler; i. e., about 1400 or 1420. He was a German. His influence in preparing the world for the Reformation under Luther was immense.

Note 38, p. 180.—Ferdinand the Catholic, king of Aragon, is chiefly interesting to Americans because he was the husband of Isabella, queen of Spain, who commissioned Columbus to undertake the voyage which ended in the discovery of America.

Note 39, p. 181.—Thomas Wolsey, an English cardinal (born 1471), is one of the most celebrated characters of history. He rose to a position of influence under Henry VIII, in which he virtually ruled even the king. He was extravagant, luxurious, ambitious, an aspirant for the papacy, and an enemy of the Reformation. He lost, but finally regained in part, the favor of Henry VIII. He died in 1530. Among his last utterances are the famous words: "If I had served my God as diligently as I have served my king, he would not have given me over to my enemies."

Note 40, p. 182.—The English Church was indeed not improved by separation ; but the separation made the improvement possible, and the improvement came.

Note 41, p. 183.—A general concept is an idea which is suitable to every individual of a class. No two horses are alike, yet every one has the general idea of a horse which enables him to distinguish a horse from other animals. The question was the relation of the general idea (*e. g.*, of a man) to the particular (*i. e.*, some particular man). Did the general idea exist independent of the particular object, or only in connection with it?

Note 42, p. 186.—St. Victor was the name of a monastery, and the learned monks took, in addition to their own names, that of the monastery, as Walter St. Victor, Richard St. Victor, etc.

Note 43, p. 190.—An example of a heathen custom perpetuated in the Roman Catholic Church is the "Feast of Fools," celebrated with grotesque rites in Europe during the Middle Ages. It was in imitation of the Roman *Saturnalia*, and was held in December, commencing with Christmas.

Note 44, p. 194.—The doctrine that one can do more in the service of God than God requires, and thereby earn merit with God—the doctrine of works of supererogation—is very old in the Church. It was upheld and defined by the Scholastics, and is now a doctrine in the Roman Catholic Church. Protestants reject it on the ground that, after we have done all that we can, we are unprofitable servants (Luke xvii, 10), and because it is contrary to the whole tenor of the Gospel.

Note 45, p. 195.—The several Ecumenical Councils held in the Lateran Church, in Rome, are distinguished by the title Lateran. The most important is the so-called Fourth, held from November 11 to November 30, 1215. It occurred during the pontificate of Innocent III, in whom the rights of the papacy reached their culmination.

Note 46, p. 197.—Cathari is a term applied to various sects in the history of the Church, and means *purists*, or *puritans*. They always claimed to strive after, or to attain to, peculiar purity of life. The *Albigenses* were Cathari, who first appeared in Southern France in the twelfth century. They were distinguished by their peculiar doctrines, and especially by opposition to the Roman Catholic Church. The *Waldenses, Valdenses*, or *Vaudois*, whose name is probably derived from Peter Waldo, who was prominently associated with them, have been confused with the Albigenses by some writers. But they are distinguished by a later origin and a purer faith. They vigorously deny and oppose the peculiarities of the Roman Church. They are now thoroughly evangelical.

NOTES TO THIRD CHAPTER.

Note 1, p. 209.—Raphael and Michael Angelo were celebrated contemporary artists. Raphael was born in 1483, and died in 1520. His Madonnas were numerous and marvelous. Greatest is his Sistine Madonna (so called from its containing a likeness of St. Sixtus) now in the Gallery at Dresden. Angelo was equally famous as sculptor and painter.

Note 2, p. 213.—Cæsar Borgia was a monster in crime, and especially an adept in murder when he could thereby better gain his ends. Yet he was a lover and patron of learning. Lucretia Borgia, his sister, was beautiful, but abandoned. It is said that for a time, in the absence of her father, Pope Alexander VI, she conducted the affairs of the chair of St. Peter. The shamelessness of the papacy of the period is seen in the fact that Alexander made no secret of being the father of his children, although as a clergyman of the Roman Church he could not marry.

Note 3, p. 213.—Machiavelli (1469–1527) was a great Italian statesman. Cæsar Borgia was taken as the model prince in his celebrated work "The Prince." "The work is a scientific account of the art of acquiring and preserving despotic power." "It exhibits an obliquity of moral principle, . . . which can only be palliated by alleging that dissimulation and treachery were universally looked upon, . . . in his day, as legitimate political weapons." Skillful crimes were generally admired by the contemporaries of Machiavelli. "As a statesman he was upright and honorable."

Note 4, p. 215.—Humanism denoted first of all the development of the human mind by education; then the study of the Greek and Latin classical authors, which were supposed to be the only means of higher education.

Note 5, p. 215.—Reuchlin and Erasmus were Humanists and rivals in learning. The great weapon of Erasmus in controversy was ridicule. In his "Praise of Folly" he ridicules the dialectics of the theologians; the filth, ignorance, and idleness of the monks; the hypocrisy of the bishops;. and the popes and the papal court for their luxurious selfishness. Erasmus was at first the friend, but finally the foe, of the Reformation.

Note 6, p. 227.—The most wonderful feature of St. Peter's, Rome, is its magnificent dome. The size of the church is very great. Yet it is so constructed within and without, as to leave the impression of littleness. Hence, except the dome, there is nothing in the architecture to suggest majesty. The decorations are inappropriate. Yet, owing to its history, the church is frequently and enthusiastically visited.

Note 7, p. 227.—The Fuggers were a family of immense wealth, which often loaned large sums of money to the emperors. They were benevolent to the poor, but bitter enemies of the Reformation. They resided in Augsburg, and during the famous Diet of Augsburg in 1530, Emperor Charles V was a guest of Antonius Fugger, of whom it is related that he "astonished the emperor by lighting a fire of cinnamon with an Imperial bond for money due him."

Note 8, p. 232.—It was at the Diet of Worms that Luther, refusing to recant because it is not safe to do anything against one's conscience, uttered the memorable words: "Here I stand; I can do no other; God help me." By an edict of May 26, 1521, Luther was outlawed. But the ban was never executed against him.

Note 9, p. 233.—The Wartburg is a castle in Thuringia, near Eisenach. On his return from Worms, Luther was taken captive by masked friends and taken to the Wartburg for safety. Here he passed under the name of Knight George. He claimed to have had here a vision of the devil, at whom he threw his inkstand. It struck the wall, and the ink-spots were formerly exhibited, but the plastering has been carried away by tourists. He finally took matters in his own hands and returned to Wittenberg.

Note 10, p. 233.—Francis of Sickingen was a knight and a friend of the Reformation. He took up arms in defense of the new doctrines, but Luther refused to sanction his course. The power of the knighthood was completely broken by his defeat and death. The Peasants' War was also opposed by Luther. The suffering it produced was terrible, nearly one-half of the peasants being killed during its progress.

Note 11, p. 233—The Reformation was seriously troubled by fanatical spirits, such as Carlstadt and Thomas Münzer. They and others stirred up the people and students of Wittenberg to disturb the public worship and cast the pictures out of the churches. Luther left the Wartburg, and preached in Wittenberg a whole week against the fanatics. He quieted them there; but they went elsewhere and wrote and worked against him, as against Romanism.

Note 12, p. 234.—The *Schmalcald League* was composed of several Protestant cities and provinces, and was formed in 1531, to protect themselves against the attacks of the enemies of the Reformation, including the emperor. The *Schmalcald Articles* were the propositions agreed upon at Schmalcald, which it was necessary to maintain at the coming proposed Ecumenical Council. The *Schmalcald War* against the Schmalcald League went in favor of the emperor, because the League itself was not really united, and because of the inefficiency of some of its leaders.

Note 13, p. 235.—The Ecumenical Council mentioned in the preceding notes was constantly postponed by the pope. The emperor therefore published (at Augsburg, 1548) certain doctrinal articles to be valid in the interim (hence called the Augsburg Interim)—that is, till the meeting of the Council. These articles were, however, agreeable neither to Protestants nor papists. They were revoked when the religious

Peace of Augsburg was agreed upon, whereby the cities and States adopting the Augsburg Confession were granted the right " to enjoy the practices of their religion in peace."

Note 14, p. 235.—The Thirty Years' War (1618–1648), or succession of wars, grew out of oppressions of the Protestants by Roman Catholics. It resulted in giving the Protestants equal rights with the Romanists in the empire. With it also ended the religious wars of Europe. Peace was concluded at Westphalia, October 24, 1648. At the battle of Lutzen, Gustavus Adolphus, king of Sweden and a Protestant, lost his life. Tilly and Wallenstein were prominent actors on the side of the Romanists.

Note 15, p. 244.—Luther was opposed to the use of arms in the defense of his faith. Zwingli had no such scruples.

Note 16, p. 253.—The duke of Alva was one of the most blood-thirsty monsters ever employed to advance the Roman Catholic cause and destroy Protestantism. He knew no mercy nor pity. He was sent by Philip II of Spain to the Netherlands, where he took bloody revenge upon all who had favored the Protestant cause.

Note 17, p. 253 —On St. Bartholomew's Day (August 24, 1572) occurred the horrible slaughter of Protestants in Paris. The most prominent of them had been invited there to celebrate the marriage of the king of Navarre and the sister of the French king, Charles IX. A solemn pledge of safety had been given them. Upon the tolling of a bell the bloody work began, and did not end until ten thousand, of all ranks, had been massacred. The massacre spread to the country, and the total number killed has been estimated at from thirty thousand to one hundred thousand—the latter estimate being that of a papist. While some

Romanists have justified it, others have attributed it to political rather than religious enmity.

Note 18, p. 267.—VOLTAIRE was one of the greatest literary men of any age. He believed in God, but was a scoffer at the Christian religion. The weapon with which he assailed it was satire. Morally, he was thoroughly bad. He did good service, however, in securing religious toleration. In a dangerous illness, just before his death, he sought reconciliation with the Church. LESSING was not less remarkable than Voltaire as a literary man, but he was far more friendly to Christianity. It is impossible to detail his history and writings here.

Note 19, p. 269.—Probabilism, allowing of the performance of an act which one believes to be wrong, on the ground that some other and recognized authority pronounces it to be right, destroys the supremacy of the individual's conscience. The degrees of probability varied according to the number of authorities favoring a given view.

Note 20, p. 271.—Pascal was equally great in mathematics and literature. With eloquence, learning, and genius, he combined virtue in a rare degree. By his ascetic practices he undermined his health and shortened his life. Pascal is best known by his "Thoughts on Religion," which was intended to show the necessity of a revelation and the truth of the Christian revelation.

Note 21, p. 271.—Achilles, the hero of Homer's "Iliad," is represented in Greek mythology as the son of Peleus, king of the Myrmidons, and the sea goddess, Thetis. The waters of the River Styx were supposed to have the property of rendering the human body invulnerable. To protect him from danger his mother dipped him in that river. She held him by the heel, which was therefore not touched by the water; hence his heel was his vulnerable spot, and "Achilles' heel" is a synonym for the same. He was afterward said to have been shot in the heel and killed.

Note 22, p. 282.—Servetus was an opponent of the doctrine of the Holy Trinity, in the time of the Reformation. He differed also in other important respects from the Reformers. He was arrested at Calvin's suggestion. Calvin also wrote the charges against him. Servetus violently attacked Calvin, and demanded that he should also be tried, and that the trial should proceed until one of them was condemned to death or other punishment. Calvin unquestionably believed that the death of Servetus was demanded in the interest of the Church. He was opposed to his being burned at the stake. We must not judge the deed alone in the light of the tolerant spirit of the present day.

Note 23, p. 283.—The Edict of Nantes, issued by Henry IV of France, 1598, granted the Protestants the right to serve God according to their own consciences, and secured them their civil rights. Louis XIV, in revoking the Edict, authorized the destruction of all Protestant churches, banished all Protestant pastors from France, and closed all Protestant schools. Four hundred thousand Protestants (Huguenots) left France, and settled in various countries of Europe and America.

Note 24, p. 294.—The story that Hengist and Horsa began the Anglo-Saxon invasion of Britain is now generally discredited. That invasion seems to have been a part of the general migration of nations.

Note 25, p. 294.—Christianity was perhaps introduced into Ireland as early as the second century. The Irish seem originally to have received their Christianity from the East, instead of from Rome. St. Patrick was a Scotchman, and became the apostle to the Irish

(432). Some Scots from Ireland settled in Scotland in 503. They had received Christianity under St. Patrick. From them Columba went forth as a missionary to the Picts.

Note 26, p. 294.—When Gregory was told that these boys were from a pagan land, and were called Angles (English), he replied that it was "sad to think that beings so full of light and brightness should be in the power of the Prince of Darkness." "Rightly," said he, "are they called Angles, for their faces are as the faces of angels, and they ought to be fellow-heirs of the angels in heaven."

Note 27, p. 294.—The possessions of the Saxons in England were divided into seven petty kingdoms (really eight), called the Heptarchy. Of these Kent was one.

Note 28, p. 295.—The chief differences between the early British and Irish opinions and those of Augustine, as derived from Rome, pertained to the method of reckoning Easter, the form of clerical tonsure, the marriage of the clergy, and the papal jurisdiction. The British bishops did not object to the marriage of the clergy, and were opposed to the jurisdiction of the popes.

Note 29, p. 295.—The Danish invasion of England began in the ninth century. Canute was the son of Sweyn, who had apostatized from Christianity. He was also king of Denmark, where he established Christianity after it had experienced a long struggle with paganism.

Note 30, p. 298.—Wordsworth's Ecclesiastical Sonnet on Wyclif is as follows:

"Once more the Church is seized with sudden fear,
And at her call is Wyclif disinhumed;
Yea, his dry bones to ashes are consumed,
And flung into the brook which travels near.
Forthwith that ancient Voice, which streams can hear,
Thus speaks (that Voice which walks upon the wind,
Though seldom heard by busy human kind):

'As thou these ashes, little Brook, wilt bear
Into the Avon, Avon to the tide •
Of Severn, Severn to the narrow seas,
Into main ocean they—this deed accurst
An emblem yields to friends and enemies
How the bold teacher's doctrine, sanctified
By truth, shall spread, throughout the world dispersed.'"

Note 31, p. 298.—Henry VIII was six times married. His first wife was Catharine of Aragon, whom he divorced. The second was Anne Boleyn, whom he beheaded. The next morning he married his third wife, Jane Seymour, who died soon after the birth of Edward (afterward King Edward VI). He next married Anne of Cleves, but she was so ugly that he soon divorced her. His fifth wife was Catharine Howard, whom he executed because she was unfaithful to him. His sixth wife was Catharine Parr, who survived him.

Note 32, p. 299.—A visitation of the monasteries in 1535 revealed a fearful state of corruption. A part of them were suppressed in 1536. Various troubles followed, and it was not until 1539 that they were all suppressed.

Note 33, p. 301.—The "Five Points" of Calvinism, as defined by the Synod of Dort, are: 1. *Of Divine Predestination*, according to which God, in his good pleasure, chose a definite number to be saved and left all others to their own obduracy. 2. *Of the Death of Christ and the Redemption of Men thereby*, according to which Christ redeemed "all those, and those only, who were from eternity chosen to salvation." 3 and 4. *Of the Corruption of Man, his Conversion to God, and the Manner thereof*, in which man's free will to turn to God and exercise faith is denied. 5. *Of the Perseverance of the Saints*, which teaches that the elect can not totally and finally fall from grace and be lost. The Lambeth Articles are practically the same. The Arminians deny all these special doctrines, and assert the reverse, although Calvinists and Arminians hold much in common.

Note 34, p. 302.—For the first offense the offender forfeited one year's income and suffered six months imprisonment. The second deprived of all spiritual promotion, and imprisoned for one year. The third imprisoned for life. By the end of Elizabeth's reign, one-third of the clergy had been deposed. If any person seventeen years of age absented himself from the established services for one month without satisfactory reason, he was imprisoned; if he refused conformity, he was banished; if he returned without permission, he was put to death.

Note 35, p. 303.—The "Gunpowder Plot" was an attempt on the part of Romanists to blow up the House of Parliament while that body was in session and the king present, and then place a Romanist on the throne. Guy Fawkes was one of the chief conspirators, although not the originator of the plot. It was happily discovered in time to prevent its execution.

Note 36, p. 303.—Knox did not finally forsake the Roman Church until 1542, although his faith had been shaken for several years. Meantime the Scottish Reformation had commenced. Knox was taken prisoner, sent to France, and made a galley slave. Upon his release he returned to England, but was compelled to return to the Continent. Upon his return to Scotland he became the leader of the Reformation there, where, owing to the efforts of Knox, it was much more swift and thorough than in England. Mary was very beautiful, but a firm Romanist. She tried all her wiles to win Knox back to Romanism, but in vain. He was to Scotland religiously what Luther was to Germany.

Note 37, p. 305.—In reality, Cromwell had not intended

the execution of the king when he first got possession of him. But as Charles wrote to his wife that he intended a rope for Cromwell and his abettors, the question became one of life and death for all concerned. Besides, in all his transactions, the king showed himself utterly unworthy of belief, and all confidence in him was lost. He was executed January 30, 1649.

Note 38, p. 305.—The Star Chamber was an old court; the High Commission was a device of Queen Elizabeth worthy of the Inquisitors. Both were employed to compel conformity or to punish non-conformists.

Note 39, p. 312.—The Unitarian and Universalist bodies have a long history. Unitarianism in America owes its reputation chiefly to the Rev. William Ellery Channing, a moral product of the system he rejected, and a man of great piety and earnestness. By carrying out his principles consistently, the Unitarians of to-day have become "freethinkers" rather than practical Christians. They lay much stress upon intelligence and morality. Many of them, however, are distinguished for practical piety.

Note 40, p. 316.—The Holy Club was made up at first of John and Charles Wesley, Mr. Morgan, and Mr. Kirkham. They fasted much, and in other ways exhibited their ascetic tendencies. They were especially diligent in visiting the sick and prisoners.

Note 41, p. 323.—John Fletcher was educated at Geneva, and was profoundly versed in philology and philosophy. He joined the Methodists in 1755, and in 1757 took orders in the Church of England. He was a diligent pastoral visitor, accomplishing thereby much good. His liberality to the poor was very great. Southey says: "No age or country has ever produced a man of more fervent piety or more perfect charity."

Note 42, p. 323.—Selina, Countess of Huntingdon, was

one of the noblest women the world has ever seen. She was a Calvinist, and when Wesley and Whitefield took separate roads on that question, she became the leader of the Calvinistic party. She was very liberal in gifts, and wise in planning the work under her care. She died in 1791, in the same year with Wesley.

Note 43, p. 327.—Wesley held that there are but two clerical orders, those of deacons and of presbyters or elders, and that the bishopric is not an order, but an office. Hence a presbyter could ordain a bishop. This is also the view held by the Methodist Episcopal Churches.

APPENDIX II.

CHRONOLOGICAL TABLES.

1. SPREAD OF CHRISTIANITY.—PERSECUTIONS.

FIRST PERIOD.

33. First Christian congregation in Jerusalem.
35– 40. In Samaria, Phœnicia, and Antioch.
45– 47. In Asia Minor; Paul's first missionary journey.
52– 53. In Greece—Corinth ; Paul's second journey.
55– 57. Third journey of Paul; two years' residence in Ephesus.

> In the apostolic period Christianity was carried to Mesopotamia, Persia, Armenia, Rome, Alexandria, and the East Indies (Thomas).

PERSECUTIONS.

64– 68. Under Nero (martyrdom of Paul and Peter).
66. The Christians flee to Pella.
81– 96. Banishment of individuals under Domitian (John to Patmos).
98–117. Under Hadrian, in Asia Minor.
138-161. Antoninus Pius protects the Christians against the rage of the people.
161–180. Persecution under Marcus Aurelius, at Smyrna (Polycarp, martyred 168), and at Lyons and Vienna (177).
193–211. Under Septimius Severus, in Egypt and Proconsular Africa.
211–217. Continuance of the persecutions under Caracalla.

362

235-238. Under Maximin I; Congregations of Toulouse and Paris.

249-251. Under Decius.

251. Gallus leaves the Christians to the rage of the people.

254-259. Under Valerian; martyrdom of Cyprian, 258.

259-268. Gallienus declares Christianity a permitted religion.

270-275. Aurelian issues an edict of persecution.

303-311. Bloody persecution under Diocletian and Galerius (4 edicts).

305. Constantius Chlorus ameliorates the lot of the Christians in Gaul, Spain, and Britain.

308-310. Maximin II persecutes the Christians in Egypt.

311. Galerius, shortly before his death, revokes the edict of persecution.

FURTHER SPREAD OF CHRISTIANITY IN ASIA, AFRICA, AND WESTERN EUROPE.

312, 313. Edicts of Constantine the Great in favor of the Christians.

314. Measures of Licinius against the Christians.

323. Constantine, sole ruler; Christianity made the religion of the State.

After 327. Christianity introduced into Abyssinia, Ethiopia, and Armenia.

337. Constantine baptized at Pentecost; dies in his baptismal garments.

After 350. The West Goths in Spain (until 553), the East Goths in Italy (until 589), the Vandals (until 534), and the Lombards (until 773) hold to the Arian form of Christianity.

After 400. The Burgundians and Franks in Gaul; orthodox after 517.

432. St. Patrick teaches in Ireland.

496. Clovis, king of the Franks, baptized.

565. Columba preaches in Scotland among the Picts.

In England Christianity is suppressed by the Anglo-Saxons.

596. Pope Gregory the Great sends Augustine to England.

597. Baptism of Ethelbert, king of Kent.

613, 614. Irish monk Gallus, missionary in Switzerland.

After 622. Spread of Christianity hindered by Mohammedanism.

696. The English monk Wilbeard preaches among the Frankish Friesians, and founds Utrecht (died 739).

After 715. Winfred, an Anglo-Saxon monk, preaches among the Friesians, 722, in Thuringia and Hesse; in 723 Gregory II ordains him bishop, under the name Boniface; Gregory III, archbishop and apostolic vicar of Germany. In 739 and 742 he founds several bishoprics, after 743 assembles Synods, after 745 maintains his archiepiscopal residence in Mayence; in 753 abdicates in favor of his pupil, Lullas; in 755 preaches anew among the Friesians, by whom he was murdered; buried in the monastery of Fulda.

Second Period.

FURTHER SPREAD OF CHRISTIANITY—CRUSADES.

820. Beginning of the conversion of the Bulgarians.

822. Ebbo of Rheims, missionary to Denmark and Northern Europe.

826–865. Ausgar (Auschar) apostle of the northern kingdoms.

848. Cyril preaches among the Chazari.

About 850. The Russians of Constantinople ask for a bishop.

861. Methodius spreads Christianity among the Bulgarians.

934. Henry I compels the Danes to tolerate Christianity.

972– 997. Duke of Geysa introduces Christianity into Hungary.

1014–1035. Canute the Great secures the position of Christianity in Denmark.

1075. Inge of Sweden forbids all idolatry (Upsala).

c096. First Crusade, under Godfrey of Bouillon.

1099. Capture of Jerusalem.

1147. Second Crusade, under Emperor Conrad and Louis VII of France.

1187. Saladin captures Jerusalem.

1189. Third Crusade, under Emperor Frederick I.

1190. Fourth Crusade, under Richard the Lionhearted and Philip Augustus of France.

After1202. Jenghiz Khan allows Christianity to be preached among the Mongolians.

1207. Godfrey of Lukina goes as missionary to the Prussians.

1218. Founding of the Church in Esthonia and Semgollen by the Knights of the Sword.

1228. Fifth Crusade, under Frederick II.

1237. The Knights of the Sword and the Teutonic Order unite to convert Prussia.

1248. Sixth Crusade, under Louis IX of France (St. Louis), against Egypt.

1270. Seventh Crusade, to Tunis and Ptolemais.

1275. Mission of Gregory IX to China.

1283. Prussia subjugated by the Teutonic Order.

1288. Nicolaus IV sends the Franciscan John of Mount Corvino to China; progress of Christianity aided by the translation of the New Testament and the Psalms into the Tartar language.

1291. Ptolemais and the supremacy of Palestine lost to the Christians.
1335. Christianity founded in Lapland.
1369. The Mongolians and Christianity expelled from China.
1453. Constantinople captured by the Turks.
1501. The power of the Moors in Spain annihilated.

2. BISHOPS AND POPES OF ROME.

(St. stands for saint, b. for blessed, m. for martyr.)

Name.	Term of Office.
1. St. Peter, m.,	42– 67
2. St. Linus, m.,	67– 78
3. St. Cletus, m.,	78– 90
4. St. Clement I, m.,	90–100
5. St. Anacletus, m.,	100–112
6. St. Evaristus, m.,	112–121
7. St. Alexander I, m.,	121–132
8. St. Sixtus I, m.,	132–142
9. St. Telesephorus, m.,	142–154
10. St. Hyginus, m.,	154–158
11. St. Pius I, m.,	158–167
12. St. Anicetus, m.,	167–175
13. St. Soterus, m.,	175–182
14. St. Eleutherius, m.,	182–193
15. St. Victor I, m.,	193–203
16. St. Zephyrinus, m.,	203–220
17. St. Calixtus I, m.,	221–227
18. St. Urban I, m.,	227–233
19. St. Pontianus, m.,	233–238
20. St. Anterus, m.,	238–239
21. St. Fabian, m.,	240–253
22. St. Cornelius, m.,	254–255
(Novatian, first rival pope.)	
23. St. Lucius I, m.,	255–257
24. St. Stephen I, m.,	257–260
25. St. Sixtus II, m.,	260–261
26. St. Dionysius,	261–272
27. St. Felix I, m.,	272–275
28. St. Eutychianus,	275–283
29. St. Caius, m.,	283–296
30. St. Marcellinus, m.,	296–304
31. St. Marcellus I, m.,	304–309
32. St. Eusebius,	309–311
33. St. Melchiades,	311–314
34. St. Sylvester,	314–337
35. St. Marcus,	337–340
36. St. Julius I,	341–352
37. St. Liberius,	352–363
38. St. Felix II,	363–365
39. St. Damasus,	366–384
(Ursicinus, rival pope.)	
40. St. Siricius,	384–398
41. St. Anastasius,	399–402
42. St. Innocent I,	402–417
43. St. Zosimus,	417–418
44. St. Boniface I,	418–423
45. St. Celestine I,	423–432
46. St. Sixtus III,	432–440
47. St. Leo I, the Great,	440–461
48. St. Hilary,	461–468
49. St. Simplicius,	468–483
50. St. Felix III,	483–492
51. St. Gelasius I,	492–496
52. St. Anastasius II,	496–498
53. St. Symmachus,	498–514
54. St. Hormisdas,	514–523
55. St. John I, m.,	523–526
56. St. Felix IV,	526–530
57. Boniface II,	530–532
58. John II,	532–535
59. St. Agapetus I,	535–536
60. St. Sylverius, m.,	536–538
61. Vigilius,	538–555
62. Pelagius I,	555–560
63. John III,	560–573
64. Benedict I,	574–578
65. Pelagius II,	578–590
66. St. Gregory I, the Great,	590–604
67. Sabinianus,	604–606
68. Boniface III,	607–607
69. St. Boniface IV,	608–615
70. St. Adeodatus I,	615–619
71. Boniface V,	619–625
72. Honorius I,	625–638

Name.	Term of Office.	Name.	Term of Office.
73. Severinus,	638–640	122. Christopher,	903– 904
74. John IV,	640–642	123. Sergius III	904– 911
75. Theodorus I,	642–649	124. Anastasius III,	911– 913
76. St. Martin I, m.,	649–655	125. Lando,	913– 914
77. St. Eugenius I,	655–656	126. John X,	915– 928
78. St. Vitalianus,	657–672	127. Leo VI,	928– 929
79. Adeodatus II,	672–676	128. Stephen VIII,	929– 931
80. Donus I,	676–678	129. John XI,	931– 936
81. St. Agathon,	678–682	130. Leo VII,	936– 939
82. St. Leo II,	682–683	131. Stephen IX,	939– 942
83. St. Benedict II,	684–685	132. Marinus II,	943– 946
84. John V,	685–686	133. Agapetus II,	946– 956
85. Conon,	686–687	134. John XII,*	956– 964
86. St. Sergius I,	687–701	(Leo VIII, rival pope.)	
87. John VI,	701–705	135. Benedict V,	964– 965
88. John VII,	705–707	136. John XIII,	965– 972
89. Sisinnius,	708–708	137. Benedict VI,	972– 973
90. Constantine,	708–715	138. Donus II,	973– 975
91. St. Gregory II,	715–731	139. Benedict VII,	975– 984
92. St. Gregory III,	731–741	140. John XIV,	984– 985
93. St. Zachary,	741–752	141. Boniface VII,	985– 985
94. St. Stephen II,	752–752	142. John XV,	985– 996
95. Stephen III,	752–757	143. John XVI,	996– 996
96. St. Paul I,	757–767	144. Gregory V,	996– 999
97. Stephen IV,	768–771	145. John XVII,	999– 999
98. Adrian I	771-795	146. Sylvester II,	999–1003
99. St. Leo III,	795–816	147. John XVIII,	1003–1003
100. Stephen V,	816–817	148. John XIX,	1003–1009
101. St. Paschal I,	817–824	149. Sergius IV,	1009–1012
102. Eugenius II,	824–827	150. Benedict VIII,	1012–1024
103. Valentinus,	827–827	151. John XX,	1024–1033
104. Gregory IV,	827–844	152. Benedict IX,	1033–1044
105. Sergius II,	844–847	153. Gregory VI,	1044–1046
106. St. Leo IV,	847–855	154. Clement II,	1046–1047
(Fabulous, rival Pope Joan.)		155. Damasus II,	1048–1048
107. Benedict III,	855–858	156. St. Leo IX,	1049–1055
108. St. Nicholas I the Great,	858–867	157. Victor II,	1055–1057
109. Adrian II,	867 872	158. Stephen X,	1057–1058
110. John VIII,	872–882	159. Benedict X,	1058–1059
111. Marinus I,	882–884	160. Nicholas II,	1059–1061
112. Adrian III,	884–885	161. Alexander II,	1061–1073
113. Stephen VI,	885–891	162. St. Gregory VII,	1073–1085
114. Formosus,	891–896	(Clement III, rival pope.)	
(Sergius, rival pope.)		163. Victor III,†	1087–1087
115. Boniface VI,	896–896	164. Urban II,	1088–1099
116. Stephen VII,	897–898	165. Paschal II,	1099–1118
117. Romanus,	898–898	(Albert and Theodoric, rival popes.)	
118. Theodorus II,	898–898	166. Gelasius II,	1118–1119
119. John IX,	898–900	167. Calixtus II,	1119–1124
120. Benedict IV,	900–903	168. Honorius II,	1124–1130
121. Leo V,	903–903		

* He was the first pope to change his name upon ascending the pontifical throne. The practice grew until it became universal. His name was Octavianus.

† He was elected in 1086, but declined. In 1087 he was, however, induced to accept the office. He died about six months later.

Name.	Term of Office.	Name.	Term of Office.
169. Innocent II,	1130-1143	212. John XXIII,	1410-1415
(Anacletus, rival pope.)		213. Martin V,	1417-1431
170. Celestine II,	1143-1144	214. Eugenius IV,	1431-1447
171. Lucius II,	1144-1145	(Felix, rival pope)	
172. B. Eugenius III,	1145-1153	215. Nicholas V,	1447-1455
173. Anastasius IV,	1153-1154	216. Calixtus III,	1455-1458
174. Adrian IV,*	1154-1159	217. Pius II,	1458-1464
175. Alexander III,	1159-1181	218. Paul II,	1464-1471
(Victor, Paschal, and Calixtus, rival popes.)		219. Sixtus IV,	1471-1484
		220. Innocent VIII,	1484-1492
176. Lucius III,	1181-1185	221. Alexander VI,	1492-1503
177. Urban III,	1185-1187	222. Pius III,	1503-1503
178. Gregory VIII,	1187-1187	223. Julius II,	1503-1513
179. Clement III,	1187-1191	224. Leo X,	1513-1521
180. Celestine III,	1191-1198	225. Adrian VI,	1522-1523
181. Innocent III,	1198-1216	226. Clement VII,	1523-1534
182. Honorius III,	1216-1227	227. Paul III,	1534-1549
183. Gregory IX,	1227-1241	228. Julius III,	1550-1555
184. Celestine IV,	1241-1241	229. Marcellus II,	1555-1555
185. Innocent IV,	1243-1254	230. Paul IV,	1555-1559
186. Alexander IV,	1254-1261	231. Pius IV,	1559-1565
187. Urban IV,	1261-1264	232. St. Pius V,	1566-1572
188. Clement IV,	1265-1269	233. Gregory XIII,	1572-1585
189. B. Gregory X,	1271-1276	234. Sixtus V,	1585-1590
190. Innocent V,	1276-1276	235. Urban VII,	1590-1590
191. Adrian V,	1276-1276	236. Gregory XIV,	1590-1591
192. John XXI,	1276-1277	237. Innocent IX,	1591-1592
193. Nicholas III,	1277-1280	238. Clement VIII,	1592-1601
194. Martin IV,	1281-1285	239. Leo XI,	1605-1605
195. Honorius IV,	1285-1287	240. Paul V,	1605-1625
196. Nicholas IV,	1288-1292	241. Gregory XV,	1621-1623
197. St. Celestine V,	1294-1294	242. Urban VIII,	1623-1644
198. Boniface VIII,	1294-1303	243. Innocent X,	1644-1655
199. B. Benedict XI,	1303-1304	244. Alexander VII,	1655-1667
200. Clement V,	1305-1314	245. Clement IX,	1667-1669
201. John XXII,	1316-1334	246. Clement X,	1670-1676
(Nicholas, rival pope.)		247. Innocent XI,	1676-1689
202. Benedict XII,	1334-1342	248. Alexander VIII,	1689-1691
203. Clement VI,	1342-1352	249. Innocent XII,	1691-1700
204. Innocent VI,	1352-1362	250. Clement XI,	1700-1721
205. B. Urban V,	1362-1370	251. Innocent XIII,	1721-1724
206. Gregory XI,	1370-1378	252. Benedict XIII,	1724-1730
207. Urban VI,	1378-1389	253. Clement XII,	1730-1740
(From 1378 to 1410 occurred the great schism, during which a rival line of popes resided at Avignon: Clement VII (1378-1394), Benedict XIII (1394-1410).		254. Benedict XIV,	1740-1758
		255. Clement XIII,	1758-1769
		256. Clement XIV,	1769-1774
		257. Pius VI,	1775-1799
		258. Pius VII,	1800-1823
		259. Leo XII,	1823-1829
208. Boniface IX,	1389-1404	260. Pius VIII,	1829-1830
209. Innocent VII,	1404-1406	261. Gregory XVI,	1831-1846
210. Gregory XII,	1406-1409	262. Pius IX,	1846-1878
211. Alexander V,	1409-1410	263. Leo XIII,	1878-

* The only Englishman ever elected pope.

3. ECUMENICAL COUNCILS (AS RECKONED BY THE ROMAN CATHOLICS).

1. The Synod of Apostles in Jerusalem (Acts xv).

2. The first Council of Nice, held 325 A. D., to assert the Catholic doctrine respecting the Son of God, in opposition to the opinions of Arius.

3. The first Council of Constantinople, convoked under the Emperor Theodosius the Great (381), to determine the Catholic doctrine regarding the Holy Ghost.

4. The first Council of Ephesus, convened under Theodosius the Younger (431), to condemn the Nestorian heresy.

5. The Council of Chalcedon, under the Emperor Marcian (451), which asserted the doctrine of the union of the divine with the human nature in Christ, and condemned the heresies of Eutyches and the Monophysites.

6. The second Council of Constantinople, under Justinian (553), which condemned the doctrines of Origen, Arius, Macedonius, and others.

7. The third Council of Constantinople, convoked under the Emperor Constantine V, Pogonatus (681), for the condemnation of the Monothelite heresy.

8. The second Council of Nice, held in the reign of the Empress Irene and her son Constantine (787), to establish the worship of images.

9. The fourth Council of Constantinople, under Basilius and Adrian (869), the principal business of which was the deposition of Photius, who had introduced himself into the See of Constantinople, and the restoration of Ignatius, its former occupant.

10. The first Lateran Council, held in Rome under the Emperor Henry V, and convoked by Pope Calixtus II (1123), to settle the dispute on investiture.

11. The second Lateran Council, under Emperor Conrad III and Pope Innocent II (1139), condemning the errors of Arnold of Brescia and others.

12. The third Lateran Council, convened by Pope Alexander III (1179), to condemn the "errors and impieties" of the Waldenses and Albigenses.

13. The fourth Lateran Council, held under Innocent III (1215), asserting, among other matters, the dogma of transubstantiation.

14. The first Ecumenical Synod of Lyon, held during the pontificate of Innocent IV (1245), to promote the Crusades, restore discipline, etc.

15. The second Ecumenical Synod of Lyon, held under Gregory X (1274), to reunite the Greek and Latin Churches.

16. The Synod of Vienne in Gaul under Clement V (1311), to suppress the Knights Templars, etc.

17. The Council of Constance, convoked at the request of the Emperor Sigismund (1414), sat four years. It asserted the superiority of the Council to the pope, and condemned the doctrines of John Huss and Jerome of Prague.

18. The Council of Basel, convoked by Pope Martin V (1430). It sat nearly ten years. It proposed to reform the discipline, and even the constitution, of the Roman Catholic Church. It was formally dissolved by the pope, and all its acts passed thereafter are regarded by the Roman Catholics as null and void.

19. The celebrated Council of Trent (1545–1563). It was opened by Paul III, and closed under the pontificate of Paul IV.

20. The Vatican Council (1869–1870), which asserted and defined the infallibility of the pope.